Landlord and Tenant Guide to Colorado Residential Leases and Evictions

4th Edition

Victor M. Grimm, Esq.
Denise E. Grimm, Certified Paralegal

BRADFORD PUBLISHING COMPANY
Denver, Colorado

DISCLAIMER

This book is intended to provide general information with regard to the subject matter covered. It is not meant to provide legal opinions or to offer advice, nor to serve as a substitute for advice by licensed, legal, or other professionals. This book is sold with the understanding that Bradford Publishing Company and the authors, by virtue of its publication, are not engaged in rendering legal or other professional services to the reader.

Bradford Publishing Company and the authors do not warrant that the information contained in this book is complete or accurate, and do not assume and hereby disclaim any liability to any person for any loss or damage caused by errors, inaccuracies or omissions, or usage of this book.

Laws, and interpretations of those laws, change frequently, and the subject matter of this book can have important legal consequences that may vary from one individual to the next. It is therefore the responsibility of the reader to know whether, and to what extent, this information is applicable to his or her situation, and if necessary, to consult legal, tax, or other counsel.

Library of Congress Cataloging-in-Publication Data

Grimm, Victor M.
Landlord and tenant guide to Colorado residential leases and evictions / Victor M. Grimm, Denise E. Grimm. -- 4th ed.
p. cm.
Rev. ed. of: Landlord & tenant guide to Colorado evictions. 3rd ed. c2005.
Includes bibliographical references.
ISBN 978-1-932779-57-8
1. Eviction--Colorado--Popular works. 2. Landlord and tenant--Colorado--Popular works. I. Grimm, Denise E. II. Grimm, Victor M. Landlord & tenant guide to Colorado evictions. III. Title.

KFC1917. G75 2009
346.78804'34--dc22

2009018864

Bradford Publishing Company
1743 Wazee Street, Denver, Colorado 80202
www.bradfordpublishing.com

PREFACE TO FOURTH EDITION (2009)

It is with great pleasure that we present the fourth edition of the *Landlord and Tenant Guide to Colorado Residential Leases and Evictions*. It is our sincere hope that the tools contained in the book, such as the forms, law, and procedural explanations help litigants be more confident, prepared, and informed in their specific cases.

In this new edition, we have added residential lease forms and helpful discussion on important provisions to assist landlords and tenants in the leasing process. We also have included a very important new law effective as of September 2008, known as the Warranty of Habitability Law. This edition contains an extensive discussion of the law and key provisions that should be included in residential leases (available through Bradford Publishing Company) to account for the new law. This new edition also contains examples of new lease forms, which are now available through Bradford Publishing Company.

Over the last several years, the Colorado legislature has been increasingly active in passing new laws aimed at tempering the sometimes harsh realities of the eviction process. Some of these measures have been more successful than others, and even newer laws contain important measures for ensuring that Colorado housing is not only "fit for human habitation" (under the new Warranty of Habitability Law), but provides remedies for the tenant to procure this standard. A full understanding of the new and revised laws is essential to both landlord and tenant involved in the litigation process. This fourth edition of the book incorporates and explains these changes and discusses the new law. This edition also contains numerous references in the text to Internet sites, which may prove a quite helpful supplement to other resources. A list of helpful websites is also now provided in the Appendix.

We trust that this book will continue to serve as a valuable guide for both the general public and legal professionals for many years to come.

Victor M. Grimm and
Denise E. Grimm

May 2009

Table of Contents

Introduction

"Landlord" . . . "Tenant" . . . "Eviction." These terms bring to mind colorful stereotypes of events and characters from our collective consciousness. A "Landlord" is imagined as a slimy-looking man with a pencil moustache, black cape and top hat, leering at the young widow demanding "You must pay the rent!" The archetypal "tenant" takes on one of two forms: (1) the hapless share-cropper, living in poverty and working 10-hour days, seven days a week, to pay the wealthy landowner the inflated annual rent on his run-down shack and square of infertile crop land; or (2) the sadistic societal leach who, after making outrageous demands for special treatment from the landlord (e.g., "The heat must remain at 85 degrees," "Fix my leaking faucet tonight, even if it is 2:00 a.m.!"), fails to pay rent, draws out eviction litigation for six months, leaves the apartment trashed, and then goes on to find his next unsuspecting victim. See the 1991 movie, *Pacific Heights*, for instance.

Unfortunately, these stereotypes also carry over into much of the legal literature on the subject. There is almost no end to the articles, seminars, and books directed at attorneys and real estate professionals focusing on leases and evictions "from the landlord's perspective," i.e., how-to throw the deadbeat out. Less common, but also present, are "Tenants' Rights Advocates" perspectives replete with shining armor and white horses. Many of these writings take an unbalanced approach, presenting only the landlord's or tenant's legal arguments. These two extremes were also evidenced in the lobbying and legislative process involved in the "Warranty of Habitability" law, which was recently enacted in Colorado. This book attempts to be a value-neutral guide for both the landlord and tenant involved in a leasing transaction or an eviction proceeding.

In Colorado there is no technical legal proceeding called an "eviction." Rather, the legal procedure under which a landlord regains possession of leased premises from a tenant is called an action for "unlawful detainer." This is a civil court action brought pursuant to Colorado's Forcible Entry and Unlawful Detainer (FED) statute (§ 13-40-101 *et seq.*, C.R.S.). The FED statute also prohibits the forcible recapture of real property and addresses the procedures involving mortgagors and mortgagees, contract purchasers and vendors, trespassers and squatters. These procedures, although similar, are outside the scope of this book and will not be discussed here. The term "eviction" will be used throughout this book because it is less cumbersome and more recognizable than "action for unlawful detainer." But remember that none of the courts or legal forms officially use the term "eviction."

How to Use This Book

The first part of this book provides an overview of the residential leasing process. These chapters include examples of residential lease forms, a discussion of some key provisions important to the leasing parties, and an in-depth discussion of Colorado's new laws implying a "Warranty of Habitability" and other rights and responsibilities for landlords and tenants.

The second part of the book addresses the eviction process. For the landlord, this book sets out in chronological order the steps that must be undertaken to legally dispossess a tenant of the leased premises—from the initial default to the sheriff physically removing the tenant. At each step of the eviction process, the landlord must follow certain procedures to avoid violating any of the tenant's legal rights, and these procedures are outlined here. Scrupulous attention to these procedures not only safeguards the tenant's legal rights, but also assures a speedier resolution and reduces the chance that the judge will dismiss the landlord's case on a "technicality."

Tenants facing an eviction are strongly encouraged to read not only the section on tenants' defenses, but also the section on the procedures the landlord must follow to accomplish the eviction. Review the landlord's actions carefully in light of the law. At best, an omission by a landlord may be a complete defense to the eviction action; at worst, it provides a basis for asking the judge for more time in which to negotiate with the landlord. Additionally, the section on tenants' defenses contains procedural and substantive information on how to oppose an eviction as well as a brief discussion on the other legal actions a tenant may file, including security deposit actions. The section on tenants' defenses should also help landlords understand what rights Colorado law gives to tenants and what defenses landlords might face in court.

The third part of this book addresses ancillary issues germane to residential leases including security deposits, domestic violence matters, and other special circumstances.

Forms

Many of the forms provided in this book may be used for either county or district court. County court deals with claims under $15,000, and it is where most residential eviction actions are heard. Thus, the examples contained in this book are for county court. All of the forms referred to in this book are printed by Bradford Publishing Company, 1743 Wazee Street, Denver, Colorado 80202, 303-292-2590. Blank forms are available from Bradford Publishing Company at its retail store or they may be purchased online for immediate downloading and use. Simply go to *www.bradfordpublishing.com*, where you can search by form number or name. A complete list of the form titles and identification numbers is included in the Appendix of this book. When ordering these forms, refer to the identification number (e.g., form number 235PA). Some Bradford forms are also available at local office supply stores.

Legal Citations

Legal citations to cases and articles are contained in endnotes. If additional explanation on an issue or support for an argument in court is required, the specific statute, case, or article may be obtained through your local law library. Almost every county in Colorado has one that is open to the public. Call your local county clerk of court for the specific location. Citations to statutory law—the Colorado Revised Statutes (C.R.S.) and the Colorado Rules of Civil Procedure (C.R.C.P.)—are contained in the endnotes. Most of these statutory citations are to the FED statute, which is officially codified as Sections 101 through 123, contained in Article 40 of Title 13 of the C.R.S. The FED statute and other relevant laws are reproduced in the Appendix of this book. These laws may also be found online at several sites. One of the easiest ways to access them is through the State of Colorado legislative website, www.leg.state.co.us.

A bibliography of sources relied on in the preparation of this book is also included in the Appendix. Parties needing further information on a particular subject are strongly urged to refer to these publications. This Appendix also includes a list of helpful websites.

Caution

This book is written so as to be comprehensible to non-lawyers. It may also be helpful to new attorneys, paralegals, and those attorneys who are in general practice or rarely represent parties in evictions. *This book should not be viewed as a substitute for professional consultation or representation in an eviction, but rather as a supplement.* Although a typical eviction is fairly straightforward, each case has its own unique set of facts, which may or may not be relevant to the case. A book such as this one, which covers general procedures, cannot address all contingencies and should not be expected to do so. We have attempted to give a good overview of the complete eviction process, but it is not an exhaustive treatise on the subject. Every possible factual scenario or legal issue that might arise in a landlord/tenant case could not be addressed here. Thus, if you are facing a situation beyond the scope of this book, please seek professional counsel at once. The law as it exists today is not necessarily the law of tomorrow. The law constantly changes as new cases and statutes expand, contract, or eliminate rights and issues.

It should be noted that this book does not address local county or municipal laws, which affect landlord/tenant relations (e.g., an ordinance exists in the City of Boulder requiring interest to be paid on security deposits). Nor does this book deal with federal laws or rules (e.g., laws that apply to the eviction of "Section 8" subsidized tenants; and bankruptcy laws). Finally, this book does not deal with mobile home park leases or evictions (see Mobile Home Park Act, §§ 38-12-200.1 *et seq.*, C.R.S.), which are quite different from evictions of a tenant residing in an apartment or house.

Chapter I. Overview of Leasing Procedures

A. Priority of Leases

The importance and priority of the written lease cannot be emphasized enough. In many instances where there is a conflict between the default provisions of the law and lease provisions, the lease will control. Therefore, before the landlord or tenant takes any type of action (such as filing a suit in court or starting eviction proceedings), *the lease should be reviewed for applicable provisions*. This is particularly important in regard to notice, security deposit, and rental liability issues. One very important exception to this statement relates to the statutory requirement to provide pre-litigation notices and imposition of minimal notice periods. Based on public policy grounds, courts will not permit waivers of such requests or reduction of minimum statutory time frames, even if explicitly set forth in the lease. Finally, Colorado law states that a lease cannot contain a waiver of any warranty of habitability or domestic violence protections because these protections are provided for by Colorado law. These protections are discussed in more detail in Chapters II and XV. Other than these types of exceptions, the terms of the lease provide the "outline" of the rights and responsibilities of the landlord and tenant and will generally be enforced by the courts. While Colorado law does not require a lease to be in writing unless the lease is for a period of more than one year,[1] almost all residential tenancies involve a written lease. And some local laws require written leases for residential tenancies, such as in the City of Boulder.[2] Always check your local laws.

Because the lease is considered a legally binding contract between the parties, it is essential that all parties read and understand the lease before signing it. It will not be an acceptable excuse in court that a signatory did not read a lease or that essential terms were not understood.[3] If there are important issues involving the tenancy, make sure they are addressed in the lease. For example, if a tenant wants to have a pet on the property this is the type of matter to address in the lease.

Most landlord/tenant transactions involve a formal pre-printed lease, but a lease can be as simple as a handwritten document specifying: (1) the parties' names; (2) the property to be leased; (3) the rights and responsibilities of the parties and terms and conditions of the agreement; (4) the rental amount; and (5) the signatures of the parties.[4]

B. Residence Lease Form (Form No. 1000)

Following is a blank residential lease, available from Bradford Publishing Company, as well as an example of a completed lease and an explanation of the key provisions of the lease to guide you in drafting the lease provisions. Remember to consult with an attorney if you have questions or if special situations arise that are not addressed in this book.

The form below is a standard residential lease. Note that several other residential lease forms are available from Bradford Publishing that are tailored to specific rental situations, including an Apartment Lease (Form No. 1001), a Condominium Lease (Form No. 1002), and two month-to-month leases (Form Nos. 757 and 1041).

EXHIBIT A (Form No. 1000)

THIS LEASE HAS IMPORTANT LEGAL CONSEQUENCES.
THE PARTIES SHOULD CONSULT LEGAL COUNSEL BEFORE SIGNING.

RESIDENCE LEASE

This Residence Lease (the "**Lease**") is made on ______❶______________ (date) and is entered into by and between Landlord (as defined below) and Tenant (as defined below). In consideration of the payment of the Rent (as defined below), other monies due the Landlord ("**Additional Rent**"), and the performance of the promises by Tenant set forth below, Landlord leases to Tenant, and Tenant accepts, the Premises described below, subject to the terms and provisions set forth in the Lease. This Lease shall be deemed to be a Rental Agreement as such term is employed in the Colorado Revised Statutes (the "**Rental Agreement**.")

PARTIES, PREMISES, AND DEFINED TERMS

1. **Landlord:** ____❷____,
a(n) ________________________________ [*Individual, Company or Type of Entity*], (the "**Landlord**").

2. **Tenants/Occupancy:** 1) ______❸__________________; 2) __________________________;
3) ____________________________________; and 4) ______________________________;
[*identify all occupants of the Premises over the age of 18*] are persons entitled under to occupy the Dwelling Unit to the exclusion of others (collectively referred to in the Lease as the "**Tenant**"). A maximum of ___❹___ people shall occupy the Premises.

3. **Premises:** The following described property situated in _______❺______________________
____________________________________, [*insert city and county*] State of Colorado, with the address of
____ [*insert street address*] described as follows:
Lot __❻________, Block ____________, ________________________________ (the "**Premises**").
The Lease ☐ includes ☐ excludes parking, specifically: Parking/Garage Space ___❼___ (the "**Parking Space**").

4. **Term:** Landlord leases the Premises to Tenant from twelve o'clock noon on the ____❽____ day of ________________, 20_____, and until 11:59 p.m. on the ___❾____ day of ______________, 20_____ (the "**Term**"). Subject to Tenant's performance of all obligations under the Lease, including without limitation, payment of Rent and other amounts, Tenant shall enjoy quiet possession of the Premises.

5. **Rent:** Rental for the entire Term is _______❿___________________________ and _____/100 Dollars ($___________) and shall be paid in monthly installments of _______⓫__________________ and _____/100 Dollars ($___________) payable in advance, on or before twelve o'clock noon on the first day of each calendar month during the term of the Lease at the location set forth below, without notice (the "**Rent**"). Unless otherwise provided in the Lease, all payments must be mailed or delivered to Landlord (or Landlord's property management company, as the case may be) at the following address:
____⓬____.

If the Term does not begin on the first day of the month, the Rent will be prorated accordingly.

6. **Security Deposit:** Before occupying the Premises, Tenant must deposit with Landlord a security, cleaning and damage deposit in the amount of _______⓭___________________________ and _____/100 Dollars ($___________) (including Pet Damage Deposit, if applicable, as defined below) as security for the return of the Premises at the expiration of the Term in as good condition as when Tenant entered the Premises, normal wear and tear excepted, as well as the faithful, timely and complete performance of all other terms, conditions and covenants of the Lease (the "**Security Deposit**").

No. 1000. Rev. 9-08. RESIDENCE LEASE © 2007 (Page 1 of 10) Initials: ______________ ______________
Landlord Tenant

Bradford Publishing, 1743 Wazee St., Denver, CO 80202 — (303) 292-2590 — www.bradfordpublishing.com

7. **Colorado Revised Statutes Definitions:** The Colorado Warranty of Habitability Law, codified at § 38-12-501 *et seq.*, C.R.S., contains the following definitions which may be applicable in conjunction with certain rights and responsibilities imposed by the law: Dwelling Unit is the structure, or the part of the structure, that is used as the home, residence, or sleeping place by Tenant (the "**Dwelling Unit**"). Common areas are the facilities and appurtenances to a Residential Premises, including the grounds, areas, and facilities held out for the use of tenants generally or whose use is promised to Tenant (the "**Common Areas**"). Residential Premises means the Dwelling Unit, the structure of which the unit is a part and the Common Areas (the "**Residential Premises**").

14 8. **Utilities:** Tenant shall be responsible for paying the following utilities, which charges shall be deemed Additional Rent: ☐ Electric ☐ Gas ☐ Water ☐ Sewer ☐ Phone ☐ Cable/Satellite T.V. ☐ Internet Access ☐ Refuse Disposal ☐ Other ____.
If the Premises shares meter facilities for utilities, the charges will be allocated to each by Landlord based on a reasonable basis and shall be considered Additional Rent. If Tenant fails to timely pay any of the above charges, it shall be deemed a Default by Tenant. If separate arrangements are made for Tenant to provide its own utilities directly from the respective service provider, then Landlord shall have no liability therefore. Landlord shall be responsible for any remaining utilities not specifically designated to be paid by Tenant.

9. **Late Payments:** If any rental installment or other payment is received later than ___15___ days after the date when due, the parties agree that Additional Rent in the amount of ☐ $___16___ or ☐ ________ percent (______%) of the outstanding sums, shall also be due and payable. The foregoing items shall be deemed Additional Rent.

10. **Repairs and Maintenance of the Premises:** The Tenant shall be responsible for maintenance of the Premises as described further in the Lease. The Landlord shall be responsible for maintenance and repair of the Premises as described further in the Lease. However, in the event that the parties agree that Tenant shall be responsible for some or all of the repairs and/or some or all of the maintenance beyond that set forth in the Lease, then the parties shall execute a separate writing consistent with the requirements of The Colorado Warranty of Habitability Law, codified at § 38-12-501 *et seq.*, C.R.S indicating such agreement. Such separate writing may be appended to this Lease as an addendum.

11. **Pets:** Pets ☐ are ☐ are not permitted on the Premises. If pets are permitted, they are limited to (number and type of pets) ___17____,
and Tenant must deposit an additional Pet Damage Deposit of $___18___ with Landlord before arrival of pet.

PREMISES

12. **Common Areas/Governing Documents:** If the Premises includes any common areas with any other properties that are subject to any declarations, covenants, conditions, or restrictions by any governing documents (the "**Governing Documents**") pertaining to the Premises, Tenant is granted a license to use those areas on the terms and conditions contained in such governing documents. All use of the Common Areas is at the sole risk of Tenant and Landlord will not be held liable for any damages or injuries occasioned by such use.

13. **Parking:** If parking is available and included on or adjacent to the Premises, the parties understand and agree that the Lease establishes a license to use the Premises for parking for Tenant's motor vehicles. All motor vehicles must be properly licensed and insured. No inoperative, stored, or "junked" motor vehicles are permitted. Landlord may cause removal of all motor vehicles or personal property not authorized or permitted, including those left on the Premises or designated Common Areas after expiration or termination of the Lease or Term. Tenant agrees to comply with any parking requirements and restrictions specified in any Governing Documents or rules and regulations governing the Premises.

14. **Check-In Inspection, Condition of Premises and Representations:** Landlord and Tenant may conduct an inspection of the Premises at the time of possession. A check-in inspection sheet may be completed at that time and the information contained in it will be sufficient and satisfactory proof of the condition of the Premises at the time of possession should a subsequent dispute arise. All systems and appliances on the Premises, including refrigerators, stoves, microwaves, dishwashers, washers, dryers, etc., will be in working condition at the commencement of the Term, unless specifically noted to the contrary on the check-in inspection sheet. As of the commencement of the Lease, Tenant acknowledges that Tenant has examined the Premises and is satisfied with the condition of the Premises, including all systems and appliances on the Premises. Taking possession of the Premises is conclusive evidence to the fact that the Premises are in good order and satisfactory condition.

Initials: ______________ ______________
Landlord Tenant

15. **Use of Premises:** Where used in this Paragraph 15, Premises includes any Common Areas and Tenant includes Tenant's licensees and invitees.

a. **Occupancy of Premises:** Tenant represents and warrants that Tenant has identified all of the individuals over the age of 18 who will occupy the Premises in Paragraph 2 of the Lease and that the Premises are to be used only as a private residence for those individuals. Landlord must approve any change to those listed as Tenants in the Lease. If Tenant desires any change or increase to those shown as Tenants in the Lease, and provided any increase is not in violation of applicable occupancy codes, those individuals desiring tenancy must complete any application and approval process required by Landlord, in advance of any change, and after Landlord's approval must execute a new Lease. If Tenant fails to obtain Landlord's approval in advance of any change in occupancy, Tenant understands that this failure constitutes a Default as described in the Lease. Landlord represents and warrants that it has obtained any rental licenses as may be required in the city or county in which the Premises are located.

b. **Legal Compliance:** Tenant is liable for the actions of Tenant's licensees and invitees. Tenant agrees to comply with and abide by all federal, state, county and municipal laws and ordinances, and any Governing Documents, if applicable, in connection with the occupancy and use of the Premises. No alcoholic beverages shall be possessed or consumed by Tenant, or Tenant's licensees or invitees, unless the person possessing or consuming alcohol is of legal age. No illegal drugs or controlled substances (unless specifically prescribed by a physician for a specific person residing or present on the Premises) are permitted on the Premises. Tenant agrees to refrain from using the Premises in any way that may result in an increase of the rate or cost of insurance on the Premises. No hazardous or dangerous activities are permitted on the Premises.

c. **Rules and Regulations:** Landlord shall provide Tenant with a copy of all rules and regulations, if any, affecting the Premises, to which Tenant agrees to abide.

d. **Safety:** Tenant must not use the Premises in a manner that may endanger the person or property of Landlord, co-tenants, or any person living on or near the Premises. Tenant agrees to limit use of the Premises to those consistent with the Premises' clean, safe, sanitary, and habitable condition.

e. **Nuisance Prohibited:** Neither Tenant nor Tenant's licensees or invitees shall be a nuisance or act in any manner that would interfere with the quiet enjoyment by adjacent property owners or other tenants (or their invitees) of their premises. This prohibition includes, but is not limited to, loud noises, loud music, noxious or unpleasant odors, and disruptive behavior or actions.

16. **Check-Out Procedure:** The parties may, at their discretion, conduct a check-out/walk-through of the Premises when, or immediately before, Tenant re-delivers the Premises at the end of the Term.

17. **Surrender of Premises:** Tenant will return the Premises to Landlord at the expiration of the Term in as good condition as when Tenant took possession of the Premises, normal wear and tear excepted. Any deterioration or damage caused by accident, abuse, carelessness, or negligence shall not be considered normal wear and tear. If Tenant fails to re-deliver the Premises in appropriate condition, Landlord may restore the Premises to appropriate condition, including repair, replacement and cleaning. The cost of any work necessitated will be deducted from the Security Deposit, and if the Security Deposit is insufficient to cover work performed, Tenant will be obliged to pay the additional balance.

18. **Subletting or Assignment:** Tenant shall neither sublet any part of the Premises nor assign the Lease, nor any interest in the Lease, without Landlord's prior written consent. Consent to a sublease or assignment shall be in the sole and absolute discretion of Landlord.

PAYMENTS

19. **Payments/Dishonored Checks:** Payments shall be deemed received when actually delivered to, and received by, Landlord at the payment location. Dishonored checks and any checks received late in the mail will be treated as late payments. Any additional bank and handling charges that are assessed in the event of a dishonored check shall be deemed Additional Rent. Landlord may require Tenant to replace any dishonored check with a money order, cashier's check, or other good funds. Landlord may further require that all subsequent payments after a dishonored check be paid with a money order, cashier's check, or other good funds.

20. **Partial Payment:** Any partial payment made by Tenant will be allocated first to the payment of Additional Rent, including, without limitation, utilities (if applicable) and other expenses, and second to unpaid Rent. Landlord's acceptance of any partial payment does not waive Landlord's right to require immediate payment

of the unpaid balance of Rent, or waive or affect Landlord's rights to institute legal proceedings including, without limitation, an eviction action.

21. **No Offset:** No assent, express or implied, to any Default of any one or more of the agreements in the Lease will be deemed or taken to be a waiver of any succeeding or other Default. The covenants set forth in the Lease are independent. Tenant shall have no right to withhold or set off any Rent due Landlord.

22. **Joint and Several Obligations of Tenant:** If more than one person comprises Tenant, it is expressly understood and agreed that each person comprising Tenant is jointly and severally liable for any and all obligations of Tenant in the Lease. This means that each and every person comprising Tenant are each, together and separately, responsible for all of Tenant's obligations. Landlord may, at its option, determine who to hold responsible.

SECURITY DEPOSIT

23. **Retention or Return of Security Deposit:** Landlord shall abide by any applicable laws or ordinances requiring interest to be paid on the Security Deposit. Landlord may retain the Security Deposit for nonpayment of Rent or Additional Rent, repair of the Premises or Common Areas, replacement of damaged or missing items on the Premises or Common Areas, and/or cleaning of the Premises or Common Areas beyond normal wear and tear incurred during the Term. Tenant may not elect to apply the Security Deposit as last month's rent. Any amount remaining from the Security Deposit, together with a written accounting for any portion retained, will be returned by mail to Tenant not more than sixty (60) days after expiration of the Term. Landlord shall mail the return or accounting to Tenant's last known address. If Tenant consists of more than one person, Tenant agrees that Landlord may provide, at Landlord's discretion, the return or accounting to one representative of Tenant or pro-rata refunds to each person.

24. **Restoration of Balance of Security Deposit:** Landlord has the right at any time, but not the obligation, to apply all or any part of the Security Deposit toward curing any Default of Tenant during the Term. If Landlord does so apply the Security Deposit, Tenant must immediately deposit with Landlord an amount equal to the amount applied so that Tenant will at all times have on deposit with Landlord the entire Security Deposit.

REPAIRS AND MAINTENANCE

25. **Tenant's Maintenance of the Premises:** In addition to the duties imposed upon Tenant by this Lease, The Colorado Warranty of Habitability Law, codified at § 38-12-501 *et seq.*, C.R.S., requires the following: Tenant has a duty to use that portion of the Premises within Tenant's control in a reasonably clean and safe manner. Tenant fails to maintain the Premises in a reasonably clean and safe manner when the Tenant substantially fails to:

a. Comply with obligations imposed upon Tenant by applicable provisions of building, health, and housing codes materially affecting health and safety;

b. Keep the Dwelling Unit reasonably clean, safe, and sanitary as permitted by the conditions of the unit;

c. Dispose of ashes, garbage, rubbish, and other waste from the Dwelling Unit in a clean, safe, sanitary, and legally compliant manner;

d. Use in a reasonable manner all electrical, plumbing, sanitary, heating, ventilating, air-conditioning, elevators, and other facilities and appliances in the Dwelling Unit;

e. Conduct himself or herself and require other persons in the Residential Premises within the Tenant's control to conduct themselves in a manner that does not disturb their neighbors' peaceful enjoyment of the neighbors' Dwelling Unit; or

f. Promptly notify Landlord if the Residential Premises is uninhabitable as defined in the Colorado Revised Statutes or if there is a condition that could result in the Premises becoming uninhabitable if not remedied.

In addition to the duties set forth in the above paragraph, Tenant shall not knowingly, intentionally, deliberately, or negligently destroy, deface, damage, impair, or remove any part of the Residential Premises or knowingly permit any person within Tenant's control to do so. Nothing in the above paragraph shall be construed to authorize a modification of Landlord's obligations under the Colorado Warranty of Habitability Law, codified at § 38-12-501 *et seq.*, C.R.S.

26. **Tenant's Notification, Restrictions, and Additional Responsibilities:** Except as may otherwise be permitted by applicable law, Tenant shall not perform or contract with third parties to perform any repairs of any

kind on the Premises or structure on which the Premises are located without the written consent of Landlord. If any repair which is the responsibility of either Tenant or Landlord becomes necessary, Tenant must notify Landlord, in writing, as soon as possible and allow reasonable time for the work to be completed. Any unauthorized work performed or contracted for by Tenant will be at Tenant's sole expense and no deductions or offsets in Rent or Additional Rent shall be permitted except to the extent explicitly permitted by the Colorado Warranty of Habitability Law, codified at § 38-12-501 *et seq.*, C.R.S.

a. **Painting/Decorating:** Tenant shall not paint the Premises or Common Areas without Landlord's prior written consent. Tenant shall not otherwise decorate or deface the Premises or Common Areas in a manner that causes damage or alteration to the Premises or Common Areas.

b. **Plumbing/Building Systems:** Tenant shall be responsible for any and all damage to the plumbing, HVAC and electrical systems caused by Tenant's intentional, reckless or negligent use, misconduct or abuse. Such actions include, without limitation, clogging and backing up of plumbing not attributable to ordinary wear and tear of the plumbing system, and plumbing system freeze-ups occasioned by Tenant's negligence.

c. **Keys/Locks:** Tenant shall not place any additional locks on the Premises, including, but not limited to, exterior and interior doors. Tenant shall not cause any of the locks or cylinders in the locks to be changed or re-keyed in any manner.

d. **Cleanliness of Premises:** Tenant must keep the Premises and the real property surrounding the Premises free and clear of all debris, garbage and rubbish.

27. **Landlord's Maintenance and Repair of the Premises:** Landlord shall be responsible for the maintenance and repair of all structural components, interior and exterior walls, floors, ceiling, roofs, sewer connections, plumbing, wiring, appliances and glass used in connection with the Premises. More specifically, (i) any repairs, replacements, restorations, or maintenance that have been necessitated by reason of ordinary wear and tear; (ii) any repairs, replacements, restorations, or maintenance that have been necessitated by sudden natural forces or acts of God, or by fire not caused by Tenant; and (iii) any repairs, improvements or maintenance that are required by applicable state and municipal rental housing codes that govern the area in which the Premises are located, including, *inter alia*, the Colorado Warranty of Habitability as set forth in § 38-12-501 *et seq.*, C.R.S. Notwithstanding the foregoing provisions of the Lease, if repairs, replacements, restorations, or maintenance have been necessitated by any other reason including, without limitation, Tenant's intentional, reckless or negligent use, misconduct or abuse of the Premises, improvements or systems then Tenant shall be responsible for the cost and expense for repairs, improvements or maintenance occasioned by such acts or omissions. In the event the parties agree in a separate writing to the contrary as specified herein for the Tenant to be responsible for certain repairs and maintenance beyond those articulated to be the Tenant's responsibility in the paragraph above, then the responsibilities of the Landlord, as set forth in this paragraph, shall be modified accordingly.

DEFAULT, NOTICE AND REMEDIES

28. **Default:** If Tenant is in arrears in the payment of any installment of Rent, any Additional Rent, or in violation of any other covenants or agreements set forth in the Lease (a "**Default**") and the Default remains uncorrected for a period of three (3) days after Landlord has given written notice of the Default to Tenant pursuant to applicable law, then Landlord may, at Landlord's option, undertake any of the following remedies without limitation: (i) declare the Term of the Lease ended; (ii) terminate Tenant's right to possession of the Premises and re-enter and repossess the Premises pursuant to applicable provisions of the Colorado Forcible Entry and Unlawful Detainer statute; (iii) recover all present and future damages, costs and other relief to which Landlord is entitled; (iv) pursue Landlord's lien remedies; (v) pursue breach of contract remedies; and/or (vi) pursue any and all available remedies in law or equity. If possession is terminated by reason of a Default before the Term expires, Tenant shall still be responsible for the Rent and Additional Rent occurring for the remainder of the Term, subject to Landlord's duty to mitigate such damages. Pursuant to §§ 13-40-104 (d.5) and (e.5), and 13-40-107.5, C.R.S., hereby incorporated by reference, if repeated or substantial Default(s) occur under the Lease, Landlord may terminate Tenant's possession upon a written Notice to Quit, without a right to cure. Upon such termination, Landlord shall have available any and all of the above-listed remedies.

29. **Abandonment:** If Tenant abandons the Premises, then Landlord may, without being obligated to do so and without terminating the Lease, retake possession of the Premises and exercise any of the remedies contained in Paragraph 30 below.

Initials: ______________ ______________
Landlord Tenant

30. **Re-Entry:** If Landlord re-enters the Premises as a result of abandonment or a Default by Tenant:

a. Tenant shall be liable for damages to Landlord for all loss sustained, including, without limitation, the balance of the Rent and Additional Rent, court costs and reasonable attorneys' fees; and

b. Tenant's personal property and the personal property of any guest, invitee, licensee or occupant may be removed from the Premises and left on the street or alley or, at Landlord's option, it may be removed and stored or disposed of at Landlord's sole discretion. Any expense related to storage of Tenant's personal property is the sole responsibility of Tenant. Landlord shall not be deemed a bailee of the removed property, and Landlord shall not be held liable for either civil or criminal action as a result of the removal. Tenant shall indemnify Landlord for any expense in defending against any claim by Tenant or third-party and for any legal expense, cost, fine or judgment awarded to any third-party as a result of Landlord's action under the term of the Lease; and

c. Landlord may attempt to re-let the Premises for such rent and under such terms as Landlord believes appropriate; and

d. Landlord may enter the Premises, clean and make repairs and charge Tenant accordingly; and

e. any money that Landlord receives from Tenant shall be applied first to Rent, Additional Rent, and other payments due; and

f. Tenant will surrender all keys and peacefully surrender and deliver up possession of the Premises.

31. **Breach of Warranty of Habitability:** In the event of a breach of the Warranty of Habitability (as further defined in Paragraph 49 of this Lease) the parties are advised to refer with the Colorado Warranty of Habitability Law, codified at § 38-12-501 *et seq.*, C.R.S. for further requirements, responsibilities and remedies.

ADDITIONAL PROVISIONS

32. **Liability Indemnification/Waiver:** Tenant shall save Landlord harmless and indemnified from all injury, loss, claim or damage to any person or property while on the Premises, or arising in any way out of Tenant's use of the Premises. Landlord and Landlord's agents, contractors, and employees shall not be liable for, and Tenant waives all claims for, damage to person or property sustained by Tenant, resulting from any accident or occurrence in or on the Premises, including, but not limited to, claims for damage resulting from: (i) any equipment or appurtenances becoming out of repair; (ii) Landlord's failure to keep the Premises in repair; (iii) injury done or occasioned by wind, water, or other natural element; (iv) any defect in, or failure of, plumbing, heating or air-conditioning equipment (including wood stoves), electric wiring or installation thereof, gas, water and steam pipes, stairs, porches, railings or walks; (v) broken glass; (vi) the backing-up of any sewer pipe or downspout; (vii) the bursting, leaking or running of any tank, tub, sink, sprinkler system, water closet, waste pipe, drain or any other pipe or tank in, on or about the Premises; (viii) the escape of steam or hot water; (ix) water, snow, or ice being on or coming through the roof, skylight, doors, stairs, walks, or any other place on or near the Premises; (x) the falling of any fixtures, plaster or stucco; (xi) fire or other casualty; (xii) any act, omission or negligence of co-tenants or of other persons or occupants of the Premises; and (xiii) any hazardous materials or conditions on the Premises. Where used in this Paragraph: (a) Premises includes any Common Areas, structures on any Common Areas, and any adjacent property; (b) Landlord includes Landlord's agents, respective successors and assigns, contractors, and employees; and (c) Tenant includes Tenant's invitees, licensees, or any other person claiming through Tenant. Nothing contained herein shall be deemed to constitute a waiver of any rights, responsibilities or remedies as may be explicitly imposed by the Colorado Warranty of Habitability Law, codified at § 38-12-501 *et seq.*, C.R.S.

33. **Insurance:** Landlord, in its sole discretion and for its sole benefit, shall cause the Premises to be insured as it deems appropriate. Tenant shall have no right or claim to any insurance or insurance proceeds. Tenant understands and agrees that Landlord has no obligation to obtain insurance for Tenant including, but not limited to, liability, hazard, or contents insurance. If Tenant desires insurance, Tenant is advised to obtain renter's insurance at Tenant's sole cost and expense, and for Tenant's sole benefit.

34. **Destruction or Condemnation of Premises:** Landlord's and Tenant's duties and responsibilities are as follows when destruction or condemnation of the Premises occurs:

a. **Partial Destruction of the Premises:** In case of partial destruction to the Premises by fire, the elements, or other casualty, Landlord, at its discretion, may repair the Premises with reasonable dispatch after notice of the partial destruction. Tenant shall still be responsible for payment of Rent. If Landlord determines that the partial destruction may not be repaired, Subparagraph (d) of this Paragraph shall be effective.

b. **Premises Untenable:** If the Premises are made totally untenable by fire, the elements or other casualty, or if the building in which the Premises are located is partially destroyed to the point where Landlord, within a reasonable time, decides not to rebuild or repair, then Subparagraph (d) of this Paragraph shall be effective.

c. **Condemnation:** If the whole or part of the Premises rented under the Lease are taken by any authority for any public or quasi-public use or purpose, then Subparagraph (d) of this Paragraph shall be effective. All damages and compensation awarded for any taking shall be the sole property of Landlord.

d. **Termination of Term:** Tenant agrees that if Landlord decides not to repair or rebuild the Premises where the destruction has occurred as described in Subparagraphs (a) and (b) of this Paragraph, the Term granted by the Lease will cease and the Rent and Additional Rent will be prorated and payable up to the time of the cessation of the Term. A refund will be given for the balance of any Rent paid in advance for which Tenant did not have use of the Premises due to the cessation of the Term under the conditions of this clause. Where the Premises have been taken due to condemnation as described in Subparagraph (c) of this Paragraph, the Term of the Lease will cease and terminate on the date that possession of the Premises is taken by the authority. Rent and Additional Rent will be prorated and payable up to the time of the cessation of the Term. Tenant shall not hold Landlord liable for any damages as a result of any of the acts or events described in this Subparagraph.

35. **Holdover:** Tenant must vacate the Premises and remove all of Tenant's personal property from the Premises before 11:59 p.m. on the date the Term expires. Landlord may immediately commence eviction proceedings at its sole discretion. If, after the Lease expires, Tenant remains in possession of the Premises and continues to pay Rent without a written agreement as to possession, then the tenancy will be regarded as a month-to-month tenancy, at a monthly rental, payable in advance, equivalent to the last month's Rent paid under the Lease, and subject to all the terms and conditions of the Lease.

36. **Entry by Landlord:** Landlord may enter the Premises at reasonable hours for reasonable purposes (such as repairs, inspections or re-letting to prospective new tenants), after giving reasonable notice to Tenant. Landlord may also enter the Premises in the event of an emergency, without notice, or in the event of vacancy of the Premises, as described in Paragraph 30.

37. **Guarantor:** If the Lease is guaranteed, the person(s) guaranteeing the Lease ("**Guarantor**") absolutely guarantees Tenant's obligations and performance under the Lease. Guarantor further agrees to be bound by the same covenants and conditions of the Lease and makes the same warranties and representations as Tenant under the Lease. If Tenant defaults in the performance of Tenant's obligations under the Lease, Guarantor will perform Tenant's obligations.

38. **Subordination:** The Lease is subordinate to all existing and future mortgages, deeds of trust and other security interests on the Premises.

39. **Notices:** All notices required to be sent under the Lease must be in writing and either be: (i) delivered as provided by applicable law, including *inter alia*, §§ 13-40-101, C.R.S., *et seq.* [Colorado Forcible Entry and Unlawful Detainer statute]; (ii) personally delivered, with proper proof of service; or (iii) sent via U.S. first class mail, postage prepaid. All notices required to be sent to Landlord must be sent or delivered to the address where the Rent is to be paid, and all notices required to be sent to Tenant must be sent or delivered to the Premises, unless otherwise specified. Notwithstanding the foregoing, all notices involving or concerning §§ 13-40-101 *et seq.*, C.R.S., and § 38-12-501 *et seq.*, C.R.S. must be delivered as provided in this law.

40. **Attorney Fees:** If either party fails to perform any of its obligations under the Lease, or if a dispute arises concerning the meaning or interpretation of any provision of the Lease, then the defaulting party or the party not prevailing in the dispute, as the case may be, must pay any and all costs and expenses incurred by the other party in enforcing or establishing its rights under the Lease, including, without limitation, court costs and reasonable attorney fees as per §13-40-123, C.R.S.

41. **Governing Law:** The Lease is governed by and construed in accordance with the laws of the State of Colorado. Venue is proper in the county in which the Premises are located.

42. **Amendments and Termination:** Unless otherwise provided in the Lease, the Lease may be amended, modified, or terminated only by a written instrument executed by Landlord and Tenant.

43. **Captions:** The Paragraph titles or captions in the Lease are for convenience only and shall not be deemed to be part of the Lease.

No. 1000. Rev. 9-08. RESIDENCE LEASE © 2007 (Page 7 of 10) Initials: ______________ ______________
Landlord Tenant

44. **Pronouns; Joint and Several Use of Certain Terms:** Whenever the terms referred to in the Lease are singular, the same shall be deemed to mean the plural, as the context indicates, and vice versa. All references to the "Landlord" mean Landlord and/or its authorized agents, contractors, or employees as may be required by the specific context. All references to "Tenant" mean each and every person comprising Tenant or an individual person or combination of persons comprising Tenant as may be required by the specific context.

45. **Waivers:** No right under the Lease may be waived except by written instrument executed by the party who is waiving that right. No waiver of any breach of any provision contained in the Lease shall be deemed a waiver of any preceding or succeeding breach of that provision or of any other provision contained in the Lease. No extension of time for performance of any obligations or acts shall be deemed an extension of the time for performance of any other obligations or acts.

46. **Severability:** If any term, covenant, condition, or provision of the Lease or the application thereof to any person or circumstance is found, at any time or to any extent, to be invalid or unenforceable, the remainder of the Lease, or the application of that term or provision to persons or circumstances other than those to which it is held invalid or unenforceable, shall not be affected thereby, and each provision of the Lease shall be valid and shall be enforced to the fullest extent permitted by law.

47. **Lead-Based Paint Disclosure Rule:** Housing built before 1978 may contain lead-based paint. Lead from paint, paint chips, and dust can pose health hazards if not managed properly. Lead exposure is especially harmful to young children and pregnant women. Before renting pre-1978 housing, landlords must disclose the presence of known lead-based paint and/or lead-based paint hazards in the dwelling. Tenant must also receive a federally approved pamphlet on lead poisoning prevention. If the Premises were constructed before 1978, Landlord must comply with the Lead-Based Paint Disclosure Rule, 42 U.S.C. § 4852(d).

48. **Other Applicable Laws:** Federal, state, county and/or municipal laws and ordinances, which are not specifically addressed in the Lease, may affect the Premises, the Lease and the Landlord/Tenant relationship. The Colorado Warranty of Habitability statute, codified at § 38-12-501 *et seq.*, C.R.S., contains explicit responsibilities and remedies for both the Landlord and Tenant concerning use, condition and occupancy of the Premises. Landlord and Tenant should consult legal counsel before executing the Lease to ascertain such information.

COLORADO WARRANTY OF HABITABILITY

49. **Colorado Warranty of Habitability Statute:** The Colorado Warranty of Habitability Law, codified at § 38-12-501 *et seq.*, C.R.S (the "**Warranty of Habitability**") imposes certain statutory obligations as to the condition of the Premises. As such, the Landlord hereby represents and warrants in this Lease, that the Residential Premises is fit for human habitation. Landlord shall be deemed to breach the aforementioned Warranty of Habitability in the event that:

a. The Residential Premises is uninhabitable as described in § 38-12-505, C.R.S., or otherwise unfit for human habitation; and

b. The Residential Premises is in a condition that is materially dangerous or hazardous to the Tenant's life, health, or safety; and

c. The Landlord has received written notice of the condition described in above and has failed to cure the problem within a reasonable time.

50. **Uninhabitable Residential Premises:** Section 38-12-505(1), C.R.S., provides that the Residential Premises is deemed uninhabitable if it substantially lacks any of the following characteristics:

a. Waterproofing and weather protection of roof and exterior walls maintained in good working order, including unbroken windows and doors;

b. Plumbing or gas facilities that conformed to applicable law in effect at the time of installation and that are maintained in good working order;

c. Running water and reasonable amounts of hot water at all times furnished to appropriate fixtures and connected to a sewage disposal system approved under applicable law;

d. Functioning heating facilities that conformed to applicable law at the time of installation and that are maintained in good working order;

e. Electrical lighting, with wiring and electrical equipment that conformed to applicable law at the time of installation, maintained in good working order;

f. Common areas and areas under the control of the Landlord that are kept reasonably clean, sanitary, and free from all accumulations of debris, filth, rubbish, and garbage and that have appropriate extermination in response to the infestation of rodents or vermin;

g. Appropriate extermination in response to the infestation of rodents or vermin throughout the Residential Premises;

h. An adequate number of appropriate exterior receptacles for garbage and rubbish, in good repair;

i. Floors, stairways, and railings maintained in good repair;

j. Locks on all exterior doors and locks or security devices on windows designed to be opened that are maintained in good working order; or

k. Compliance with all applicable building, housing, and health codes, which, if violated, would constitute a condition that is dangerous or hazardous to Tenant's life, health, or safety.

It is further understood that no deficiency in the Common Area shall render the Residential Premises uninhabitable as set forth in the Warranty of Habitability, unless it materially and substantially limits the Tenant's use of his or her Dwelling Unit. Notwithstanding the foregoing, when any condition described above is caused by misconduct of the Tenant, a member of the Tenant's household, a guest or invitee of the Tenant, or a person under the Tenant's direction or control, the condition shall not constitute a breach of the Warranty of Habitability. It shall not be misconduct by a victim of domestic violence or domestic abuse under § 38-12-503(3), C.R.S., if the condition is the result of domestic violence or domestic abuse and the Landlord has been given written notice and evidence of domestic violence or domestic abuse as described in § 38-12-402(2)(a), C.R.S.

19 51. **Opt-Out:** If the Dwelling Unit is contained within a mobile home park, or if the Dwelling Unit is contained in a structure where there are four or fewer dwelling units sharing common walls and are located on the same parcel of property and are owned by the same owner, or if the Dwelling Unit is a single-family residential premises, and the opt-out is not inconsistent with any obligations imposed upon the Landlord by a governmental entity for the receipt of a subsidy for the Premises, then the Warranty of Habitability Law provides that the parties may opt-out of certain maintenance obligations of the Landlord and provide that the Tenant shall undertake such maintenance obligations. Provided that the Dwelling Unit is located in a type of residential premises qualifying for such opt-out provisions, the parties hereby opt-out of the following items, which have been checked, and agree that the Tenant shall be responsible for same. In the event that no items are checked, then this opt-out provision shall not be applicable. The Tenant shall be responsible for maintenance of the following: ☐ Common areas and areas under the control of the Landlord that are kept reasonably clean, sanitary, and free from all accumulations of debris, filth, rubbish, and garbage and that have appropriate extermination in response to the infestation of rodents or vermin; ☐ Appropriate extermination in response to the infestation of rodents or vermin throughout the Residential Premises; and/or ☐ An adequate number of appropriate exterior receptacles for garbage and rubbish, in good repair.

52. **Additional Provisions:** If there are any additional agreements between the parties or provisions with respect to the Premises, an Addendum may be attached to the Lease, which will be incorporated by this reference as a part of the Lease. An Addendum containing additional provisions ☐ is ☐ is not attached.

Initials: ______________ ______________
Landlord Tenant

THE PARTIES SHOULD INITIAL EACH PAGE OF THE LEASE AND SIGN BELOW. EACH PARTY SHOULD RECEIVE A SIGNED COPY OF THE LEASE AND ANY ADDENDA.

TENANT:

20 ______________________
Signature

21 ______________________
Print Name

Date: 22 ______________________

20 ______________________
Signature

21 ______________________
Print Name

Date: 22 ______________________

20 ______________________
Signature

21 ______________________
Print Name

Date: 22 ______________________

20 ______________________
Signature

21 ______________________
Print Name

Date: 22 ______________________

GUARANTOR **(if applicable):**

29 ______________________
Signature

30 ______________________
Print Name

Date: 31 ______________________

LANDLORD:

AN ENTITY:

23 ______________________, a(n)

24 ______________________
Type of Entity

By: 25 ______________________
Signature

26 ______________________
Print Name

Its: 27 ______________________

Date: 28 ______________________

Or **AN INDIVIDUAL:**

25 ______________________
Signature

26 ______________________
Print Name

Date: 28 ______________________

C. Instructions for Filling Out the Residence Lease (Form No. 1000)

The blank Residence Lease form (Exhibit A) provided above was drafted by the authors and is available through Bradford Publishing Company for use in standard residential circumstances. For apartments and condominiums specifically, please refer to Bradford Publishing Company for these additional forms. However, the Residence Lease may be used for all residential situations. Other documents (addenda), as referenced and further explained in the lease, may be attached to the lease and will become a part of the lease. An example of a completed Residence Lease (Exhibit B) is provided below for additional guidance.

Blank 1: Insert the date the parties are signing the lease.

Blank 2: Insert the landlord's name – if the landlord is a corporation, limited liability company, partnership, or other business entity, please specify the type of business entity. If the landlord is an individual (or several individuals), indicate that.

Blank 3: Insert the names of all tenants, as shown.

Blank 4: Insert the maximum number of tenants to occupy the premises. Note that certain municipalities have maximum occupancy laws; therefore, it is advisable to consult with the respective municipality to make sure the lease complies with local law.

Blank 5: Insert the city, county, and street address of the property to be leased.

Blank 6: Insert the legal description of the property to be leased.

Blank 7: Insert the parking space number, if applicable.

Blank 8: Insert the date the lease will begin (commence).

Blank 9: Insert the date the lease will end (terminate).

Blank 10: Insert the dollar amount of the annual rent (12 monthly payments x monthly amount).

Blank 11: Insert the dollar amount of the monthly payments.

Blank 12: Insert the address where the tenant or tenants are to send the rent payments.

Blank 13: Insert the amount of the security deposit, if any, including any pet damage deposit being requested. Please note that certain municipalities may require interest to be paid on the security deposit. It is therefore advisable to consult with the respective municipality to make sure the lease complies with local law.

Blank 14: Check off all the utilities for which the tenant will be responsible to pay, as applicable.

Blank 15: Insert the number of days after which the rent will be deemed late (the "grace period"). Five days is a typically reasonable time period for the grace period, but the parties are free to agree on the number of days.

Blank 16: Insert the dollar amount of the late fee tenant is required to pay if the rent is paid late, followed by the percentage of the rent this amount represents. Note that if the amount of the late fee is excessive, courts will typically disallow such award of late fees in the event of an eviction. A reasonable percentage is typically no more than five percent (5%) of the rent.

Blank 17: Choose whether or not pets will be allowed on the premises; include the type and number of pets. If the type or number is to be determined but the parties wish to allow for pets, this should be also be noted—for example, *two dogs not to exceed fifty pounds each.*

Blank 18: Insert the amount of the pet damage deposit required, if it is being requested.

Blank 19: Read Chapter II, J, for a description of the Opt-Out provisions of the Act before making a selection in #51.

Blank 20: This is the line on which the tenant signs the lease.

Blank 21: Insert the tenant's name.

Blank 22: Insert the date of the tenant's signature.

Blank 23: Insert the landlord's name.

Blank 24: If the landlord is a business entity, specify the type of entity (corporation, limited liability company, partnership). If the landlord is an individual, use the next line as shown for an individual's signature.

Blank 25: This is the line on which the landlord signs the lease.

Blank 26: Insert the name of the person signing the lease on behalf of the landlord.

Blank 27: Insert the title of the person signing the lease on behalf of the landlord.

Blank 28: Insert the date of the landlord's signature.

Blank 29: If a guarantor is signing the lease, the guarantor's signature should be placed in this blank. The landlord may request that a guarantor sign the lease to guarantee the tenant's payment of rent and the satisfaction of other lease obligations. For instance, tenants under the age of 21 may be asked to provide a guarantor.

Blank 30: Insert the guarantor's name, if applicable.

Blank 31: Insert the date the guarantor is signing the lease.

D. Important Lease Provisions to be Addressed

As discussed earlier, the lease is the agreement between the landlord and tenant that governs their relationship, and it plays an important role in the event of conflicts. While courts apply current statutory and case law to eviction and damage rulings, they will give deference to the terms of the respective lease because it reflects an agreement between the parties in addition to and in accordance with applicable law. The lease is therefore an important document.

1. Warranty of Habitability

As will be explained in more detail below, Colorado has recently enacted a new Warranty of Habitability Law, which affects all residential lease situations. The Residence Lease provided in this book contains an extensive discussion of the new law, as well as explicit requirements that the parties must follow in the event of a breach of the Warranty of Habitability. Please pay careful attention to this language throughout the lease, and review the section discussing this new law below.

2. Documentation of Condition of Premises at the Time of Occupancy and During the Tenancy

In the beginning of a tenancy, parties are typically in an amiable and friendly relationship, eager and enthusiastic about the tenancy, optimistic and hopeful that anything unspoken will be reasonably addressed in the future, trusting that all issues will iron themselves out as they arise. While many realities reveal this to be true, others do not, and the parties wind up in bitter disputes in court with a version of "he said–she said" stories. It is wise and sound business practice, for all parties involved, to document the condition of the premises at the time of occupancy, and to document in writing all issues arising during the course of the tenancy. Written documentation concerning the condition of the premises is useful because: (1) it will help clarify any verbal communications made between the parties during the tenancy; and (2) should the parties end up in court, it will provide the court with solid evidence of any issues and any communications between the parties, so the judge will not be forced to discern the credibility and veracity of the parties' various versions of events told through testimony. This practice will also be helpful in light of the new Warranty of Habitability Law. Readers should refer to Paragraph 14 of the Residence Lease to familiarize themselves with this inspection provision.

Videotaping, photographing, walk-through inspections (where all parties are present), or simply documenting the condition of the premises before the tenant takes occupancy will be helpful. Any damage to the property should also be documented. Plumbing leaks, roof collapses, mold occurrences, damaged carpet (a major source of contention in security deposit damage disputes), marred hardwood flooring, broken windows, missing door locks—all these types of damage should be documented and timely addressed before the tenant takes possession of the premises to prevent any future confusion. At the end of the tenancy, a walk-through inspection of the premises, with accompanying documentation, photographing or even videotaping (again, with all parties present) will also prove helpful in the event of a dispute over damage to the property or return of the security deposit.

3. Offsets

Many tenants are under a misconception that problems arising with the property may be handled by withholding rent from the landlord. This misperception not only leads to confusion and frustration for all parties involved, but often gives rise to eviction actions. Readers should refer to Paragraphs 21, 26 and 27 of the Residence Lease to familiarize themselves with this provision. Tenants are under a continuing obligation to pay rent regardless of any problems or circumstances that may arise. In situations where the Warranty of Habitability has been violated, a tenant must follow specific procedures and adhere to certain timeframes to terminate the lease and be relieved of any further obligations to the landlord.

4. Joint and Several Obligations of Tenant

In leases where more than one individual over the age of 18 is responsible for paying the rent, the lease may provide for "joint and several liability" (see ¶ 22 of the Residence Lease, explicitly requiring that "each and every person comprising Tenant are each, together and separately, responsible for all of Tenant's obligations"). A popular misconception among tenants is that their obligation to pay rent has been met if they have paid their share of the rent, even though another roommate fails to tender his or her portion of the rent. In fact, if the entire monthly rent is not timely paid, a default will exist even if some of the parties paid the rent. A clear understanding of this provision will help prevent misunderstandings, unnecessary pre-litigation notices, and frustration among the parties.

5. Handling of Security Deposits

Chapter XIV of this book contains a thorough discussion of the submission, maintenance, retention, and return of security deposits (see ¶¶ 6, 23, and 24 of the Residence Lease). Landlords should pay careful attention to the state and local law regarding security deposits because they easily become points of dispute and litigation if a problem arises. Typically, tenants give a security deposit to the landlord to secure the performance of the lease obligations. Often, security deposits are equal to the amount of one month's rent. Pet damage deposits may also be requested (¶ 6 of the Residence

Lease) to cover any damage occasioned by a tenant's pet (i.e., chewed doors and drywall, stained carpet). It is worthwhile to repeat that "normal wear and tear" is a standard adopted by the courts, supported by case law, which will guide the return of security deposits. Old carpets further damaged by a tenant's teething Rottweiler puppy, for example, will no doubt be rejected as a claim for new carpet replacement under a landlord's claim against a tenant, for example. Courts typically view retention of security deposits by the landlord with conservative scrutiny, and the parties are cautioned to be reasonable in their treatment of damages deducted for under the deposit.

6. Insurance

In a majority of the cases (with rare exception), the landlord carries property insurance protecting the landlord from certain occurrences on the property and damage to the property. *This insurance will not extend to the tenant, however, and tenants are advised to procure their own renter's insurance for valuables and items of concern.* Paragraph 33 of the Residence Lease discusses this situation.

7. Lead-Based Paint Disclosure

The Residence Lease (see ¶ 47) provides for disclosure of any possible existence of lead-based paint on housing erected prior to 1978, as required under federal law. If the property being leased was built before 1978, landlords must provide tenants with a lead-based paint information pamphlet at the time of signing of the lease. Additional information about lead-based paint and a copy of the pamphlet, which is entitled "Protect Your Family From Lead in Your Home," are available from Bradford Publishing or on the U.S. Environmental Protection Agency's website at http://www.epa.gov/lead/pubs/leadbase.htm.

8. Additional Provisions

The reader may notice that the Residence Lease contains a section entitled "Additional Provisions" (see ¶ 51). Completing this section is optional: if any additional terms, conditions, promises, agreements or provisions exist between the parties, the details of these arrangements should be inserted in detail here, and will become a part of the lease. Examples of these kinds of provisions include special arrangements for early move-in, exceptions on rental obligations, pets to be determined at a later date, parking arrangements or limitations, or any other imaginable custom arrangement in accordance with applicable law that reflects an agreement between the parties. Please note that in situations addressing maintenance of the premises, special requirements and restrictions exist concerning the Warranty of Habitability Law, which will require an entirely separate addenda. For further details, please refer to Chapter II, Section J, discussing this new law.

E. Example of a Completed Residence Lease

EXHIBIT B

THIS LEASE HAS IMPORTANT LEGAL CONSEQUENCES.
THE PARTIES SHOULD CONSULT LEGAL COUNSEL BEFORE SIGNING.

RESIDENCE LEASE

This Residence Lease (the "**Lease**") is made on January 1st, 2009 (date) and is entered into by and between Landlord (as defined below) and Tenant (as defined below). In consideration of the payment of the Rent (as defined below), other monies due the Landlord ("**Additional Rent**"), and the performance of the promises by Tenant set forth below, Landlord leases to Tenant, and Tenant accepts, the Premises described below, subject to the terms and provisions set forth in the Lease. This Lease shall be deemed to be a Rental Agreement as such term is employed in the Colorado Revised Statutes (the "**Rental Agreement**.")

PARTIES, PREMISES, AND DEFINED TERMS

1. **Landlord:** Celtic Park, Inc., a(n) Colorado corporation [*Individual, Company or Type of Entity*], (the "**Landlord**").

2. **Tenants/Occupancy:** 1) Stephen McManus; 2) Jan Vennegoor of Hesselink; 3) Shunsuke Nakamura; and 4) Artur Boruc; [*identify all occupants of the Premises over the age of 18*] are persons entitled under to occupy the Dwelling Unit to the exclusion of others (collectively referred to in the Lease as the "**Tenant**"). A maximum of Four (4) people shall occupy the Premises.

3. **Premises:** The following described property situated in the Town of Milleken, County of Weld, [*insert city and county*] State of Colorado, with the address of 1967 Glasgow Way, Milleken, Colorado [*insert street address*] described as follows: Lot 13, Block 69 Stracchan's Addition to the Town of Milleken (the "**Premises**"). The Lease ☒ includes ☐ excludes parking, specifically: Parking/Garage Space 10 (the "**Parking Space**").

4. **Term:** Landlord leases the Premises to Tenant from twelve o'clock noon on the 1st day of January, 2009, and until 11:59 p.m. on the 31st day of December, 2009 (the "**Term**"). Subject to Tenant's performance of all obligations under the Lease, including without limitation, payment of Rent and other amounts, Tenant shall enjoy quiet possession of the Premises.

5. **Rent:** Rental for the entire Term is Sixty Thousand and No /100 Dollars ($ 60,000.00) and shall be paid in monthly installments of Five Thousand and No /100 Dollars ($ 5,000.00) payable in advance, on or before twelve o'clock noon on the first day of each calendar month during the term of the Lease at the location set forth below, without notice (the "**Rent**"). Unless otherwise provided in the Lease, all payments must be mailed or delivered to Landlord (or Landlord's property management company, as the case may be) at the following address: 19 Sauchiehall Street, Denver, Colorado 80209.

If the Term does not begin on the first day of the month, the Rent will be prorated accordingly.

6. **Security Deposit:** Before occupying the Premises, Tenant must deposit with Landlord a security, cleaning and damage deposit in the amount of Five Thousand Two Hundred and No /100 Dollars ($ 5,200.00) (including Pet Damage Deposit, if applicable, as defined below) as security for the return of the Premises at the expiration of the Term in as good condition as when Tenant entered the Premises, normal wear and tear excepted, as well as the faithful, timely and complete performance of all other terms, conditions and covenants of the Lease (the "**Security Deposit**").

7. **Colorado Revised Statutes Definitions:** The Colorado Warranty of Habitability Law, codified at § 38-12-501 *et seq.*, C.R.S., contains the following definitions which may be applicable in conjunction with certain rights and responsibilities imposed by the law: Dwelling Unit is the structure, or the part of the structure, that is used as the home, residence, or sleeping place by Tenant (the "**Dwelling Unit**"). Common areas are the facilities and appurtenances to a Residential Premises, including the grounds, areas, and facilities held out for the use of tenants generally or whose use is promised to Tenant (the "**Common Areas**"). Residential Premises means the Dwelling Unit, the structure of which the unit is a part and the Common Areas (the "**Residential Premises**").

8. **Utilities:** Tenant shall be responsible for paying the following utilities, which charges shall be deemed Additional Rent: ☒ Electric ☒ Gas ☒ Water ☒ Sewer ☐ Phone ☐ Cable/Satellite T.V. ☐ Internet Access ☐ Refuse Disposal ☐ Other ______________________________.
If the Premises shares meter facilities for utilities, the charges will be allocated to each by Landlord based on a reasonable basis and shall be considered Additional Rent. If Tenant fails to timely pay any of the above charges, it shall be deemed a Default by Tenant. If separate arrangements are made for Tenant to provide its own utilities directly from the respective service provider, then Landlord shall have no liability therefore. Landlord shall be responsible for any remaining utilities not specifically designated to be paid by Tenant.

9. **Late Payments:** If any rental installment or other payment is received later than __Five (5)__ days after the date when due, the parties agree that Additional Rent in the amount of ☒ $__100.00__ or ☐ ________ percent (______%) of the outstanding sums, shall also be due and payable. The foregoing items shall be deemed Additional Rent.

10. **Repairs and Maintenance of the Premises:** The Tenant shall be responsible for maintenance of the Premises as described further in the Lease. The Landlord shall be responsible for maintenance and repair of the Premises as described further in the Lease. However, in the event that the parties agree that Tenant shall be responsible for some or all of the repairs and/or some or all of the maintenance beyond that set forth in the Lease, then the parties shall execute a separate writing consistent with the requirements of The Colorado Warranty of Habitability Law, codified at § 38-12-501 *et seq.*, C.R.S indicating such agreement. Such separate writing may be appended to this Lease as an addendum.

11. **Pets:** Pets ☒ are ☐ are not permitted on the Premises. If pets are permitted, they are limited to (number and type of pets) __Two (2) Border Collies and Two (2) Ferrets__, and Tenant must deposit an additional Pet Damage Deposit of $__200.00__ with Landlord before arrival of pet.

PREMISES

12. **Common Areas/Governing Documents:** If the Premises includes any common areas with any other properties that are subject to any declarations, covenants, conditions, or restrictions by any governing documents (the "**Governing Documents**") pertaining to the Premises, Tenant is granted a license to use those areas on the terms and conditions contained in such governing documents. All use of the Common Areas is at the sole risk of Tenant and Landlord will not be held liable for any damages or injuries occasioned by such use.

13. **Parking:** If parking is available and included on or adjacent to the Premises, the parties understand and agree that the Lease establishes a license to use the Premises for parking for Tenant's motor vehicles. All motor vehicles must be properly licensed and insured. No inoperative, stored, or "junked" motor vehicles are permitted. Landlord may cause removal of all motor vehicles or personal property not authorized or permitted, including those left on the Premises or designated Common Areas after expiration or termination of the Lease or Term. Tenant agrees to comply with any parking requirements and restrictions specified in any Governing Documents or rules and regulations governing the Premises.

14. **Check-In Inspection, Condition of Premises and Representations:** Landlord and Tenant may conduct an inspection of the Premises at the time of possession. A check-in inspection sheet may be completed at that time and the information contained in it will be sufficient and satisfactory proof of the condition of the Premises at the time of possession should a subsequent dispute arise. All systems and appliances on the Premises, including refrigerators, stoves, microwaves, dishwashers, washers, dryers, etc., will be in working condition at the commencement of the Term, unless specifically noted to the contrary on the check-in inspection sheet. As of the commencement of the Lease, Tenant acknowledges that Tenant has examined the Premises and is satisfied with the condition of the Premises, including all systems and appliances on the Premises. Taking possession of the Premises is conclusive evidence to the fact that the Premises are in good order and satisfactory condition.

15. **Use of Premises:** Where used in this Paragraph 15, Premises includes any Common Areas and Tenant includes Tenant's licensees and invitees.

a. **Occupancy of Premises:** Tenant represents and warrants that Tenant has identified all of the individuals over the age of 18 who will occupy the Premises in Paragraph 2 of the Lease and that the Premises are to be used only as a private residence for those individuals. Landlord must approve any change to those listed as Tenants in the Lease. If Tenant desires any change or increase to those shown as Tenants in the Lease, and provided any increase is not in violation of applicable occupancy codes, those individuals desiring tenancy must complete any application and approval process required by Landlord, in advance of any change, and after Landlord's approval must execute a new Lease. If Tenant fails to obtain Landlord's approval in advance of any change in occupancy, Tenant understands that this failure constitutes a Default as described in the Lease. Landlord represents and warrants that it has obtained any rental licenses as may be required in the city or county in which the Premises are located.

b. **Legal Compliance:** Tenant is liable for the actions of Tenant's licensees and invitees. Tenant agrees to comply with and abide by all federal, state, county and municipal laws and ordinances, and any Governing Documents, if applicable, in connection with the occupancy and use of the Premises. No alcoholic beverages shall be possessed or consumed by Tenant, or Tenant's licensees or invitees, unless the person possessing or consuming alcohol is of legal age. No illegal drugs or controlled substances (unless specifically prescribed by a physician for a specific person residing or present on the Premises) are permitted on the Premises. Tenant agrees to refrain from using the Premises in any way that may result in an increase of the rate or cost of insurance on the Premises. No hazardous or dangerous activities are permitted on the Premises.

c. **Rules and Regulations:** Landlord shall provide Tenant with a copy of all rules and regulations, if any, affecting the Premises, to which Tenant agrees to abide.

d. **Safety:** Tenant must not use the Premises in a manner that may endanger the person or property of Landlord, co-tenants, or any person living on or near the Premises. Tenant agrees to limit use of the Premises to those consistent with the Premises' clean, safe, sanitary, and habitable condition.

e. **Nuisance Prohibited:** Neither Tenant nor Tenant's licensees or invitees shall be a nuisance or act in any manner that would interfere with the quiet enjoyment by adjacent property owners or other tenants (or their invitees) of their premises. This prohibition includes, but is not limited to, loud noises, loud music, noxious or unpleasant odors, and disruptive behavior or actions.

16. **Check-Out Procedure:** The parties may, at their discretion, conduct a check-out/walk-through of the Premises when, or immediately before, Tenant re-delivers the Premises at the end of the Term.

17. **Surrender of Premises:** Tenant will return the Premises to Landlord at the expiration of the Term in as good condition as when Tenant took possession of the Premises, normal wear and tear excepted. Any deterioration or damage caused by accident, abuse, carelessness, or negligence shall not be considered normal wear and tear. If Tenant fails to re-deliver the Premises in appropriate condition, Landlord may restore the Premises to appropriate condition, including repair, replacement and cleaning. The cost of any work necessitated will be deducted from the Security Deposit, and if the Security Deposit is insufficient to cover work performed, Tenant will be obliged to pay the additional balance.

18. **Subletting or Assignment:** Tenant shall neither sublet any part of the Premises nor assign the Lease, nor any interest in the Lease, without Landlord's prior written consent. Consent to a sublease or assignment shall be in the sole and absolute discretion of Landlord.

PAYMENTS

19. **Payments/Dishonored Checks:** Payments shall be deemed received when actually delivered to, and received by, Landlord at the payment location. Dishonored checks and any checks received late in the mail will be treated as late payments. Any additional bank and handling charges that are assessed in the event of a dishonored check shall be deemed Additional Rent. Landlord may require Tenant to replace any dishonored check with a money order, cashier's check, or other good funds. Landlord may further require that all subsequent payments after a dishonored check be paid with a money order, cashier's check, or other good funds.

20. **Partial Payment:** Any partial payment made by Tenant will be allocated first to the payment of Additional Rent, including, without limitation, utilities (if applicable) and other expenses, and second to unpaid Rent. Landlord's acceptance of any partial payment does not waive Landlord's right to require immediate payment

of the unpaid balance of Rent, or waive or affect Landlord's rights to institute legal proceedings including, without limitation, an eviction action.

21. **No Offset:** No assent, express or implied, to any Default of any one or more of the agreements in the Lease will be deemed or taken to be a waiver of any succeeding or other Default. The covenants set forth in the Lease are independent. Tenant shall have no right to withhold or set off any Rent due Landlord.

22. **Joint and Several Obligations of Tenant:** If more than one person comprises Tenant, it is expressly understood and agreed that each person comprising Tenant is jointly and severally liable for any and all obligations of Tenant in the Lease. This means that each and every person comprising Tenant are each, together and separately, responsible for all of Tenant's obligations. Landlord may, at its option, determine who to hold responsible.

SECURITY DEPOSIT

23. **Retention or Return of Security Deposit:** Landlord shall abide by any applicable laws or ordinances requiring interest to be paid on the Security Deposit. Landlord may retain the Security Deposit for nonpayment of Rent or Additional Rent, repair of the Premises or Common Areas, replacement of damaged or missing items on the Premises or Common Areas, and/or cleaning of the Premises or Common Areas beyond normal wear and tear incurred during the Term. Tenant may not elect to apply the Security Deposit as last month's rent. Any amount remaining from the Security Deposit, together with a written accounting for any portion retained, will be returned by mail to Tenant not more than sixty (60) days after expiration of the Term. Landlord shall mail the return or accounting to Tenant's last known address. If Tenant consists of more than one person, Tenant agrees that Landlord may provide, at Landlord's discretion, the return or accounting to one representative of Tenant or pro-rata refunds to each person.

24. **Restoration of Balance of Security Deposit:** Landlord has the right at any time, but not the obligation, to apply all or any part of the Security Deposit toward curing any Default of Tenant during the Term. If Landlord does so apply the Security Deposit, Tenant must immediately deposit with Landlord an amount equal to the amount applied so that Tenant will at all times have on deposit with Landlord the entire Security Deposit.

REPAIRS AND MAINTENANCE

25. **Tenant's Maintenance of the Premises:** In addition to the duties imposed upon Tenant by this Lease, The Colorado Warranty of Habitability Law, codified at § 38-12-501 *et seq.*, C.R.S., requires the following: Tenant has a duty to use that portion of the Premises within Tenant's control in a reasonably clean and safe manner. Tenant fails to maintain the Premises in a reasonably clean and safe manner when the Tenant substantially fails to:

a. Comply with obligations imposed upon Tenant by applicable provisions of building, health, and housing codes materially affecting health and safety;

b. Keep the Dwelling Unit reasonably clean, safe, and sanitary as permitted by the conditions of the unit;

c. Dispose of ashes, garbage, rubbish, and other waste from the Dwelling Unit in a clean, safe, sanitary, and legally compliant manner;

d. Use in a reasonable manner all electrical, plumbing, sanitary, heating, ventilating, air-conditioning, elevators, and other facilities and appliances in the Dwelling Unit;

e. Conduct himself or herself and require other persons in the Residential Premises within the Tenant's control to conduct themselves in a manner that does not disturb their neighbors' peaceful enjoyment of the neighbors' Dwelling Unit; or

f. Promptly notify Landlord if the Residential Premises is uninhabitable as defined in the Colorado Revised Statutes or if there is a condition that could result in the Premises becoming uninhabitable if not remedied.

In addition to the duties set forth in the above paragraph, Tenant shall not knowingly, intentionally, deliberately, or negligently destroy, deface, damage, impair, or remove any part of the Residential Premises or knowingly permit any person within Tenant's control to do so. Nothing in the above paragraph shall be construed to authorize a modification of Landlord's obligations under the Colorado Warranty of Habitability Law, codified at § 38-12-501 *et seq.*, C.R.S.

26. **Tenant's Notification, Restrictions, and Additional Responsibilities:** Except as may otherwise be permitted by applicable law, Tenant shall not perform or contract with third parties to perform any repairs of any

kind on the Premises or structure on which the Premises are located without the written consent of Landlord. If any repair which is the responsibility of either Tenant or Landlord becomes necessary, Tenant must notify Landlord, in writing, as soon as possible and allow reasonable time for the work to be completed. Any unauthorized work performed or contracted for by Tenant will be at Tenant's sole expense and no deductions or offsets in Rent or Additional Rent shall be permitted except to the extent explicitly permitted by the Colorado Warranty of Habitability Law, codified at § 38-12-501 *et seq.*, C.R.S.

a. **Painting/Decorating:** Tenant shall not paint the Premises or Common Areas without Landlord's prior written consent. Tenant shall not otherwise decorate or deface the Premises or Common Areas in a manner that causes damage or alteration to the Premises or Common Areas.

b. **Plumbing/Building Systems:** Tenant shall be responsible for any and all damage to the plumbing, HVAC and electrical systems caused by Tenant's intentional, reckless or negligent use, misconduct or abuse. Such actions include, without limitation, clogging and backing up of plumbing not attributable to ordinary wear and tear of the plumbing system, and plumbing system freeze-ups occasioned by Tenant's negligence.

c. **Keys/Locks:** Tenant shall not place any additional locks on the Premises, including, but not limited to, exterior and interior doors. Tenant shall not cause any of the locks or cylinders in the locks to be changed or re-keyed in any manner.

d. **Cleanliness of Premises:** Tenant must keep the Premises and the real property surrounding the Premises free and clear of all debris, garbage and rubbish.

27. **Landlord's Maintenance and Repair of the Premises:** Landlord shall be responsible for the maintenance and repair of all structural components, interior and exterior walls, floors, ceiling, roofs, sewer connections, plumbing, wiring, appliances and glass used in connection with the Premises. More specifically, (i) any repairs, replacements, restorations, or maintenance that have been necessitated by reason of ordinary wear and tear; (ii) any repairs, replacements, restorations, or maintenance that have been necessitated by sudden natural forces or acts of God, or by fire not caused by Tenant; and (iii) any repairs, improvements or maintenance that are required by applicable state and municipal rental housing codes that govern the area in which the Premises are located, including, *inter alia*, the Colorado Warranty of Habitability as set forth in § 38-12-501 *et seq.*, C.R.S. Notwithstanding the foregoing provisions of the Lease, if repairs, replacements, restorations, or maintenance have been necessitated by any other reason including, without limitation, Tenant's intentional, reckless or negligent use, misconduct or abuse of the Premises, improvements or systems then Tenant shall be responsible for the cost and expense for repairs, improvements or maintenance occasioned by such acts or omissions. In the event the parties agree in a separate writing to the contrary as specified herein for the Tenant to be responsible for certain repairs and maintenance beyond those articulated to be the Tenant's responsibility in the paragraph above, then the responsibilities of the Landlord, as set forth in this paragraph, shall be modified accordingly.

DEFAULT, NOTICE AND REMEDIES

28. **Default:** If Tenant is in arrears in the payment of any installment of Rent, any Additional Rent, or in violation of any other covenants or agreements set forth in the Lease (a "**Default**") and the Default remains uncorrected for a period of three (3) days after Landlord has given written notice of the Default to Tenant pursuant to applicable law, then Landlord may, at Landlord's option, undertake any of the following remedies without limitation: (i) declare the Term of the Lease ended; (ii) terminate Tenant's right to possession of the Premises and re-enter and repossess the Premises pursuant to applicable provisions of the Colorado Forcible Entry and Unlawful Detainer statute; (iii) recover all present and future damages, costs and other relief to which Landlord is entitled; (iv) pursue Landlord's lien remedies; (v) pursue breach of contract remedies; and/or (vi) pursue any and all available remedies in law or equity. If possession is terminated by reason of a Default before the Term expires, Tenant shall still be responsible for the Rent and Additional Rent occurring for the remainder of the Term, subject to Landlord's duty to mitigate such damages. Pursuant to §§ 13-40-104 (d.5) and (e.5), and 13-40-107.5, C.R.S., hereby incorporated by reference, if repeated or substantial Default(s) occur under the Lease, Landlord may terminate Tenant's possession upon a written Notice to Quit, without a right to cure. Upon such termination, Landlord shall have available any and all of the above-listed remedies.

29. **Abandonment:** If Tenant abandons the Premises, then Landlord may, without being obligated to do so and without terminating the Lease, retake possession of the Premises and exercise any of the remedies contained in Paragraph 30 below.

Initials: ______________ ______________
Landlord Tenant

30. **Re-Entry:** If Landlord re-enters the Premises as a result of abandonment or a Default by Tenant:

a. Tenant shall be liable for damages to Landlord for all loss sustained, including, without limitation, the balance of the Rent and Additional Rent, court costs and reasonable attorneys' fees; and

b. Tenant's personal property and the personal property of any guest, invitee, licensee or occupant may be removed from the Premises and left on the street or alley or, at Landlord's option, it may be removed and stored or disposed of at Landlord's sole discretion. Any expense related to storage of Tenant's personal property is the sole responsibility of Tenant. Landlord shall not be deemed a bailee of the removed property, and Landlord shall not be held liable for either civil or criminal action as a result of the removal. Tenant shall indemnify Landlord for any expense in defending against any claim by Tenant or third-party and for any legal expense, cost, fine or judgment awarded to any third-party as a result of Landlord's action under the term of the Lease; and

c. Landlord may attempt to re-let the Premises for such rent and under such terms as Landlord believes appropriate; and

d. Landlord may enter the Premises, clean and make repairs and charge Tenant accordingly; and

e. any money that Landlord receives from Tenant shall be applied first to Rent, Additional Rent, and other payments due; and

f. Tenant will surrender all keys and peacefully surrender and deliver up possession of the Premises.

31. **Breach of Warranty of Habitability:** In the event of a breach of the Warranty of Habitability (as further defined in Paragraph 49 of this Lease) the parties are advised to refer with the Colorado Warranty of Habitability Law, codified at § 38-12-501 *et seq.*, C.R.S. for further requirements, responsibilities and remedies.

ADDITIONAL PROVISIONS

32. **Liability Indemnification/Waiver:** Tenant shall save Landlord harmless and indemnified from all injury, loss, claim or damage to any person or property while on the Premises, or arising in any way out of Tenant's use of the Premises. Landlord and Landlord's agents, contractors, and employees shall not be liable for, and Tenant waives all claims for, damage to person or property sustained by Tenant, resulting from any accident or occurrence in or on the Premises, including, but not limited to, claims for damage resulting from: (i) any equipment or appurtenances becoming out of repair; (ii) Landlord's failure to keep the Premises in repair; (iii) injury done or occasioned by wind, water, or other natural element; (iv) any defect in, or failure of, plumbing, heating or air-conditioning equipment (including wood stoves), electric wiring or installation thereof, gas, water and steam pipes, stairs, porches, railings or walks; (v) broken glass; (vi) the backing-up of any sewer pipe or downspout; (vii) the bursting, leaking or running of any tank, tub, sink, sprinkler system, water closet, waste pipe, drain or any other pipe or tank in, on or about the Premises; (viii) the escape of steam or hot water; (ix) water, snow, or ice being on or coming through the roof, skylight, doors, stairs, walks, or any other place on or near the Premises; (x) the falling of any fixtures, plaster or stucco; (xi) fire or other casualty; (xii) any act, omission or negligence of co-tenants or of other persons or occupants of the Premises; and (xiii) any hazardous materials or conditions on the Premises. Where used in this Paragraph: (a) Premises includes any Common Areas, structures on any Common Areas, and any adjacent property; (b) Landlord includes Landlord's agents, respective successors and assigns, contractors, and employees; and (c) Tenant includes Tenant's invitees, licensees, or any other person claiming through Tenant. Nothing contained herein shall be deemed to constitute a waiver of any rights, responsibilities or remedies as may be explicitly imposed by the Colorado Warranty of Habitability Law, codified at § 38-12-501 *et seq.*, C.R.S.

33. **Insurance:** Landlord, in its sole discretion and for its sole benefit, shall cause the Premises to be insured as it deems appropriate. Tenant shall have no right or claim to any insurance or insurance proceeds. Tenant understands and agrees that Landlord has no obligation to obtain insurance for Tenant including, but not limited to, liability, hazard, or contents insurance. If Tenant desires insurance, Tenant is advised to obtain renter's insurance at Tenant's sole cost and expense, and for Tenant's sole benefit.

34. **Destruction or Condemnation of Premises:** Landlord's and Tenant's duties and responsibilities are as follows when destruction or condemnation of the Premises occurs:

a. **Partial Destruction of the Premises:** In case of partial destruction to the Premises by fire, the elements, or other casualty, Landlord, at its discretion, may repair the Premises with reasonable dispatch after notice of the partial destruction. Tenant shall still be responsible for payment of Rent. If Landlord determines that the partial destruction may not be repaired, Subparagraph (d) of this Paragraph shall be effective.

b. **Premises Untenable:** If the Premises are made totally untenable by fire, the elements or other casualty, or if the building in which the Premises are located is partially destroyed to the point where Landlord, within a reasonable time, decides not to rebuild or repair, then Subparagraph (d) of this Paragraph shall be effective.

c. **Condemnation:** If the whole or part of the Premises rented under the Lease are taken by any authority for any public or quasi-public use or purpose, then Subparagraph (d) of this Paragraph shall be effective. All damages and compensation awarded for any taking shall be the sole property of Landlord.

d. **Termination of Term:** Tenant agrees that if Landlord decides not to repair or rebuild the Premises where the destruction has occurred as described in Subparagraphs (a) and (b) of this Paragraph, the Term granted by the Lease will cease and the Rent and Additional Rent will be prorated and payable up to the time of the cessation of the Term. A refund will be given for the balance of any Rent paid in advance for which Tenant did not have use of the Premises due to the cessation of the Term under the conditions of this clause. Where the Premises have been taken due to condemnation as described in Subparagraph (c) of this Paragraph, the Term of the Lease will cease and terminate on the date that possession of the Premises is taken by the authority. Rent and Additional Rent will be prorated and payable up to the time of the cessation of the Term. Tenant shall not hold Landlord liable for any damages as a result of any of the acts or events described in this Subparagraph.

35. **Holdover:** Tenant must vacate the Premises and remove all of Tenant's personal property from the Premises before 11:59 p.m. on the date the Term expires. Landlord may immediately commence eviction proceedings at its sole discretion. If, after the Lease expires, Tenant remains in possession of the Premises and continues to pay Rent without a written agreement as to possession, then the tenancy will be regarded as a month-to-month tenancy, at a monthly rental, payable in advance, equivalent to the last month's Rent paid under the Lease, and subject to all the terms and conditions of the Lease.

36. **Entry by Landlord:** Landlord may enter the Premises at reasonable hours for reasonable purposes (such as repairs, inspections or re-letting to prospective new tenants), after giving reasonable notice to Tenant. Landlord may also enter the Premises in the event of an emergency, without notice, or in the event of vacancy of the Premises, as described in Paragraph 30.

37. **Guarantor:** If the Lease is guaranteed, the person(s) guaranteeing the Lease ("**Guarantor**") absolutely guarantees Tenant's obligations and performance under the Lease. Guarantor further agrees to be bound by the same covenants and conditions of the Lease and makes the same warranties and representations as Tenant under the Lease. If Tenant defaults in the performance of Tenant's obligations under the Lease, Guarantor will perform Tenant's obligations.

38. **Subordination:** The Lease is subordinate to all existing and future mortgages, deeds of trust and other security interests on the Premises.

39. **Notices:** All notices required to be sent under the Lease must be in writing and either be: (i) delivered as provided by applicable law, including *inter alia*, §§ 13-40-101, C.R.S., *et seq*. [Colorado Forcible Entry and Unlawful Detainer statute]; (ii) personally delivered, with proper proof of service; or (iii) sent via U.S. first class mail, postage prepaid. All notices required to be sent to Landlord must be sent or delivered to the address where the Rent is to be paid, and all notices required to be sent to Tenant must be sent or delivered to the Premises, unless otherwise specified. Notwithstanding the foregoing, all notices involving or concerning §§ 13-40-101 *et seq*., C.R.S., and § 38-12-501 *et seq*., C.R.S. must be delivered as provided in this law.

40. **Attorney Fees:** If either party fails to perform any of its obligations under the Lease, or if a dispute arises concerning the meaning or interpretation of any provision of the Lease, then the defaulting party or the party not prevailing in the dispute, as the case may be, must pay any and all costs and expenses incurred by the other party in enforcing or establishing its rights under the Lease, including, without limitation, court costs and reasonable attorney fees as per §13-40-123, C.R.S.

41. **Governing Law:** The Lease is governed by and construed in accordance with the laws of the State of Colorado. Venue is proper in the county in which the Premises are located.

42. **Amendments and Termination:** Unless otherwise provided in the Lease, the Lease may be amended, modified, or terminated only by a written instrument executed by Landlord and Tenant.

43. **Captions:** The Paragraph titles or captions in the Lease are for convenience only and shall not be deemed to be part of the Lease.

Initials: ____________ ____________
Landlord Tenant

44. **Pronouns; Joint and Several Use of Certain Terms:** Whenever the terms referred to in the Lease are singular, the same shall be deemed to mean the plural, as the context indicates, and vice versa. All references to the "Landlord" mean Landlord and/or its authorized agents, contractors, or employees as may be required by the specific context. All references to "Tenant" mean each and every person comprising Tenant or an individual person or combination of persons comprising Tenant as may be required by the specific context.

45. **Waivers:** No right under the Lease may be waived except by written instrument executed by the party who is waiving that right. No waiver of any breach of any provision contained in the Lease shall be deemed a waiver of any preceding or succeeding breach of that provision or of any other provision contained in the Lease. No extension of time for performance of any obligations or acts shall be deemed an extension of the time for performance of any other obligations or acts.

46. **Severability:** If any term, covenant, condition, or provision of the Lease or the application thereof to any person or circumstance is found, at any time or to any extent, to be invalid or unenforceable, the remainder of the Lease, or the application of that term or provision to persons or circumstances other than those to which it is held invalid or unenforceable, shall not be affected thereby, and each provision of the Lease shall be valid and shall be enforced to the fullest extent permitted by law.

47. **Lead-Based Paint Disclosure Rule:** Housing built before 1978 may contain lead-based paint. Lead from paint, paint chips, and dust can pose health hazards if not managed properly. Lead exposure is especially harmful to young children and pregnant women. Before renting pre-1978 housing, landlords must disclose the presence of known lead-based paint and/or lead-based paint hazards in the dwelling. Tenant must also receive a federally approved pamphlet on lead poisoning prevention. If the Premises were constructed before 1978, Landlord must comply with the Lead-Based Paint Disclosure Rule, 42 U.S.C. § 4852(d).

48. **Other Applicable Laws:** Federal, state, county and/or municipal laws and ordinances, which are not specifically addressed in the Lease, may affect the Premises, the Lease and the Landlord/Tenant relationship. The Colorado Warranty of Habitability statute, codified at § 38-12-501 *et seq.*, C.R.S., contains explicit responsibilities and remedies for both the Landlord and Tenant concerning use, condition and occupancy of the Premises. Landlord and Tenant should consult legal counsel before executing the Lease to ascertain such information.

COLORADO WARRANTY OF HABITABILITY

49. **Colorado Warranty of Habitability Statute:** The Colorado Warranty of Habitability Law, codified at § 38-12-501 *et seq.*, C.R.S (the "**Warranty of Habitability**") imposes certain statutory obligations as to the condition of the Premises. As such, the Landlord hereby represents and warrants in this Lease, that the Residential Premises is fit for human habitation. Landlord shall be deemed to breach the aforementioned Warranty of Habitability in the event that:

a. The Residential Premises is uninhabitable as described in § 38-12-505, C.R.S., or otherwise unfit for human habitation; and

b. The Residential Premises is in a condition that is materially dangerous or hazardous to the Tenant's life, health, or safety; and

c. The Landlord has received written notice of the condition described in above and has failed to cure the problem within a reasonable time.

50. **Uninhabitable Residential Premises:** Section 38-12-505(1), C.R.S., provides that the Residential Premises is deemed uninhabitable if it substantially lacks any of the following characteristics:

a. Waterproofing and weather protection of roof and exterior walls maintained in good working order, including unbroken windows and doors;

b. Plumbing or gas facilities that conformed to applicable law in effect at the time of installation and that are maintained in good working order;

c. Running water and reasonable amounts of hot water at all times furnished to appropriate fixtures and connected to a sewage disposal system approved under applicable law;

d. Functioning heating facilities that conformed to applicable law at the time of installation and that are maintained in good working order;

e. Electrical lighting, with wiring and electrical equipment that conformed to applicable law at the time of installation, maintained in good working order;

f. Common areas and areas under the control of the Landlord that are kept reasonably clean, sanitary, and free from all accumulations of debris, filth, rubbish, and garbage and that have appropriate extermination in response to the infestation of rodents or vermin;

g. Appropriate extermination in response to the infestation of rodents or vermin throughout the Residential Premises;

h. An adequate number of appropriate exterior receptacles for garbage and rubbish, in good repair;

i. Floors, stairways, and railings maintained in good repair;

j. Locks on all exterior doors and locks or security devices on windows designed to be opened that are maintained in good working order; or

k. Compliance with all applicable building, housing, and health codes, which, if violated, would constitute a condition that is dangerous or hazardous to Tenant's life, health, or safety.

It is further understood that no deficiency in the Common Area shall render the Residential Premises uninhabitable as set forth in the Warranty of Habitability, unless it materially and substantially limits the Tenant's use of his or her Dwelling Unit. Notwithstanding the foregoing, when any condition described above is caused by misconduct of the Tenant, a member of the Tenant's household, a guest or invitee of the Tenant, or a person under the Tenant's direction or control, the condition shall not constitute a breach of the Warranty of Habitability. It shall not be misconduct by a victim of domestic violence or domestic abuse under § 38-12-503(3), C.R.S., if the condition is the result of domestic violence or domestic abuse and the Landlord has been given written notice and evidence of domestic violence or domestic abuse as described in § 38-12-402 (2) (a), C.R.S.

51. **Opt-Out:** If the Dwelling Unit is contained within a mobile home park, or if the Dwelling Unit is contained in a structure where there are four or fewer dwelling units sharing common walls and are located on the same parcel of property and are owned by the same owner, or if the Dwelling Unit is a single-family residential premises, and the opt-out is not inconsistent with any obligations imposed upon the Landlord by a governmental entity for the receipt of a subsidy for the Premises, then the Warranty of Habitability Law provides that the parties may opt-out of certain maintenance obligations of the Landlord and provide that the Tenant shall undertake such maintenance obligations. Provided that the Dwelling Unit is located in a type of residential premises qualifying for such opt-out provisions, the parties hereby opt-out of the following items, which have been checked, and agree that the Tenant shall be responsible for same. In the event that no items are checked, then this opt-out provision shall not be applicable. The Tenant shall be responsible for maintenance of the following: ☐ Common areas and areas under the control of the Landlord that are kept reasonably clean, sanitary, and free from all accumulations of debris, filth, rubbish, and garbage and that have appropriate extermination in response to the infestation of rodents or vermin; ☐ Appropriate extermination in response to the infestation of rodents or vermin throughout the Residential Premises; and/or ☐ An adequate number of appropriate exterior receptacles for garbage and rubbish, in good repair.

52. **Additional Provisions:** If there are any additional agreements between the parties or provisions with respect to the Premises, an Addendum may be attached to the Lease, which will be incorporated by this reference as a part of the Lease. An Addendum containing additional provisions ☐ is ☒ is not attached.

a. The parties understand and agree that Tenant's use of the Premises shall include, at no additional expense, unrestricted and exclusive use of the soccer pitches immediately adjacent to the Premises. All soccer nets may be erected by the Tenant and shall become the sole and exclusive property of the Landlord after such erection, and Tenant shall have no further claim thereto. The parties further agree that any and all injuries, incidents or claims for damages that may arise as a result of Tenant's soccer matches upon the pitches are the sole and exclusive responsibility of the Tenant, and Landlord shall be held harmless from any claims, demands or liabilities relative to such incidents. Tenants shall take all necessary precautions to prevent all acts of hooligan activity from occurring upon the Premises, and such raucous activity shall be restricted to the soccer pitches. Any tailgate parties occurring upon the Common Areas may be permitted within reasonable hours, and may include festive activities such as dancing, and impromptu tailgate barbeques. Tenants agree to be diligent in such tailgate activities in exercising discretion and caution so as not to disturb any neighboring tenants or other property owners, and further, to conduct themselves in such prudent manner so as not to involve the authorities in such events.

Initials: ____________ Landlord ____________ Tenant

b. ***The parties further agree that McManus' two Border Collies shall be allowed nonexclusive access to the dog daycare spa provided upon the Premises, at no additional charge. Further, Boruc's two Ferrets may be permitted upon all Common Areas on the Premises, at Boruc's reasonable discretion. Boruc will make all reasonable efforts to clean up any ferret excrement left upon the Premises, at his sole cost and expense. Boruc's failure to clean up such matters may be remedied by the Landlord cleaning up such matters and charging Boruc an additional reasonable fee for such service.***

THE PARTIES SHOULD INITIAL EACH PAGE OF THE LEASE AND SIGN BELOW. EACH PARTY SHOULD RECEIVE A SIGNED COPY OF THE LEASE AND ANY ADDENDA.

TENANT:

[Stephen McManus]
Signature
Stephen McManus
Print Name
Date: **January 1st, 2009**

[Jan Vennegoor]
Signature
Jan Vennegoor of Hesselink
Print Name
Date: **January 1st, 2009**

[Shunsuke Nakamura]
Signature
Shunsuke Nakamura
Print Name
Date: **January 1st, 2009**

[Artur Boruc]
Signature
Artur Boruc
Print Name
Date: **January 1st, 2009**

LANDLORD:

AN ENTITY:

Celtic Park, Inc., a(n)
Colorado corporation
Type of Entity

By: *[Gordon Stracchan]*
Signature
Gordon Stracchan
Print Name
Its: **President**

Date: ____________

Or **AN INDIVIDUAL:**

____
Signature

____
Print Name
Date: ____________

GUARANTOR (if applicable):

____
Signature

____
Print Name
Date: ____________

Chapter II. Overview of Warranty of Habitability Law

A. What is the Implied Warranty of Habitability?

For many years, Colorado had a *laissez faire* philosophy with respect to rental housing matters, allowing for standards of suitability to be left up to the property owner's discretion. That philosophy has changed, however. In 2008, tenant advocacy groups and apartment owners engaged in a mediated process to address housing issues.[5] Colorado is the 49th state in the nation to enact this type of law ensuring minimal housing standards.[6]

The new Warranty of Habitability Law (referred to in this book as the "Act" or the "Warranty of Habitability") took effect on September 1, 2008 and created an implied warranty of habitability affecting residential tenancy and a landlord's duty to provide housing that is "fit for human habitation."[7] With few exceptions,[8] the new law requires that landlords must be in compliance with the law before they lease residential premises. According to the Act, the landlord must also maintain these conditions throughout the tenancy. Questions may arise as to exactly what the new requirements are—these answers may be found in the Act itself, which specifically identifies the physical characteristics of a property that must be maintained by the landlord in order to be in compliance. If a landlord fails to follow the new law, very specific remedies are available to the tenant.[9] These remedies can include terminating an existing lease agreement, an award by the court of "actual damages" (money), and in some cases, injunctive relief.[10] If a tenant is attempting to terminate a lease agreement based on a breach, the tenant should obtain advice from an attorney before commencing such a course of action.

Landlords are not alone in being required to perform new duties under the Act—the Act imposes new duties on a tenant to maintain housing in good, safe, and reasonable condition.[11] In certain circumstances, a tenant and a landlord may agree that a tenant can undertake some responsibilities that a landlord would otherwise handle, providing certain statutory preconditions are met.[12] Such arrangements can come in handy in cases where, for example, a landlord is out of state and no property manager is on the premises. Once again, before proceeding under this new law and attempting to draft such an agreement, a careful understanding of the law is both necessary and advisable. Exhibit G, found later in this chapter, is an example of an agreement that may be used in these circumstances.

As with any new law, not every situation is foreseeable and not every circumstance can be accounted for. The ambitious reader may notice that certain ambiguity in the Act exists regarding notice periods, and undefined terms, such as "reasonable time," and "condition that is materially dangerous or hazardous to a tenant's life, health or safety" are not explained anywhere in the Act. Such matters are addressed in light of specific fact situations as tempered by the common law (the law as created by earlier legal cases). In contentious and hotly disputed litigation, the reader is advised to research further case law to support his or her argument, rather than merely relying on the general information presented here.

B. What Constitutes a Breach of the Warranty of Habitability?

As already explained, the Act first and primarily provides that in every rental agreement for residential premises[13] a landlord is deemed to warrant that the premises are fit for human habitation.[14] Three elements must be satisfied in order to constitute a breach of the Warranty of Habitability. A breach has occurred if:

1. The residential premises is **uninhabitable** as defined in § 38-12-505(1), C.R.S. or otherwise unfit for human habitation; and
2. The residential premises is in a condition that is **materially dangerous** or hazardous to the tenant's life, health, or safety; and
3. The landlord has received **written notice** of the condition described in above and has **failed to cure** the problem within a reasonable time.[15]

As explained further below, the specific conditions rendering a residential premises "uninhabitable" are spelled out by the Colorado legislature. However, the conditions giving rise to "materially dangerous or hazardous to the tenant's life, health or safety" are not identified in the Act.[16] It must also be noted that the elements are listed in the conjunctive, thus, it is very important to appreciate that *all* elements must be satisfied before a landlord is considered to have breached the Warranty of Habitability.[17]

1. What Constitutes "Uninhabitable" under the Act?

The Act gives a specific meaning as to what can be defined as "uninhabitable" in order to find a claim for breach of the Warranty of Habitability. Under § 38-12-505(1), C.R.S., residential premises are deemed uninhabitable if they "substantially lack" any of the following qualities or characteristics:

- Waterproofing and weather protection of roof and exterior walls maintained in good working order, including unbroken windows and doors;
- Plumbing or gas facilities that conformed to applicable law in effect at the time of installation and that are maintained in good working order;

- Running water and reasonable amounts of hot water at all times furnished to appropriate fixtures and connected to a sewage disposal system approved under applicable law;
- Functioning heating facilities that conformed to applicable law at the time of installation and that are maintained in good working order;
- Electrical lighting, with wiring and electrical equipment that conformed to applicable law at the time of installation, maintained in good working order;
- Common areas and areas under the control of the landlord that are kept reasonably clean, sanitary, and free from all accumulations of debris, filth, rubbish, and garbage and that have appropriate extermination in response to the infestation of rodents or vermin;
- Appropriate extermination in response to the infestation of rodents or vermin throughout the residential premises;
- An adequate number of appropriate exterior receptacles for garbage and rubbish, in good repair;
- Floors, stairways, and railings maintained in good repair;
- Locks on all exterior doors and locks or security devices on windows designed to be opened that are maintained in good working order; or
- Compliance with all applicable building, housing, and health codes, which, if violated, would constitute a condition that is dangerous or hazardous to the tenant's life, health, or safety.[18]

In addition to issues listed above, uninhabitability can also exist if the premises are "otherwise unfit for human habitation."[19] The Act gives no further explanation for this term, however, and the reader pursuing a claim under the new law is advised to further research on his or her own or consult with legal counsel well-versed with the new law.

2. What Constitutes "Dangerous or Hazardous" under the Act?

As explained earlier, the Act gives three elements that must all be complied with for a court to find breach of the Warranty of Habitability. It is insufficient simply to satisfy the requirement that the premises are uninhabitable. Tenants must also show that the premises are "materially dangerous or hazardous to the tenant's life, health, or safety."[20] Once again no further detail is provided by the lawmakers as to what is or is not materially dangerous or hazardous. With this explicit second element it seems apparent that a merely uninhabitable premises is insufficient to invoke the Act, it must be both uninhabitable and also dangerous or hazardous.

3. What Constitutes the "Written Notice" and "Failed to Cure" Elements Under the Act?

Finally, a tenant must show a third element in order to satisfy the new law. This third element is actually comprised of two parts: (i) a landlord must receive written notice of the condition and (ii) a landlord fails to cure the problem within a reasonable period of time.[21] The form of the notice and method of service is not explained by the Act, and there is also no guidance given as to what is a reasonable period of time to cure a problem.[22] A sample notice for a tenant to use when a breach of the Warranty of Habitability is suspected is provided at Exhibit C. The tenant is cautioned that all situations differ factually and that this form must be completed on a case-by-case basis.

EXHIBIT C

NOTICE OF UNINHABITABLE CONDITION

STATE OF COLORADO
} ss.
COUNTY OF ____❶____
County where property is located

TO: ____❷____
Landlord
____❸____
____
Landlord address

RE: ____❹____
Address and unit no., if applicable, of leased residential premises (the "Residential Premises")

Pursuant to the Colorado Warranty of Habitability Law, codified at §§ 38-12-501, C.R.S., *et seq.*, you are hereby notified by the undersigned Tenant that, as further detailed herein, an uninhabitable condition exists with respect to the above Residential Premises.

Specifically, (a) the Residential Premises is deemed uninhabitable as described in § 38-12-505(1), C.R.S., as it substantially lacks one or more of the following characteristics as indicated below:

❺ ☐ Waterproofing and weather protection of roof and exterior walls maintained in good working order, including unbroken windows and doors, specifically: ______________ ______________ ______________;

☐ Plumbing or gas facilities that conformed to applicable law in effect at the time of installation and that are maintained in good working order, specifically: ______________ ______________ ______________;

☐ Running water and reasonable amounts of hot water at all times furnished to appropriate fixtures and connected to a sewage disposal system approved under applicable law, specifically: ______________ ______________ ______________;

☐ Functioning heating facilities that conformed to applicable law at the time of installation and that are maintained in good working order, specifically: ______________ ______________ ______________;

☐ Electrical lighting, with wiring and electrical equipment that conformed to applicable law at the time of installation, maintained in good working order, specifically: ______________ ______________ ______________;

☐ Common areas and areas under the control of the Landlord that are kept reasonably clean, sanitary, and free from all accumulations of debris, filth, rubbish, and garbage and that have appropriate extermination in response to the infestation of rodents or vermin, specifically: ______________ ______________ ______________;

☐ Appropriate extermination in response to the infestation of rodents or vermin throughout the Residential Premises, specifically: ____
____
____;

☐ An adequate number of appropriate exterior receptacles for garbage and rubbish, in good repair, specifically: ____
____
____;

☐ Floors, stairways, and railings maintained in good repair, specifically: ____________________
____
____;

☐ Locks on all exterior doors and locks or security devices on windows designed to be opened that are maintained in good working order, specifically: ____________________________
____
____;

☐ Compliance with all applicable building, housing, and health codes, which, if violated, would constitute a condition that is dangerous or hazardous to Tenant's life, health, or safety, specifically: ________
____
____

☐ OR otherwise unfit for human habitation, specifically: ____________________________
____
____
____.

AND

(b) the Residential Premises is in a condition that is materially dangerous or hazardous to the Tenant's life, health or safety.

AND

(c) The Landlord is hereby notified by this written notice of the condition described in paragraphs (a) and (b) above, and the Tenant further hereby demands that the Landlord cure the problem within a reasonable period of time.

In the event the Landlord fails to cure the above specified problem, the Landlord shall be deemed to breach the Warranty of Habitability imposed by applicable law and Tenant may avail him/herself of the remedies as specified in § 38-12-507, C.R.S.

6 ____________________________
Tenant's signature

7 ____________________________
Date

CERTIFICATE OF SERVICE

STATE OF COLORADO } ss.
COUNTY OF ___❶___ }

I hereby certify that I provided the within Notice of Uninhabitable Condition on this ___❽___ day of ____________, 20 _______ by:

❾ ☐ Hand delivering a true copy to ____________________

☐ Delivering a true copy to ____________________ via U.S. First Class Mail, postage prepaid, to the following address: ____________________

____

☐ Overnight or express courier, to ____________________ to the following address:

____

☐ Other ____________________

___❻___
Tenant's signature

C. Filling Out the Notice of Uninhabitable Condition (Form No. 992)

The Notice of Uninhabitable Condition (Exhibit C) was drafted by the authors and is available through Bradford Publishing Company for use in standard residential circumstances where an alleged breach of the Warranty of Habitability has occurred. For additional guidance, we have provided Exhibit D, which is an example of a completed Notice of Uninhabitable Condition.

Blank 1: Insert the county where the rental property is located.

Blank 2: Insert the landlord's name.

Blank 3: Insert the landlord's address.

Blank 4: Insert the address (including the unit number, if applicable) of the rented property.

Blank 5: Check any and all characteristics that the property lacks which give rise to a claim for breach of the warranty of habitability.

Blank 6: Insert the tenant's signature.

Blank 7: Insert the date.

Blank 8: Insert the date on which the Notice was delivered.

Blank 9: Insert the method of delivery – choose only one.

EXHIBIT D

NOTICE OF UNINHABITABLE CONDITION

STATE OF COLORADO }
} ss.
COUNTY OF WELD }
County where property is located

TO: CELTIC PARK, INC., a Colorado corporation
Landlord
19 Sauchiehall Street

Denver, Colorado 80209
Landlord address

RE: 1967 Glasgow Way, Milleken, Colorado
Address and unit no., if applicable, of leased residential premises (the "Residential Premises")

Pursuant to the Colorado Warranty of Habitability Law, codified at §§ 38-12-501, C.R.S., *et seq.*, you are hereby notified by the undersigned Tenant that, as further detailed herein, an uninhabitable condition exists with respect to the above Residential Premises.

Specifically, (a) the Residential Premises is deemed uninhabitable as described in § 38-12-505(1), C.R.S., as it substantially lacks one or more of the following characteristics as indicated below:

☐ Waterproofing and weather protection of roof and exterior walls maintained in good working order, including unbroken windows and doors, specifically: ______________________;

☐ Plumbing or gas facilities that conformed to applicable law in effect at the time of installation and that are maintained in good working order, specifically: ______________________;

☒ Running water and reasonable amounts of hot water at all times furnished to appropriate fixtures and connected to a sewage disposal system approved under applicable law, specifically: The Residential Premises lack running cold or hot water in kitchen, bathroom and laundry room; Tenants have been forced to haul in water from nearby outdoor watering facilities adjacent to soccer pitches in order to supply themselves with bathing water. Tenants have also been forced to heat water manually for bathing and washing dishes;

☒ Functioning heating facilities that conformed to applicable law at the time of installation and that are maintained in good working order, specifically: The Residential Premises lack modern heating facilities, Tenants have been forced to chop wood and gather kindling for wood stove hauled in by McManus in order to stay warm during the first part of January 2009;

☒ Electrical lighting, with wiring and electrical equipment that conformed to applicable law at the time of installation, maintained in good working order, specifically: The Residential Premises further lack proper "on the grid" electricity – Tenants have been asked to make do with solar photovoltaic electricity, which is neither in conformity with applicable law at the time of installation, nor has this been maintained in good working order. Tenants have been forced to do without their espresso makers and hair dryers and further, have been asked to find their way through the darkness by oil lanterns;

☐ Common areas and areas under the control of the Landlord that are kept reasonably clean, sanitary, and free from all accumulations of debris, filth, rubbish, and garbage and that have appropriate extermination in response to the infestation of rodents or vermin, specifically: ________________
____;

☐ Appropriate extermination in response to the infestation of rodents or vermin throughout the Residential Premises, specifically: ____
____;

☐ An adequate number of appropriate exterior receptacles for garbage and rubbish, in good repair, specifically: ____
____;

☐ Floors, stairways, and railings maintained in good repair, specifically: ____________________
____;

☐ Locks on all exterior doors and locks or security devices on windows designed to be opened that are maintained in good working order, specifically: ______________________________________
____;

☐ Compliance with all applicable building, housing, and health codes, which, if violated, would constitute a condition that is dangerous or hazardous to Tenant's life, health, or safety, specifically: ________
____

☐ OR otherwise unfit for human habitation, specifically: ______________________________
____
____.

AND

(b) the Residential Premises is in a condition that is materially dangerous or hazardous to the Tenant's life, health or safety.

AND

(c) The Landlord is hereby notified by this written notice of the condition described in paragraphs (a) and (b) above, and the Tenant further hereby demands that the Landlord cure the problem within a reasonable period of time.

In the event the Landlord fails to cure the above specified problem, the Landlord shall be deemed to breach the Warranty of Habitability imposed by applicable law and Tenant may avail him/herself of the remedies as specified in § 38-12-507, C.R.S.

[Artur Boruc]

[Stephen McManus]

[Jan Vennegoor of Hesselink]

[Shunsuke Nakamura]

Tenant's signature

February 14th, 2009

Date

CERTIFICATE OF SERVICE

STATE OF COLORADO
} ss.
COUNTY OF Weld

I hereby certify that I provided the within Notice of Uninhabitable Condition on this 15th day of February, 20 09 by:

☒ Hand delivering a true copy to 19 Sauchiehall Street, Denver, Colorado 80209

☐ Delivering a true copy to ______________________ via U.S. First Class Mail, postage prepaid, to the following address: ______________________

____

☐ Overnight or express courier, to ______________________ to the following address:

____

☐ Other ______________________

[*Jan Vennegoor of Hesselink*]
Tenant's signature

No. 992. NOTICE OF UNINHABITABLE CONDITIONS (Page 3 of 3)

D. What are the Landlord's Responsibilities in the Event of a Breach?

Under the Act, a landlord must remedy a condition of uninhabitability or materially dangerous condition which may threaten the life, health, or safety of a tenant within a reasonable time after the tenant gives written notice of the condition to the landlord. In the aforementioned example, Celtic Park, Inc. has the duty to restore the electricity, plumbing, and heating to standards in conformity with applicable law in response to the Notice of Uninhabitable Condition received by the landlord from the tenants. The landlord also has the option of moving the tenant to a comparable unit, so long as the landlord bears the cost of the tenant's moving expenses.[23] Whether or not a landlord chooses to relocate a tenant is, according to the new law, up to the landlord's discretion—hence, a cost-benefit analysis should be considered before undertaking such a course of action. Based on the language of the Act, it does not appear that the tenant has a say in the matter if the landlord chooses to relocate the tenant. Landlords who choose to relocate a tenant should bear in mind that the landlord has the continuing responsibility to bring the unsuitable premises up to standards "fit for human habitation" prior to reletting to another tenant, or else the landlord will find itself in exactly the same situation as before—in breach of the warranty of habitability, but with a different tenant this time.

E. What Happens in the Event of a Breach of the Warranty of Habitability?

1. Tenant's Remedies

If the landlord breaches the Warranty of Habitability, several remedies are available to a tenant. First, the tenant can surrender possession of the premises in a timely manner (as described below) and terminate the rental agreement if: (1) the tenant has given adequate and timely legal notice to the landlord; *and* (2) the landlord has refused to remedy the problem; *and* (3) the tenant has waited the appropriate period of time (as discussed in more detail below). Second, the tenant may pursue a claim for injunctive relief. Third, a tenant may seek monetary damages from the landlord.

2. Termination of Tenancy

The new law provides that after giving the landlord five business days from the receipt of a (second) written notice to remedy the yet unremedied breach, a tenant may terminate the rental agreement by surrendering possession of the dwelling unit between 10 and 30 days after giving notice.[24] It cannot be emphasized enough that this timely surrender is important—a tenant may not remain in the unsuitable premises for several months after providing notice without payment of rent to a landlord, then suddenly vacate and expect that a court will support termination of the rental agreement. Doing so will only open a tenant up to damages sought by a landlord for breach of the rental agreement and a host of other legal complications. As the old saying goes, "timing is everything."

To terminate a tenancy in the presence of a breach of Warranty of Habitability (as defined in § 38-12-503(2), C.R.S.) the Act requires:

> (a) upon no less than ten and no more than thirty days written notice to the landlord specifying the condition alleged to breach of the warranty of habitability and giving the landlord five business days from the receipt of the written notice to remedy the breach, a tenant may terminate the rental agreement by surrendering possession of the dwelling unit.[25]

A conservative and safe interpretation of this new law would seem to indicate that before a tenant can terminate the rental agreement by surrendering possession, the tenant must provide the landlord with *two* notices: (1) an initial written notice providing the landlord with a reasonable time to remedy the problem (under § 38-12-503(2)(c), C.R.S.) ; and (2) a notice providing the landlord with one last five-day period in which to remedy the problem (under § 38-12-507(1)(a), C.R.S.). A strict reading of the Act would also seem to indicate that the statement in § 38-12-507, C.R.S. stating that "if there is a breach of the Warranty of Habitability as set forth in Section 38-12-503(2)" [which allows for the initial notice, and the landlord to act "within a reasonable time"] implies that this additional *second notice* is in fact required before a tenant can terminate the rental agreement by surrendering possession of the residential premises. Bearing all of this in mind, a tenant may use the following Notice Terminating Tenancy (see Exhibit E) to provide this second notice to a landlord.

When a landlord receives such a notice, the landlord has five days from receipt to remedy the breach, or the tenant may terminate the tenancy as set forth in the notice.[26]

EXHIBIT E

NOTICE TO REMEDY BREACH AND NOTICE OF TERMINATION FOR BREACH OF WARRANTY OF HABITABILITY

STATE OF COLORADO }
COUNTY OF ____❶____ } ss.
County where property is located

TO: ____❷____
Landlord
____❸____

____
Landlord address

RE: ____❹____
Address and unit no., if applicable, of leased residential premises (the "Residential Premises")

Pursuant to the Colorado Warranty of Habitability Law, codified at §§ 38-12-501, C.R.S., *et seq.*, Tenant previously provided to Landlord a Notice of Uninhabitable Condition, more specifically, such Notice was tendered to Landlord on or about ____❺____ (date).

The aforementioned Notice of Uninhabitable Condition advised the Landlord pursuant to § 38-12-503(2), C.R.S., that the Residential Premises were uninhabitable as described in the Notice, and the Residential Premises were in a condition that was materially dangerous or hazardous to the Tenant's life, health or safety AND the Landlord received such written notice AND was provided a reasonable time to cure the problem.

The Landlord has failed to cure the problem within such reasonable time.

NOW, THEREFORE, THE LANDLORD IS HEREBY NOTIFIED THAT THE LANDLORD IS IN BREACH OF THE WARRANTY OF HABITABILITY FOR THE REASONS SPECIFIED IN THE PRIOR NOTICE, SPECIFICALLY: ____❻____
____
____

The Landlord is further notified that the Tenant intends to terminate the rental agreement by and between the Landlord and the Tenant for the Residential Premises on ____❼____ (date) *(no less than ten and not more than thirty days from this Notice)* by surrendering possession of the Residential Premises, UNLESS the Landlord remedies the aforementioned breach by repairs, the payment of damages, or otherwise AND the Landlord adequately remedies the breach within five (5) business days of receipt of this Notice.

____❽____
Tenant's signature

____❾____
Date

CERTIFICATE OF SERVICE

STATE OF COLORADO }
COUNTY OF ____❶____ } ss.

I hereby certify that I provided the within Notice to Remedy Breach and Notice of Termination on this ❿__________ day of ____________________, 20 ______ by:

⓫ ☐ Hand delivering a true copy to ____________________

☐ Delivering a true copy to ____________________ via U.S. First Class Mail, postage prepaid, to the following address: ____________________
____

☐ Overnight or express courier, to ____________________ to the following address:
____

☐ Other ____________________

____❽____
Tenant's signature

F. Filling Out the Notice to Remedy Breach and Notice of Termination for Breach of Warranty of Habitability (Form No. 993)

The Notice to Remedy Breach and Notice of Termination for Breach of Warranty of Habitability (Exhibit E) was drafted by the authors and is available through Bradford Publishing Company for use in standard residential circumstances where an alleged breach of the Warranty of Habitability has occurred and a landlord has failed to remedy the problem in accordance with the time periods and requirements under the Act. For additional guidance, we have provided Exhibit F, which is an example of a completed Notice to Remedy Breach and Notice of Termination for Breach of Warranty of Habitability.

Blank 1: Insert the county where the rental property is located.

Blank 2: Insert the landlord's name.

Blank 3: Insert the landlord's address.

Blank 4: Insert the address (including unit number, if applicable) of the rented property.

Blank 5: Insert the date on which the original Notice of Uninhabitable Condition was provided to the Landlord (see Exhibit C).

Blank 6: Insert the characteristics that the property lacks, which give rise to a claim for breach, as previously identified in the original Notice of Uninhabitable Condition. (Note: The tenant is strongly advised to list only the original characteristics that were complained of in the original Notice of Uninhabitable Condition. If the tenant inserts new characteristics in this form, the entire process should be repeated because it will trigger new opportunities for remedy and cure, with applicable time periods.).

Blank 7: Insert the date on which the tenant intends to surrender possession and terminate the rental agreement. This date must be no less than 10 and not more than 30 days from the second Notice, as interpreted under the Act.

Blank 8: Insert the tenant's signature.

Blank 9: Insert the date.

Blank 10: Insert the date on which the Notice is being served or delivered.

Blank 11: Insert the method of delivery – choose only one.

EXHIBIT F

NOTICE TO REMEDY BREACH AND NOTICE OF TERMINATION FOR BREACH OF WARRANTY OF HABITABILITY

STATE OF COLORADO
} ss.
COUNTY OF **WELD**
County where property is located

TO: **CELTIC PARK, INC.**
Landlord
19 Sauchiehall Street

Denver, Colorado 80209
Landlord address

RE: **1967 Glasgow Way, Milleken, Colorado**
Address and unit no., if applicable, of leased residential premises (the "Residential Premises")

Pursuant to the Colorado Warranty of Habitability Law, codified at §§ 38-12-501, C.R.S., *et seq*., Tenant previously provided to Landlord a Notice of Uninhabitable Condition, more specifically, such Notice was tendered to Landlord on or about **February 15th, 2009** (date).

The aforementioned Notice of Uninhabitable Condition advised the Landlord pursuant to § 38-12-503(2), C.R.S., that the Residential Premises were uninhabitable as described in the Notice, and the Residential Premises were in a condition that was materially dangerous or hazardous to the Tenant's life, health or safety AND the Landlord received such written notice AND was provided a reasonable time to cure the problem. **More specifically, Landlord was provided until February 27th, 2009 to cure the problem.**
The Landlord has failed to cure the problem within such reasonable time.

NOW, THEREFORE, THE LANDLORD IS HEREBY NOTIFIED THAT THE LANDLORD IS IN BREACH OF THE WARRANTY OF HABITABILITY FOR THE REASONS SPECIFIED IN THE PRIOR NOTICE, SPECIFICALLY:

Running water and reasonable amounts of hot water at all times furnished to appropriate fixtures and connected to a sewage disposal system approved under applicable law, specifically: **The Residential Premises lack running cold or hot water in kitchen, bathroom and laundry room; Tenants have been forced to haul in water from nearby outdoor watering facilities adjacent to soccer pitches in order to supply themselves with bathing water. Tenants have also been forced to heat water manually for bathing and washing dishes;**

Functioning heating facilities that conformed to applicable law at the time of installation and that are maintained in good working order, specifically: **The Residential Premises lack modern heating facilities. Tenants have been forced to chop wood and gather kindling for wood stove hauled in by McManus in order to stay warm during the first part of January, 2009;**

Electrical lighting, with wiring and electrical equipment that conformed to applicable law at the time of installation, maintained in good working order, specifically: **The Residential Premises further lack proper "on the grid" electricity – Tenants have been asked to make do with solar photovoltaic electricity, which is neither in conformity with applicable law at the time of installation, nor has this been maintained in good working order. Tenants have been forced to do without their espresso makers and hair dryers and further, have been asked to find their way through the darkness by oil lanterns;**

The Landlord is further notified that the Tenant intends to terminate the rental agreement by and between the Landlord and the Tenant for the Residential Premises on **March 31st, 2009** (date) *(no less than ten and not more than thirty days from this Notice)* by surrendering possession of the Residential Premises, UNLESS the Landlord remedies the aforementioned breach by repairs, the payment of damages, or otherwise AND the Landlord adequately remedies the breach within five (5) business days of receipt of this Notice.

[*Artur Boruc*]

[*Stephen McManus*]

[*Jan Vennegoor of Hesselink*]

[*Shunsuke Nakamura*]
Tenant's signature

March 5th, 2009
Date

CERTIFICATE OF SERVICE

STATE OF COLORADO
} ss.
COUNTY OF **Weld**

I hereby certify that I provided the within Notice to Remedy Breach and Notice of Termination on this **5th** day of **March**, 20 **09** by:

☒ Hand delivering a true copy to **19 Sauchiehall Street, Denver, Colorado 80209**

☐ Delivering a true copy to __________ via U.S. First Class Mail, postage prepaid, to the following address: __________

☐ Overnight or express courier, to __________ to the following address: __________

☐ Other __________

[*Jan Vennegoor of Hesselink*]
Tenant's signature

PLEASE NOTE: In the preceding example, the original Notice of Uninhabitable Condition was provided on February 15, 2009. The landlord was provided until March 5, 2009 (18 days), which could be interpreted as a reasonable period of time in which to remedy the problems complained of. The second notice was provided on March 5, 2009, providing the landlord with an additional five days, exclusive of the day served, Saturdays, Sundays, and holidays (until March 12, 2009) to remedy the problems complained of or relocate the tenant to a comparable unit, at the landlord's expense. Should the landlord fail to take any action as required, then the tenants have provided that they will vacate the premises within 26 days (no less than 10, nor more than 30 days) of the date of the second Notice, or on March 31, 2009.

G. Tenant's Injunctive Relief

Injunctive relief is a judicial remedy (available through the court system) pursuant to C.R.C.P. 65. Injunctive relief is used in extreme circumstances where a showing of "immediate and irreparable injury, loss, or damage will result"[27] if the relief is not granted. Litigants are cautioned to employ legal counsel when seeking injunctive relief because the complexities and requirements can prove daunting in the lap of a pro se party (an individual representing himself or herself). Factors that a court must consider when granting injunctive relief include: (1) whether there is a danger of real, immediate, and irreparable injury to the plaintiff which is preventable by the injunction; (2) whether the plaintiff has an adequate legal remedy; (3) whether the injunction will preserve the status quo during the time before the trial; (4) whether there is a reasonable probability that plaintiff will succeed on the merits; (5) whether the public interest would be served by the injunction; and (6) whether the balance of equities favors the injunction.[28] Notwithstanding the strict, extreme, and drastic requirements for a successful award of injunctive relief, the Act provides for injunctive relief under certain terms and conditions. But the requirements for obtaining this relief, as discussed in the new law, are a bit ambiguous. First, the Act provides that a tenant may seek injunctive relief for breach of the Warranty of Habitability.[29] This relief may be sought in any "court of competent jurisdiction,"[30] but in light of the limited injunctive relief available in county courts, it seems that injunctive relief is actually only available in a district court action.[31] The aggrieved litigant is again directed to conduct further research on the standards for injunctive relief prior to proceeding, as the new law contains insufficient guidance as to how to proceed.

If the court grants a tenant an injunction as a remedy for the landlord's breach of the Warranty of Habitability, the court also may order the landlord to pay monetary damages to the tenant.[32] However, if the landlord pays the damages to the court within two business days of the court's order, the landlord will not be subject to the court's injunctive order.[33] In that situation, a tenant may then apply to the court for immediate release of the damages paid into the court by the landlord. The provisions with regard the assessment and tender of actual damages would appear to contradict the basic elements for injunctive relief under the *Rathke* case that there be no plain, speedy, and adequate remedy at law prior to imposition of the relief.[34]

If the premises complained of are vacated by the tenant because of the breach of the Warranty of Habitability, the landlord must comply with the Warranty of Habitability law before reletting the premises.[35]

Before a tenant can successfully obtain injunctive relief concerning materially dangerous conditions that threaten the tenant's life, safety, or health, the tenant must give notice to the applicable local government where the property is located, identifying the underlying materially dangerous or hazardous conditions to the tenant's life, health, or safety giving rise to the breach.[36] It is advisable to obtain a copy of this notice and provide it to the court, when asked to do so.

1. When is Injunctive Relief Not Available?

Injunctive relief is not always available for a tenant under the Act. In cases where the conditions are beyond the landlord's control and the landlord has taken reasonable and timely measures to remedy an uninhabitable condition, the new law limits the tenant's remedies to termination of the rental agreement if the uninhabitable or materially dangerous condition is caused by a third party or tenant in another dwelling unit not under the landlord's direction and control.[37]

2. Damages

A tenant can also recover damages (a monetary judgment) as a remedy for damage which directly arose from a breach of the warranty of habitability.[38] The monetary judgment may also include "reduction in the fair rental value of the dwelling unit."[39]

3. Attorney Fees

A very common question arising in the course of a lawsuit is the issue of attorney fees. The Act does not provide for automatic recovery of attorney fees and, in fact, modifies the previous FED law providing for automatic recovery of attorney fees. In cases where a reciprocal award of attorney fees is made in the rental agreement, the Act allows that the prevailing party in any action under the agreement is entitled to recovery of reasonable attorney fees and costs.[40]

4. Breach of Warranty of Habitability Used as a Tenant Counterclaim or Defense to Eviction

A breach of the Warranty of Habitability does not preclude a landlord from bringing an eviction action.[41] As noted in the discussion concerning monetary defaults under a tenancy later in this book, if a landlord brings an eviction action for a breach of a rental agreement against a tenant for failure to pay rent (or other monetary obligation) under the lease, a tenant may assert breach of the Warranty of Habitability as a defense. An important caveat, however: at the time of filing the tenant's answer, the court is required to order the tenant pay into the registry of the court all or part of the rent accrued. The court may reduce this sum based on expenses incurred by tenant arising from the alleged breach by the landlord.[42] Referring back to the example shown in Exhibit C, for instance, tenant-incurred expenses may include temporary heaters, water containers, or the like that were necessary to provide the tenants with adequate heating, plumbing and electricity during the breach of the Warranty of Habitability. Award of these expenses is up to the court's discretion, however.

If the landlord's case against the tenant involves a nonmonetary default under the lease, or is based on a notice to vacate or notice to quit, the tenant cannot assert a breach of the Warranty of Habitability as a defense to the eviction action.[43] Finally, "[o]nly parties to the rental agreement or other adult residents listed on the rental agreement who are also lawfully residing in the dwelling unit may assert a claim for a breach of the warranty of habitability."[44] These limitations are further discussed in the eviction section of this book.

H. Landlord Defenses

Landlords may be wondering what defenses they have available to them in the event they are notified of a breach of Warranty of Habitability. The Act makes available certain defenses to the landlord.[45] First, if a tenant's actions or inactions have prevented the landlord from repairing the underlying conditions giving rise to the breach, that is a defense for the landlord.[46] Second, if the conditions surrounding the breach are the result of the action or inaction of a tenant in another dwelling unit or third party not under the landlord's control and direction, and the landlord has taken reasonable, timely, and necessary steps to abate the condition and is unable to do so, then the tenant will only be allowed to terminate the rental agreement.[47] These landlord defenses are also further discussed in the eviction section of this book.

I. Tenant's Responsibilities Under the Act

The tenant also has new duties under the Act to maintain the premises "within the tenant's control" in a "reasonably clean and safe manner,"[48] and can be deemed to have failed to do so if a tenant does not:

(a) Comply with obligations imposed upon tenants by applicable provisions of building, health, and housing codes materially affecting health and safety;

(b) Keep the dwelling unit reasonably clean, safe, and sanitary as permitted by the conditions of the unit;

(c) Dispose of ashes, garbage, rubbish, and other waste from the dwelling unit in a clean, safe, sanitary, and legally compliant manner;

(d) Use in a reasonable manner all electrical, plumbing, sanitary, heating, ventilating, air-conditioning, elevators, and other facilities and appliances in the dwelling unit;

(e) Conduct himself or herself and require other persons in the residential premises within the tenant's control to conduct themselves in a manner that does not disturb their neighbors' peaceful enjoyment of the neighbors' dwelling unit; or

(f) Promptly notify the landlord if the residential premises is uninhabitable as defined in § 38-12-505, C.R.S. or if there is a condition that could result in the premises becoming uninhabitable if not remedied.[49]

Further, the new law requires that "a tenant shall not knowingly, intentionally, deliberately, or negligently destroy, deface, damage, impair, or remove any part of the residential premises or knowingly permit any person within his or her control to do so."[50]

These duties are in addition to any duties imposed on the tenant by a lease, but do not excuse or modify the landlord's duties under the Act.[51]

J. Opt-Out Provisions of the Act

1. Opt-Out for Maintenance

By implication, the Act requires that the landlord be responsible for all repairs and maintenance not detailed as the tenant's responsibilities in a lease. However, the landlord and tenant may wish to agree that the tenant be responsible for certain maintenance of the residential premises, as individual circumstances may warrant. For tenants in small scale tenancies, the new law allows a tenant to assume certain responsibilities such as maintenance, alterations, and remodeling of a residential premises, as long as the agreement with the landlord for the tenant to do so: (1) does not conflict with any of the landlord's responsibilities under any governmental subsidy (e.g., Section 8) housing agreements;

(2) the work is not necessary to cure any failures to comply with the Warranty of Habitability; and (3) the agreement does not affect any of the landlord's obligations to other tenants' premises.[52]

In some circumstances, a tenant may also agree to assume obligations for: (1) common areas and areas under the control of the landlord, to keep them reasonably clean, sanitary, and free from all accumulations of debris, filth, rubbish and garbage, and to have those areas remain free of rodent or vermin infestation by employing extermination services;[53] or (2) appropriate extermination in response to infestation of rodents or vermin throughout a residential premises;[54] or (3) by providing or maintaining an adequate number of appropriate exterior receptacles for garbage and rubbish, in good repair.[55]

The Act allows for this type of "opt-out" if the premises are: (1) within mobile home parks; (2) contain four or fewer dwelling units sharing common walls located on the same parcel; or (3) single-family residential premises.[56] In such situations, the landlord and tenant may enter into a separate signed agreement, supported by adequate consideration, in which the tenant agrees to perform certain obligations, such as repairs, maintenance, and remodeling.[57] For garbage and extermination matters only, the agreement need not be separate or written.[58] It is important to reiterate, again, that under this particular provision in the new law, it is not permissible for a tenant to assume an obligation for repair, maintenance, or improvement of a condition to cure a defect giving rise to a breach of Warranty of Habitability. As written elsewhere in the Act, it is clearly indicated that it is the landlord's responsibility to let the premises in suitable condition from the outset, with one exception for single-family residences, as explained below.

2. Opt-Out for Single Family Residences

In situations involving single-family residences, special maintenance and repair conditions may also arise. Unlike other requirements for dwellings units, in single-family residence situations, a landlord and tenant may agree in writing that a tenant may perform specific repairs, maintenance tasks, alterations and remodeling necessary to cure a failure to comply with § 38-12-505(3), C.R.S. (that the premises be "fit for human habitation") before leasing to the tenant, except in situations where a tenant is receiving Section 8 housing assistance.[59] The landlord and tenant may only enter into this kind of agreement if: (1) a separate, good faith agreement exists supported by adequate consideration; (2) the tenant has the requisite skills to perform the work required to cure a failure to comply with the Warranty of Habitability; and (3) the tenant assumes the obligation for the "uninhabitable" characteristics.[60]

An example of an agreement where a qualified tenant performs repairs and maintenance, as set forth above, is shown below as Exhibit G.

EXHIBIT G

AGREEMENT CONCERNING MAINTENANCE OR REPAIR OF RESIDENTIAL PREMISES BY TENANT

THIS AGREEMENT is entered into as of this ❶ ________ day of ________________ (date) by and between ❷ ________________________________ (the "Landlord") and ❸ ________________________________ (the "Tenant") concerning the property commonly known as ❹ ________________________________ ________________________________ (the "Premises"). The Landlord and Tenant have entered into a separate Rental Agreement, which is governed by the Colorado Implied Warranty of Habitability Law, codified at § 38-12-501, *et seq.*, C.R.S. (the "Implied Warranty of Habitability"). The purpose of this Agreement is confirm and agree that the parties hereto are agreeing that certain obligations for repairs and/or maintenance of the Premises imposed by the Implied Warranty of Habitability upon the Landlord shall instead be performed by Tenant. Such obligations are supported by adequate consideration. The Landlord represents and warrants that the Landlord does not receive a subsidy from any governmental source, and this Agreement does not affect the obligation of the Landlord to other tenant's residential premises.

NOW, THEREFORE, in consideration of the foregoing, the parties hereto agree as follows:

The Tenant agrees to perform the following specific repairs, maintenance tasks, alterations and/or remodeling*:[61]

❺ ________________________________

____

____

____

(Attach additional sheets as necessary)

The adequate consideration supporting the above obligations of Tenant is:

❻ ________________________________

____

IN WITNESS WHEREOF, the parties have entered into this Agreement as of the day and date first above written.

LANDLORD: TENANT:

❼ ____________________ ❽ ____________________

* The work must not be necessary to cure a failure to comply with § 38-12-505 (3) C.R.S. [initial condition of Premises which fails to comply with the Implied Warranty of Habitability]. However if Premises is a single family residence and the Tenant has the requisite skills to perform the work required to cure a failure to comply with § 38-12-505 (3) C.R.S. then the parties may agree to Tenant's performance of such work.

K. Filling Out the Agreement Concerning Maintenance or Repair of Single-Family Residential Premises by Tenant (the "Agreement to Opt-Out") (Form No. 994)

The Agreement to Opt-Out (Exhibit G) was drafted by the authors and is available through Bradford Publishing Company for use in single-family residence circumstances where the landlord and tenant have agreed that a qualified tenant will perform certain repairs, maintenance tasks, alterations, and/or remodeling obligations. For additional guidance, we have provided Exhibit H, which is an example of a completed Agreement to Opt-Out.

Blank 1: Insert the date.

Blank 2: Insert the name of the landlord.

Blank 3: Insert the name of the tenant.

Blank 4: Insert the common address of the premises.

Blank 5: Insert the specific repairs, maintenance tasks, alterations and/or remodeling obligations agreed to be performed by the tenant.

Blank 6: Insert the compensation (consideration) to be paid by the landlord to the tenant for the performance of the work. Consideration may also be in the form of a credit for rent or reduction of rent, for example.

Blank 7: Insert the landlord's signature.

Blank 8: Insert the tenant's signature.

EXHIBIT H

AGREEMENT CONCERNING MAINTENANCE OR REPAIR OF RESIDENTIAL PREMISES BY TENANT

THIS AGREEMENT is entered into as of this **1st** day of **March, 2009** (date) by and between **TRUMP TOWERS, LLC, a Colorado limited liability company** (the "Landlord") and **Troy Tulowitzki, an individual** (the "Tenant") concerning the property commonly known as **2001 Blake Street, Denver, Colorado 80205** (the "Premises"). The Landlord and Tenant have entered into a separate Rental Agreement, which is governed by the Colorado Implied Warranty of Habitability Law, codified at § 38-12-501, *et seq.*, C.R.S. (the "Implied Warranty of Habitability"). The purpose of this Agreement is confirm and agree that the parties hereto are agreeing that certain obligations for repairs and/or maintenance of the Premises imposed by the Implied Warranty of Habitability upon the Landlord shall instead be performed by Tenant. Such obligations are supported by adequate consideration. The Landlord represents and warrants that the Landlord does not receive a subsidy from any governmental source, and this Agreement does not affect the obligation of the Landlord to other tenant's residential premises.

NOW, THEREFORE, in consideration of the foregoing, the parties hereto agree as follows:

The Tenant agrees to perform the following specific repairs, maintenance tasks, alterations and/or remodeling*: [62]

Tenant agrees that he will replace all broken windows and doors on the first floor of the residence. Tenant further agrees that he will waterproof all exterior walls and install weather protection (materials provided at landlord's expense). Tenant represents and warrants that he is a qualified carpenter with the requisite skills to perform the aforementioned tasks. The parties further agree that the aforementioned tasks will be performed no later than the 1st of April, 2009 and that tenant shall take occupancy of the single-family residence immediately thereafter.

(Attach additional sheets as necessary)

The adequate consideration supporting the above obligations of Tenant is:

Three Thousand and no/100 Dollars ($3,000.00), to be paid at completion of the job.

IN WITNESS WHEREOF, the parties have entered into this Agreement as of the day and date first above written.

LANDLORD:

TRUMP TOWERS, LLC, a Colorado limited liability company

By: ***[Donald Trump]***
Donald Trump
Its: Manager

TENANT:

[Troy Tulowitzki]
Troy Tulowitzki, an individual

* The work must not be necessary to cure a failure to comply with § 38-12-505 (3) C.R.S. [initial condition of Premises which fails to comply with the Implied Warranty of Habitability]. However if Premises is a single family residence and the Tenant has the requisite skills to perform the work required to cure a failure to comply with § 38-12-505 (3) C.R.S. then the parties may agree to Tenant's performance of such work.

No. 994. AGREEMENT CONCERNING MAINTENANCE OF RESIDENTIAL PREMISES © 2009

Bradford Publishing, 1743 Wazee St., Denver, CO 80202 — (303) 292-2590 — www.bradfordpublishing.com

L. Other Provisions of the Act

1. Victims of Domestic Violence: An Exception Excusing the Tenant from Liability

Consistent with the provisions in the revised FED law (in 2007) concerning domestic violence, the Act provides for an exception to tenant's misconduct in events of domestic violence. In cases where the tenant is a victim of domestic violence or abuse and the condition of the premises is a result of such abuse or violence, it shall not be deemed to be a result of tenant misconduct and thus not an available defense for the landlord.[63] In cases of domestic violence or abuse, the landlord must have been provided with written notice and evidence of such violence or abuse.[64]

2. Prohibition on Landlord Retaliation

The Act prohibits a landlord from retaliating against a tenant if the tenant has alleged a breach of the Warranty of Habitability. Under the new law, a landlord is prohibited from "discriminatorily increasing rent or decreasing services or . . . bringing or threatening to bring an action for possession in response to the tenant having made a good faith complaint to the landlord or a governmental agency alleging a breach of the warranty of habitability."[65] If the landlord has the right to increase the rent or decrease services at the end of the lease term, and the landlord chooses to do so, a "rebuttable presumption" exists in favor of the landlord that the landlord has not acted in retaliation by exercising such right.[66] The law places the burden of proof on the tenant for such acts of retaliation and further provides that in FED actions for possession, timing alone is insufficient proof for an act of retaliation.[67]

3. Prohibition on Self-Help/Clarification of Abandonment

The Act, clarifying FED law previously issued by Colorado courts, prohibits a landlord from exercising self-help remedies and evicting the tenant from the premises without resort to "court process." More specifically, it is illegal to physically bar a tenant from entry upon the leased premises while the premises are still subject to a lease agreement, unless certain conditions have occurred. Landlord behavior that constitutes a self-help remedy includes the physical removal of the tenant's personal property, physical changing of door or window locks, or termination of vital heating, gas, plumbing, or other essential services. The law provides remedies for the tenant to pursue damages against a landlord if the landlord has undertaken self-help remedies without resort to appropriate court process.[68] Additional discussion on self-help by a landlord can also be found in Chapter III, Section F.

To find that a tenant has abandoned the premises, physical evidence of the abandonment must be present, such as substantial removal of the tenant's personal property, extended absence of the tenant while the rent remains unpaid, or return of the keys.[69] Mutual consent between the parties concerning the tenant's termination of the lease agreement would also support a landlord's removal of the tenant from the dwelling unit.[70] In such cases, it is advisable to reduce the agreement to a writing to avoid confusion and misunderstanding.

M. Carbon Monoxide Safety Act

The "Lofgren and Johnson Families Carbon Monoxide Safety Act", § 38-45-101 *et seq.*, C.R.S. is effective July 1, 2009. The new law requires carbon monoxide detectors to be installed in residences, under certain circumstances, and § 38-45-104, C.R.S. specifically requires that all rental units be equipped with carbon monoxide detectors. The law provides further detail as to when these detectors must be serviced and replaced and also provides that once installed and maintained properly by the landlord, it is the tenant's responsibility to assure that the detectors are functioning properly and if not, to notify the landlord promptly. The law does not detail any specific penalties for violation of the Act. The law does, however, provide that if the property owner or other responsible party complies with the Act, then no action may be brought against the property owner or other responsible party for any malfunction of the detector, thus creating a type of "safe harbor" for those in compliance with the Act.

Chapter III. Overview of Eviction Procedure

A. Basic Steps in the Eviction Process

The eviction process can be broken down into three fundamental steps: (1) pre-litigation notice; (2) litigation; and (3) post-litigation execution.

1. Pre-Litigation Notice

Absent certain exceptions that are clearly delineated in the statutes, all eviction cases must be preceded by a notice from the landlord served on the tenant. Depending on the situation, this may be: (a) Demand for Compliance or Possession (also known as a Three Day Notice); (b) Notice to Vacate (also known as a Ten Day Notice); (c) Notice to Quit (Repeat Violation of Covenant); (d) Notice to Quit (Substantial Violation); and/or (e) notice as set forth in the lease. This notice basically serves to give the tenant notice that a problem exists and may (depending on the situation) give the tenant options relating to the tenancy to cure the problem.

2. Litigation

After the proper notice is given, the appropriate time has passed, and the problem is not remedied by the tenant (if applicable), the formal court proceedings are commenced by the filing and serving of a complaint and a summons. The complaint is the landlord's request to the court for relief in recovering possession and/or damages from the tenant. The summons requires the tenant to participate in court proceedings or face a default judgment. The filing of a complaint opens a file with the court; the file is assigned a "civil action number."

After being served with the complaint, the tenant is given until a specified time, "the return date," to file an Answer. The answer sets forth the tenant's response to the complaint and summons, including defenses and counterclaims against the landlord. If the tenant has a claim for breach of the Warranty of Habitability, this defense must be asserted in the answer. This defense may only be used with respect to monetary defaults. If a tenant seeks injunctive relief as compensation for the breach of the Warranty of Habitability, the action must be removed to district court because county court is limited in the nature of injunctive relief. The reader is advised to carefully review Chapter II for further understanding of this type of defense.

After an answer has been received by the court, a trial date is then set. At the trial, the court hears the landlord's and tenant's cases and renders a decision or judgment.

3. Post-Litigation Execution

If the trial results in a judgment against the tenant for possession of the leased premises, or if a tenant fails to answer and a default judgment is entered, a Writ of Restitution will be issued after 48 hours. This writ orders the sheriff to remove the tenant and the tenant's possessions from the premises. If necessary, the sheriff will then physically remove the tenant and supervise removal by a third party of the tenant's possessions if the tenant does not cooperate by leaving voluntarily. Pragmatically speaking, an evicting landlord should obtain the services of a mover or other capable person to remove the personal property because the sheriff merely acts as a civil standby in such circumstances. One should not expect the sheriff to help move lamps and dressers to the curb.

B. Approximate Time Frame

Contrary to the popular perception, eviction proceedings are relatively expeditious. From pre-litigation notice through recovery of possession, an eviction can take anywhere from three days to three months, depending on numerous factors. If an appeal occurs, years can be added. However, the average contested eviction takes approximately three to five weeks.

C. Approximate Cost

Eviction actions may be brought either in the county court or the district court. Different filing fees apply to the different courts. Cases involving amounts under $15,000, which include almost all eviction actions, are brought in the county court. The parameters of the fees are set by the state law.[71] However, counties may have some variance in fees, especially sheriff fees. Fees tend to change periodically, so check with your county's clerk of court and sheriff for specific fee amounts. The current fees for county court are set forth below.

Clerk	
Complaint filing fee:	$80
Answer (no Counterclaim):	$75
Answer with Counterclaim:	$79
Jury Demand:	$98
Sheriff	
Service of Process:	$35 (may be less, not more) + mileage fees ($.36 per mile or more)

Writ of Restitution: $200 plus additional expenses in excess of $200 (if any) and actual transportation costs[72]

D. Negotiation and Meditation

Settling a landlord/tenant dispute outside of court through negotiation or mediation is almost always preferable to seeking a judgment through court proceedings. This is true for numerous reasons:

- Parties who reach resolution "on their own" tend to be more cooperative in carrying out their respective resolution (e.g., vacation of premises, payment of rent).
- The procedure of negotiation or mediation is less costly.
- Negotiation or mediation is usually more expeditious.
- Parties who reach a negotiated or mediated settlement "feel better" about themselves, each other, and the resolution process than those who must go through the legal system.
- Negotiating and mediating "minor" disputes leaves the overburdened court system available to resolve "major" disputes.
- If the parties fail to resolve the dispute through mediation or negotiation and then pursue their legal remedies in court, the judge will know the parties attempted to work it out before running to the courthouse.
- Some judges actually require that certain disputes be taken to mediation before allowing the case to proceed in court.

Numerous mediation programs exist throughout Colorado. Some programs have special mediators who handle nothing other than landlord/tenant disputes. Increasingly, many courts are providing mediators at the return date and encouraging the parties to resolve the matter "on the courthouse steps" rather than insisting on a trial.[73] A partial list of mediation programs is contained in Appendix E. If an agreement is reached, it should always be memorialized in writing.[74]

E. Self-Help, Abandonment, and the Landlord's Lien

One of the most common questions to arise when a landlord/tenant problem occurs is whether self-help is available or if a landlord must resort to the court for remedies. Two other related questions are: What can a landlord do if a tenant abandons the premises; and Can a landlord take a tenant's personal property through a "Landlord's

Lien"? The answers to all these questions are inextricably tied to both factual and legal issues.

1. Self-Help

One sure way for a landlord to turn the bad situation of a defaulting tenant into a worse situation is to undertake a self-help remedy without carefully and thoroughly considering the lease, the law, and the facts involved in the particular case. In landlord/tenant disputes self-help is the practice of "taking the law into your own hands" and attempting to enforce a lease without court assistance. The case reports are filled with horror stories of landlords who wrongfully entered the leased premises and were held liable for such wrongful acts as trespass, conversion, and outrageous conduct.[75] Several of these cases resulted in large punitive damages being assessed against the landlord.[76]

Many leases contain provisions allowing the landlord to undertake self-help remedies.[77] In the past, commentators and case law were divided as to whether such self-help was permissible under Colorado law.[78] The legislature has recently resolved this issue, at least with respect to residential tenancies. As of September 1, 2008, self help (including lock-outs and related actions) are illegal and subject to serious legal recourse, except in very specific circumstances. There are only three circumstances in which a landlord may use self-help to re-take possession of the premises:

- When it is done with the mutual consent of the landlord and tenant.
- When the premises are being used for an illegal drug laboratory (e.g., meth lab) and the landlord has been notified by a peace officer or government agency.
- When the tenant has abandoned the premises.[79]

Self-help measures includes the willful termination of utilities or the willful removal of doors, windows, or locks to the premises other than as required for repair or maintenance. If the landlord willfully and unlawfully removes the tenant from the premises or willfully and unlawfully causes the termination of heat, running water, hot water, electric, gas, or other essential services, the tenant may seek any remedy available under the law.[80]

2. Abandonment

According to the Act, an "abandonment" of the premises by the tenant is deemed to have occurred if the tenant engages in any of the following behavior, "which would cause a reasonable person to believe the tenant had permanently surrendered possession of the dwelling unit":[81]

- The return of keys.

- The substantial removal of the tenant's personal property.[82]
- Notice by the tenant.
- The extended absence of the tenant while rent remains unpaid.[83]

The Act appears to have been drafted with an eye toward the existing case law concerning abandonment. The case law standards may not be totally eclipsed by the Act, and an understanding of these cases may assist in the application of the Act.[84] As evidenced by a review of these cases, abandonment is sometimes in the eye of the beholder.[85] The requisite facts for the establishment of an abandonment are very case-sensitive.[86] If an abandonment is not established, the landlord may once again be held liable for various torts and be subjected to severe penalties.[87]

Case law sets forth two requirements that must be met before an abandonment exists: (1) an act of abandonment; and (2) an intent to relinquish the premises.[88]

The words and conduct of the tenant are primary indicators in meeting these requirements.[89]

Example:

Application of the abandonment test can be very confusing. For example, in one case[90] a butcher closed his business for approximately 10 days. The tenant had failed to pay one month's rent, and the landlord entered the leased premises, "smelled a distinct odor," and changed the locks. The landlord assumed an abandonment had occurred. The court, however, ruled that an abandonment had not occurred and that the landlord had breached the lease, relieving the tenant from any further obligation under the lease. In another case,[91] a tenant told his landlord that he was leaving for two or three days to go to Montana, but did not return for eight weeks although he called the landlord during his absence and assured the landlord that he intended to return and pay the back rent owed. Despite the apparent intent not to abandon the premises, the court held an abandonment did occur and the landlord was entitled to undertake remedial actions.

One commentator suggests that despite the fact that the self-help remedy may be recognized by the courts in isolated situations, the much more prudent action would be to file an eviction proceeding with the court to eliminate even the possibility of a wrongful eviction claim.[92]

3. Landlord's Lien

Colorado statutes create a lien in favor of a landlord upon certain personal property of the tenant for the value of unpaid rent, plus other costs.[93] The law is quite detailed and specifically excepts certain personal property from the lien. Section 38-20-102, C.R.S. provides: "The lien shall be upon the household furniture, goods, appliances and other personal property . . . upon the rental premises . . . but exclusive of small kitchen appliances, cooking utensils, beds, bedding, necessary wearing apparel, personal or business records and documents, and the personal effects of the tenant and the members of his household." Very specific requirements exist as to the assertion of the lien.[94] Enforcement of this lien requires the institution of a court foreclosure action and sale procedures. The statute sets strict time limits and provides for the loss of lien and/or damages if the time limits are not complied with. This procedure is complicated, costly, and riskier than an eviction action. It is also arguably unconstitutional.[95] The landlord is strongly urged to hire an attorney before filing a landlord lien action.

However, one section of the landlord lien statute, § 38-20-116, C.R.S., merits brief discussion. In a situation where a tenant abandons personal property at the leased premises, the landlord may dispose of the personal property if the landlord follows these guidelines:

1. The property is presumed abandoned if the tenant has failed to contact the landlord for over thirty days and landlord has no knowledge that the tenant intends to claim the property;
2. Fifteen days before selling or disposing of the abandoned property, the landlord must notify the tenant of the proposed disposition;
3. The notice must contain the manner and date of the disposition, and it must be sent to the tenant's last known address by registered or certified mail, return receipt requested, to be signed by the addressee only; and
4. If the notice is returned to the landlord, a notice must be published.

A landlord must follow the above requirements when disposing of abandoned property. Unlike the other provisions of the landlord lien statute, no court proceedings are required. The above provisions apply only to residential tenants; commercial tenants are not covered by this provision.[96]

4. Special Laws for Employees Who Occupy the Premises of Employers

Parties who have both an employer/employee relationship and a possible "landlord/tenant" relationship should be aware of the "Employee Occupancy Law."[97] Popular situations in which this dual relationship might occur include ski area employees living on property owned by the ski area, maintenance professionals living on the premises, and motel managers living on-site. The Employee Occupancy Law provides that, in certain situations, a "landlord" who is also an employer need not follow normal eviction procedures to dispossess a terminated employee who has been occupying the premises of an employer as a condition of employment. Rather, the employer may avail itself of a summary process, in which the employee receives three days' written notice to vacate; and if the employee refuses, then the county sheriff can summarily remove the tenant. The rationale behind the Employee Occupancy Law is that the employee does not enjoy a true tenancy relationship with his or her employer, but rather, is occupying the premises as a "licensee," who is granted much less protection under the law. It is unclear whether the new Warranty of Habitability law would be applicable to this law, however, because no provision specifically addresses the Employee Occupancy Law.

Certain requirements and procedures are set forth in the Employee Occupancy Law:[98]

1. The employer/landlord and employee/tenant must have signed a written agreement which provides:
   a. The names of the employer and employee;
   b. A statement that the employer is granting the employee a license to occupy certain premises and that this license is provided to the employee as part of the employee's compensation and is subject to termination at any time after the employment relationship ceases;
   c. The address of the premises; and
   d. The signature of the employer and employee.
2. If the employee is terminated and the employer desires to terminate the employee's occupancy, then the employer must provide a "Notice of Termination" to the employee. The Notice of Termination must comply with the following requirements:
   a. The notice must be written;
   b. The notice must describe the premises;

c. The notice must set forth the time when the employee's licensee to occupy the premises will terminate (a minimum three days after service of the notice); and

d. The notice must be signed by the employer or employer's agent or attorney.

3. If the employee then fails to vacate the premises within three days after the receipt of the Notice of Termination, then the employer may then contact the county sheriff, who is authorized to remove the employee and any personal property of the employee.

Chapter IV. Pre-litigation Notice: Default; Demand for Compliance or Possession

A. Distinguishing Between Default and Termination

There are three basic situations that give rise to an eviction action. The first situation is known as a "default" and occurs when: (a) the tenant fails to pay rent required under the terms of tenancy; or (b) the tenant acts in a manner violating a covenant or condition under the terms of the tenancy (e.g., keeps a llama in a studio apartment when the lease states "No Pets Allowed"). The second common scenario giving rise to an eviction occurs when: (a) the tenant has done nothing wrong; and (b) the terms of tenancy provide for a termination at certain time intervals or upon a certain notice; and (c) the landlord desires to terminate the tenancy. This is known as "termination of tenancy." A third situation involving pre-litigation notice arises in circumstances where repeated violation of a covenant occurs or substantial (usually criminal) violations of the lease or applicable law transpire. These are called "special default notices." The distinction between these three situations is important, not only because lawyers and judges love to distinguish, classify, and label different situations, but also because there are different procedures for dealing with each type of problem. The default situation will be addressed first.

B. Default

1. Failure to Pay Rent

Nearly all evictions are commenced because of defaults under the terms of tenancy. The most common default is the failure to pay rent.[99] The law requires that before the tenant is technically guilty of an unlawful detention and subject to eviction, the tenant must be served with a document known as a "Written Demand," also known as a "Demand for Possession," a "Three Day Notice," or "Demand for Compliance or Possession."[100] The Demand for Compliance or Possession must give the tenant three days to either: (a) pay the rent due and owing, or (b) vacate the premises.

Example:

It is important to note that the failure of a tenant to pay rent on the first of the month (or other date as set forth in the agreement) does not automatically mean that a default has occurred. Prior to determining a default, the landlord must examine the lease and see if it contains some grace period within which a tenant may pay before a default occurs. A typical provision might read as follows:

> "Tenant shall pay rent to landlord on or before the first of each month during the term of this tenancy. If tenant defaults in the payment of rent, landlord may give tenant notice of such default and if tenant does not cure such default within seven days, landlord may terminate this lease on not less than three days notice."

In the above scenario, a landlord would be obliged to give two notices: a "Seven Day Notice" as set forth by the lease and then, after the seven days expire, a Three Day Notice. If the landlord does not comply with this provision, it is not a proper default for an eviction action. Note, however, that unlike the Three Day Notice, additional notices in the lease may be waived (given up) by the tenant or the tenant's agent.

Finally, while no specific Colorado cases exist on this point, if a landlord provides a tenant with a Demand for Compliance or Possession, granting a longer period to cure than three days, the court may determine that this longer notice subsumes and replaces the notice set forth in § 13-40-104(1)(d), C.R.S., and an additional notice is not required.101

Another problem to look out for when determining a default is known as "waiver" or "estoppel." A "waiver" is the voluntary and intentional relinquishment of a known right. If the landlord has repeatedly accepted late or partial rent payments over a period of time, for example, the landlord may be said to have waived his or her right to receive timely or full rental payments. The court may also determine that the tenant had detrimentally relied on the fact that the landlord was willing to accept late or partial payments and rule that the landlord is "estopped" (legally precluded by virtue of past behavior) from declaring a default.[102]

If waiver or estoppel appears to be a problem, it is not the end of the world: (a) many leases contain non-waiver clauses, and although these may not be controlling, they certainly help and should be brought to the attention of the court if a tenant raises waiver or estoppel as a defense; and (b) prompt payment requirements may be "revived" after periods of accepting late payments. This can be accomplished by sending a notice of revival in letter form (citing the specific lease provisions). This will put the tenant on notice that the landlord will no longer accept late payments. Then prospectively (not retroactively), the tenant will be required to make timely payments. If the tenant fails to do so, the landlord may then proceed to declare a default.

2. Violation of Covenant or Condition

The second type of default occurs when a tenant violates a condition, rule, or covenant of the tenancy other than nonpayment of rent. Conditions and rules are limitless. Some common examples are: "No dogs allowed," "No waste/desecration of premises," "No loud parties," etc.

> **Example:**
>
> I remember two such covenants vividly because, working as a teenager in my grandfather's real estate office, one of my tasks was to imprint leases with a large rubber stamp stating: "NO DOGS, CATS OR REPTILES. NO WATER BEDS." While I was stamping those leases, I would theorize: If one of my grandfather's tenants signed such a lease and proceeded to cohabitate (or cohibernate) with his well-behaved and lovable Gila monster, he would be in violation of a covenant or condition and would be in default under the lease. If, however, the tenant's soulmate was a Great White Salamander, he might well argue that no condition has been violated by virtue of the fact that a salamander is an amphibian and the lease is silent as to such animals. The situation could keep two of my brethren in the legal profession (who, matter-of-factly, have been referred to in similar zoological terms) busy with arguments and counter-arguments for many billable hours. However, the important point that must be made is that a violation of a covenant or condition must generally refer to a violation of a specific provision contained in a written lease.

Many pre-printed leases contain vague catchall covenants. For example, one lease states: "[Tenant shall not] commit, permit or suffer any objectionable or disorderly conduct, noise or nuisance whatsoever about the premises . . . or commit, permit or suffer anything to be done . . . that will disturb or interfere with the rights, comforts or conveniences of other tenants." "Objectionable or disorderly conduct" could mean many different things to many people. When a landlord cites this kind of catchall provision as the provision breached by the tenant, a court will usually apply a "reasonable man" standard to determine whether a breach has occurred. In other words, the court will look at the facts and determine whether a reasonable person would find the tenant's behavior acceptable. Therefore, when saying which provision of the lease the tenant violated, it is always better to cite to a specific provision over a general catchall provision.

There is no requirement that the covenant or condition be in a written lease. The covenant could very well be contained in a verbal agreement. However, the conditions of a verbal agreement will be very difficult to prove in court. Further, the tenant and landlord are likely to remember the agreement a little or quite differently.

The Warranty of Habitability Act also imposes additional covenants that the tenant must comply with, and the tenant's failure to comply with them may be the basis of a default.[103]

The law's requirements regarding a default for breach of a covenant or condition are almost identical to those regarding nonpayment of rent.[104] The tenant must be served with a Demand for Compliance or Possession and be given three days to alternatively comply with the condition or vacate the premises. If the tenant complies and subsequently violates the same condition or covenant, a non-curable Notice to Quit may then be provided three days prior to litigation.[105]

The legislature has also enacted special laws which are applicable to all tenancies in Colorado, making significantly disruptive, dangerous, and criminal actions by a tenant grounds for eviction without the necessity for a Demand for Compliance or Possession.[106]

3. Demand for Compliance or Possession

The Demand for Compliance or Possession (Demand), also known as the "Three Day Notice," must be served (and the requisite time period must have elapsed) before beginning a default eviction proceeding. The case will be thrown out of court if this requirement is not met.[107] Therefore, it is essential that the statutory requirements be satisfied. The Demand is a simple one-page document that notifies the tenant that within three days from receipt of the notice, the tenant must either: (a) cure the respective default, or (b) vacate the premises. A 1982 Colorado Supreme Court case had previously ruled that a tenant may waive his or her right to a demand in the lease.[108] However, this holding has since been overturned by a 1983 amendment to the Colorado Statutes: Section 13-40-104(1)(d), C.R.S. states that no lease agreement can contain a waiver by the tenant of the three-day notice requirement.[109] Therefore, a demand must be served even if contrary language exists in the lease.[110] The form and contents of the demand are mandated by statute and have been elaborated upon by various cases.

4. Checklist for Filling Out the Demand for Compliance or Possession (Form No. 235PA)

- [x] Must be in writing.[111]
- [x] Must be addressed to the tenant or lessee.[112]
- [x] Demand *in the alternative* for: (1) payment of rent[113] or compliance with condition,[114] *or* (2) possession of premises.
- [x] Description of the premises[115] (preferably a legal description and the street address including the apartment/unit number).
- [x] Specific grounds for the demand for possession[116] (i.e., nonpayment of rent, breach of a condition).
- [x] Time when compliance or possession shall be delivered up.[117]
- [x] Signed by either: all persons claiming possession (e.g., all owners, husband and wife if jointly owned property) or an authorized agent or attorney.[118]

Exhibit I is a sample demand for compliance or possession, which, if completed properly, will meet all of the above requirements. This form, as well as almost all other forms in this book, are printed by Bradford Publishing Company, 1743 Wazee Street, Denver, Colorado 80202, 303-292-2590. Blank forms are available from Bradford Publishing Company at its retail store or they may be purchased online for immediate downloading and use. Simply go to *www.bradfordpublishing.com*, where you can search by form number or name. Exhibit J is an example of a properly completed demand for default due to unpaid rent. Exhibit K is an example of a properly completed demand for default for violation of condition.

EXHIBIT I

DEMAND FOR COMPLIANCE OR POSSESSION

TO: ❶ ______________________________ (Tenant)

The Landlord set forth below hereby demands that you shall, within three days of the time this notice is served upon you, either comply with the covenant/condition stated below or deliver to the Landlord the possession of the premises known as: Street Address ❷ ______________________________

Lot(s) No. ❸ ____________, Block No. ❸ ____________, Addition/Subdivision ❸ ____________

______________________, in the ❹ ____________ * County of ❺ ____________,

State of Colorado.

❻ The covenant/condition with which you are to comply is: (Check either or both, as applicable)

ⓐ ☐ The payment to the Landlord in the sum of $____________ being the past due rent owed to the Landlord from ____________________ (date) to ____________________ (date).

ⓑ ☐ Other covenant of the lease being violated: ______________________________

____

The covenant/condition checked above constitutes a default under the terms of the Lease, which default entitles the Landlord to possession of the premises.

The rental for said premises is $❼ ____________ per ❽ ____________.

Dated this ❾ ______ day of ____________, 20____.

❿ ______________________________
Landlord

By: ⓫ ______________________________
Agent or Attorney

CERTIFICATE OF SERVICE

State of Colorado)
) ss.
❶ ________ County of ❷ ____________)

I hereby certify that I served the within Demand for Compliance or Possession on ❸ ____________ (date) by:

❹ ☐ delivering a true copy to ______________________________

☐ the tenant ☐ other person occupying such premises

☐ leaving a true copy with ______________________________, a member of the tenant's family over the age of fifteen, residing on or in charge of the premises

☐ posting a true copy in a conspicuous place on the premises (describe) ____________________

____________________ at ❺ ______________________________

in the ❻ ____________ County of ❼ ____________________, Colorado.

❽ ______________________________

* Insert "City and" where applicable. Signature

Bradford Publishing, 1743 Wazee St., Denver, CO 80202 — 303-292-2500 — www.bradfordpublishing.com

5. Filling Out the Demand for Compliance or Possession (Form No. 235PA)

The same form of Demand for Compliance or Possession may be used for either a nonpayment of rent default or a violation of condition default. Completed forms for both situations are provided in Exhibit J (Non-Payment of Rent) and Exhibit K (Violation of Condition).

Blank 1: Insert all the tenants' names that appear on the lease, as well as any parties you believe are on the premises who are not named in the lease. If you believe that there may be others occupying the premises or if you do not have the names of all of the parties, add the phrase "and any other parties occupying the premises commonly known as . . . " to the identified tenants.

Blank 2: Insert the street address, including the unit or apartment number (e.g., "1444 Wazee Street, Denver, Colorado").

Blank 3: Insert the legal description of the premises (if available); this can be found in your deed or mortgage for the property. You can also contact your county clerk and recorder to obtain this information.

Blank 4: Insert the city or village (e.g., "Golden") (except in Denver or Broomfield, insert "City and").

Blank 5: Insert the county in which the property is located.

Box 6:

a) This box should be checked if the default is NON-PAYMENT OF RENT. Insert the amount of rent past due (usually monthly rent); the date when rent is due (usually the first of the month); and the end of the rental period (usually the last of month).

Note: If the period is more than one month, the entire period should be included, e.g., "Payment to the landlord in the sum of $900.00 being past due rent owed to landlord from April 1, 2009 to May 31, 2009." This would represent two month's rent at $450.00 per month. Additionally, if any late rent fees or charges are due, then you may insert these amounts.

CAUTION: Some courts may determine that certain fees or charges are penalties and will decline to enforce them if considered unreasonable.

---

b) This box should be checked if the default is a violation of a covenant or condition in the lease. Fill in the specific provision of lease violated and cite applicable language, e.g., "Page 2, Paragraph 5(a) prohibiting band practice after 2:00 a.m."

Note: If the tenant is in default under both A and B, both boxes may and should be checked and completed.

Blank 7: Insert the periodic rent (usually monthly rent), e.g., "$600."

Blank 8: Insert the period of rental payments (usually monthly), e.g., "month."

Blank 9: Insert the date when notice is served. Note: The date when the demand is actually served controls over the date that was inserted in the demand, if different.

Blank 10: Signatures of all owners; print or type names below the signatures.

or

Blank 11: Signature of the attorney or agent. Note: The agent or attorney must have authority to act for all owners.[119]

EXHIBIT J

DEMAND FOR COMPLIANCE OR POSSESSION

TO: Transpersonal Tenant [and any other parties occupying the premises commonly known as 620 West Surf, Apartment 5, Denver, Colorado (Tenant)

The Landlord set forth below hereby demands that you shall, within three days of the time this notice is served upon you, either comply with the covenant/condition stated below or deliver to the Landlord the possession of the premises known as: Street Address 620 West Surf, Apartment 5, Denver, Colorado 80209

Lot(s) No. 1, Block No. 6, Addition/Subdivision Salmon Run

________________, in the City and * County of Denver, State of Colorado.

The covenant/condition with which you are to comply is: (Check either or both, as applicable)

☒ The payment to the Landlord in the sum of $ 750.00 being the past due rent owed to the Landlord from February 1, 2009 (date) to February 28, 2009 (date).

☐ Other covenant of the lease being violated: ________________

The covenant/condition checked above constitutes a default under the terms of the Lease, which default entitles the Landlord to possession of the premises.

The rental for said premises is $ 750.00 per month.

Dated this 10th day of February, 20 09.

/s/
Landlord Laconic Landlord

By: ________________
Agent or Attorney

CERTIFICATE OF SERVICE

State of Colorado
County of ________ } ss.

I hereby certify that I served the within Demand for Compliance or Possession on ________ (date) by:

☐ delivering a true copy to:
☐ the tenant ☐ other person occupying such premises.

☐ leaving a true copy with ________, a member of the tenant's family over the age of fifteen, residing on or in charge of the premises.

☐ posting a true copy in a conspicuous place on the premises, described as:
________ at ________
in the ________ County of ________, Colorado.

* Insert "City and" where applicable ________ Signature

No. 235PA. Rev. 5-05. DEMAND FOR COMPLIANCE OR POSSESSION

Bradford Publishing, 1743 Wazee St., Denver, CO 80202 — 303-292-2590 — www.bradfordpublishing.com

EXHIBIT K

DEMAND FOR COMPLIANCE OR POSSESSION

TO: **Transpersonal Tenant [and any other parties occupying the premises commonly known as 620 West Surf, Apartment 5, Denver, Colorado** (Tenant)

The Landlord set forth below hereby demands that you shall, within three days of the time this notice is served upon you, either comply with the covenant/condition stated below or deliver to the Landlord the possession of the premises known as: Street Address **620 West Surf, Apartment 5, Denver, Colorado 80209**

Lot(s) No. **1**, Block No. **6**, Addition/Subdivision **Salmon Run**

________, in the **City and** * County of **Denver**, State of Colorado.

The covenant/condition with which you are to comply is: (Check either or both, as applicable)

☐ The payment to the Landlord in the sum of $________ being the past due rent owed to the Landlord from ________ (date) to ________ (date).

☒ Other covenant of the lease being violated: **Paragraph 11 of the Lease prohibits pets exceeding 50 pounds; Tenant is maintaining a bull mastiff upon the premises, which dog weighs approximately 150 pounds.**

The covenant/condition checked above constitutes a default under the terms of the Lease, which default entitles the Landlord to possession of the premises.

The rental for said premises is $ **750.00** per **month**.

Dated this **10th** day of **February**, 20**09**.

/s/
Landlord **Laconic Landlord**

By: ________
Agent or Attorney

CERTIFICATE OF SERVICE

State of Colorado
County of ________ } ss.

I hereby certify that I served the within Demand for Compliance or Possession on ________ (date) by

☐ delivering a true copy to ________
☐ the tenant ☐ other person occupying such premises.

☐ leaving a true copy with ________ a member of the tenant's family over the age of fifteen, residing on or in charge of the premises.

☐ posting a true copy in a conspicuous place on the premises, (describe) ________

in the ________ County of ________, Colorado.

6. Service of Demand for Compliance or Possession

The law specifically sets forth how service of the demand must be made.[120] It is important that these guidelines be followed; otherwise, the notice will be deemed defective and your eviction case will probably be thrown out of court.[121] The three methods of service are personal, abode (house), and constructive (posting). Each is described below, along with tips for effective service:

- To effect *personal service*, the landlord must personally deliver a copy of the notice to the tenant "or other person occupying such premises."[122] If more than one tenant resides on the premises, it is a good idea to deliver copies of the notice to all of them. Although the issue of multiple tenants is often overlooked by the courts, if a tenant fails to get any notice the eviction may be deemed wrongful. Because the notice must be served on someone living on the premises, it is not sufficient to give the notice to, for example, an in-law who is visiting and happens to answer the door that day.
- To effect abode service, the landlord must personally deliver a copy to a member of the tenants' family who is: (i) above the age of 15 years old, and (ii) residing on or in charge of the premises.[123]
- If no one is on the premises when service is attempted, the notice may be "posted in some conspicuous place on the premises."[124] This is known as *constructive service*. If posting is the method used, be sure to securely tape, staple, or otherwise affix the notice. Also, attempt to place it in a conspicuous place where the tenant will see it. If the tenant rents an entire house, place the notice on the front door and on any other doors known to be used by the tenant (to avoid arguments such as: "You knew I only use the back entrance."). If the tenant rents an apartment unit, place the notice on the apartment unit's door. If the notice is removed or vandalized, there may be an argument that proper notice was not given. Sliding the notice under a door probably is not adequate—the law says "posting"!

Unlike service of process (i.e., the summons and complaint), the law does not require that service of the notice be made by a non-party.[125] Therefore, the landlord or the landlord's representative, agent, or employee may serve the notice. No clear age requirement exists as to who may serve, but it is suggested that the party be over 18 years old.[126]

CAUTION: Remember to make photocopies of the notice before you serve it. Proper notice and proof of notice are essential to your case.

EXHIBIT L

DEMAND FOR COMPLIANCE OR POSSESSION

TO: ____❶____ (Tenant)

The Landlord set forth below hereby demands that you shall, within three days of the time this notice is served upon you, either comply with the covenant/condition stated below or deliver to the Landlord the possession of the premises known as: Street Address ____❷____

Lot(s) No. ____❸____, Block No. ____❸____, Addition/Subdivision ____❸____

____________, in the ____❹____ * County of ____❺____,

State of Colorado.

❻ The covenant/condition with which you are to comply is: (Check either or both, as applicable)

ⓐ ☐ The payment to the Landlord in the sum of $ ____________ being the past due rent owed to the Landlord from ____________ (date) to ____________ (date).

ⓑ ☐ Other covenant of the lease being violated: ____________

The covenant/condition checked above constitutes a default under the terms of the Lease, which default entitles the Landlord to possession of the premises.

The rental for said premises is $____❼____ per ____❽____.

Dated this ____❾____ day of ____________, 20____

____❿____
Landlord

By: ____⓫____
Agent or Attorney

CERTIFICATE OF SERVICE

State of Colorado

____❶____ County of ____❷____ } ss.

I hereby certify that I served the within Demand for Compliance or Possession on ____❸____ (date) by:

❹

☐ delivering a true copy to ____________

☐ the tenant ☐ other person occupying such premises.

☐ leaving a true copy with ____________, a member of the tenant's family over the age of fifteen, residing on or in charge of the premises.

☐ posting a true copy in a conspicuous place on the premises, (describe) ____________

____________, at ____❺____,

in the ____❻____ County of ____❼____, Colorado.

____❽____
Signature

* Insert "City and" where applicable.

No. 235PA. Rev. 5-05. DEMAND FOR COMPLIANCE OR POSSESSION ©

Bradford Publishing, 1743 Wazee St., Denver, CO 80202 — 303-292-2590 — www.bradfordpublishing.com

7. Filling Out the Proof of Service (Bottom of Form No. 235PA)

On the lower portion of the Demand, there is a form for Proof of Service. This should be filled out on your copy after service. See Exhibits L and M.

Blank 1: Leave this blank unless the premises are in Denver or Broomfield; if the premises are in Denver or Broomfield, insert "City and."

Blank 2: Insert the name of the county.

Blank 3: Insert the date when notice was served, including the time of day.

Blank 4: If personal service was the means by which the tenant was served, check the first box. If the tenant was served by abode service, check the second box and then insert name of person served, along with a brief physical description of that person. If service was by posting, check the third box and specify the exact place of posting.

Blank 5: Address of service.

Blank 6: Insert the city where the premises are located; if the premises are in Denver or Broomfield, insert "City and."

Blank 7: Insert the name of the county.

Blank 8: Signature of the person delivering the notice.

If the party delivering the notice will not be able to testify at trial (or default hearing), it is advisable to prepare an affidavit (a sworn statement in writing). This can be done simply by adding some language to the form, signing the document in the presence of a notary public, and having the notary public notarize it. If you anticipate that proper service of the notice will be contested, then you are urged to arrange for the party who delivered the notice to be available at the court hearing for possible testimony.

EXHIBIT M

DEMAND FOR COMPLIANCE OR POSSESSION

TO: (1) ______________________________ (Tenant)

The Landlord set forth below hereby demands that you shall, within three days of the time this notice is served upon you, either comply with the covenant/condition stated below or deliver to the Landlord the possession of the premises known as: Street Address (2) ______________________________

Lot(s) No. (3) __________, Block No. (3) __________, Addition/Subdivision (3) __________

______________________________, in the (4) __________ * County of (5) __________

State of Colorado.

(6) The covenant/condition with which you are to comply is: (Check either or both, as applicable)

(A) ☐ The payment to the Landlord in the sum of $__________, being the past due rent owed to the Landlord from __________ (date) to __________ (date).

(B) ☐ Other covenant of the lease being violated: ______________________________

____

The covenant/condition checked above constitutes a default under the terms of the Lease, which default entitles the Landlord to possession of the premises.

The rental for said premises is $ (7) __________ per (8) __________

Dated this (9) ____ day of __________, 20__.

(10) ______________________________
Landlord

By: (11) ______________________________
Agent or Attorney

CERTIFICATE OF SERVICE

State of Colorado
City and County of **Denver** } ss.

I hereby certify that I served the within Demand for Compliance or Possession on **February 10, 2009** (date) by:

☐ delivering a true copy to ______________________________
☐ the tenant ☐ other person occupying such premises.

☐ leaving a true copy with ______________________________, a member of the tenant's family over the age of fifteen, residing on or in charge of the premises.

☒ posting a true copy in a conspicuous place on the premises, (describe) **at the front and back door**, at **620 West Surf, Apartment 5, Denver, Colorado 80209**, in the **City and** County of **Denver**, Colorado.

/s/
Signature **Activator Agent, on behalf of Laconic Landlord**

* Insert "City and" where applicable.

No. 235PA. Rev. 5-05. DEMAND FOR COMPLIANCE OR POSSESSION ©
Bradford Publishing, 1743 Wazee St., Denver, CO 80202 — 303-292-2590 — www.bradfordpublishing.com

8. Timing of Notice

There is confusion regarding which days to count and which days not to count in calculating the three-day period. However, conservative construction of the applicable law yields the following rules of thumb:

- The day the notice was served does not count.
- Saturdays, Sundays, and legal holidays are excluded.
- The last day of the period (i.e., third day) is included.[127]

A demand served on a Friday must give the tenant until the following Wednesday to pay the rent or surrender possession. A demand served on a Monday must give the tenant until Thursday. It is always better to err on the side of giving more than three days, rather than less. If the tenant cures the default within the three-day period, then your case is over before it begins. If, however, the three-day period passes without a cure, you may then proceed to the litigation stage of the process (see Chapter VII). The conservative construction of counting only "business days" with regard to the three-day period is also supported by a 2004 amendment to the FED law providing that "business" and not "calendar" days are to be used when determining the minimum period for the service of a summons in an FED proceeding.[128]

Chapter V. Pre-litigation Notice: Special Defaults

Common events of default usually require the landlord to permit a three-day cure period. However, two special types of defaults exist in which no cure period is allowed. After one of these special defaults occurs, the landlord must serve on the tenant a Notice to Quit, which simply alerts the tenant that a special violation has occurred and orders the tenant to leave the premises, period. If the tenant does not comply, then the landlord may proceed to an eviction action.

The first type of special default concerns a repeat violation of a lease covenant after the tenant had previously been notified to cease such violations. The second special default involves actions by a tenant, or others on the property, which endanger persons or property and/or constitute serious criminal violations. Each of these defaults is discussed in detail below.

A. Repeat Violation of Covenant

1. Notice to Quit (Repeat Violation) (Form 219R)

A provision of the FED law modifies the rights of tenants and the duties of landlords relative to repeated violations of lease covenants. The law provides: (a) if the landlord had previously issued a Demand for Compliance or Possession to a tenant relative to a certain violation of a covenant; and (b) the tenant had cured the violation; and (c) the tenant subsequently commits a second violation of the same covenant, then the landlord need not provide a Demand for Compliance or Possession, but rather may provide a "Three Day Notice to Quit" which does not give the tenant the opportunity to cure, and then the landlord may pursue an eviction action.[129]

This Notice to Quit is served in the same manner as the Demand for Compliance or Possession (see Chapter IV). The same conservative construction of the three-day rule discussed in the last chapter is suggested.

Example:

An example of the application of this law would be as follows:

Transcendental Tenant, a psychology student with an affection for punk rock, has a one-year written lease with Lama Landlord for a studio apartment near the famed Myopia Institute in Boulder, Colorado. The lease provides: "No amplified music shall be played between the hours of 7:00 p.m. and 7:00 a.m." After a particularly angst-ridden marathon class on Nietzsche which lets out at 11:00 p.m., Transcendental retires to her abode. She takes solace in the music of the "Remaindermen," a particularly raucous punk band comprised of disillusioned officers of the court. The next morning, she receives a Demand for Compliance or Possession from Lama Landlord specifying a violation of the "No amplified music" covenant in the Lease. Several months pass without incident. Late one night, Transcendental, after contemplating Sartre's philosophy of choice, decides she will express her existence by choosing to crank "No Exit," an existentialist "grunge" band at 2:00 a.m. The next morning, she receives a Notice to Quit from Lama. This Notice specifies the prior violation of the "No amplified music" covenant and the most recent violation. She ceases to play music. Lama subsequently files an eviction action. Transcendental argues that she has ceased playing music and, in fact, has now adopted a philosophy that abstains from all entertainment, including music. The court nonetheless rules against Transcendental and evicts her in a manner she likens to *The Trial* by her favorite author, Franz Kafka.

The court in the above example correctly applied the Notice to Quit provision for repeat violations. Because this statute is relatively new, no case law or articles relative to its application exist yet at the time of the writing of this book. A form, premised on the language of the statute and previously adopted forms, follows the Checklist below.

2. Checklist for Notice to Quit (Repeat Violation of Condition/ Covenant) (Form No. 219R)

- [x] Must be in writing.
- [x] Must be addressed to the tenant or lessee.
- [x] Description of the premises.
- [x] Specification of the covenant or condition violated by the tenant.
- [x] Date of the first violation.
- [x] Date when the Demand for Compliance or Possession was sent.
- [x] Date of the subsequent violation.

- [x] Statement that the Lease shall terminate.
- [x] Date when the termination is effective.
- [x] Signed by the landlord or the landlord's agent or attorney.[130]

CAUTION: A prior Demand for Compliance or Possession must have been sent for the same violation before a landlord may use this Notice to Quit. Also, this form cannot be used for repeat rental defaults, but only for violations of "other covenants."

Exhibit N is a sample form of this Notice to Quit, which will satisfy all statutory requirements.

EXHIBIT N

NOTICE TO QUIT
(Repeat Violation of Covenant/Condition)

TO: ❶ ____

Pursuant to Title 13-40-104(1)(e.5), Colorado Revised Statutes, you are notified by the undersigned owner that on ❷ ____________________, 20______, you were served with a Demand for Compliance or Possession by reason of a violation of a covenant or condition under the terms of the Lease, specifically:
❸ ____
____
____

You have subsequently violated the same covenant or condition on ❹ ____________________, 20____.

THEREFORE, your tenancy of the lands and premises described below is hereby terminated as of ❺ ____________________, 20______, and you are accordingly notified to quit said premises and surrender possession on or before said date.

Street Address ❻ ____
Lot(s) No. ❼ ______________, Block No. ❽ ______________, Addition/Subdivision ❾ ______________
______________________________, in the ❿ ______________ * County of ⓫ ______________,
State of Colorado.

Dated this ________ day of ⓬ ____________________, 20______.

⓭ ______________________________
Owner

By: ⓮ ______________________________
Agent

CERTIFICATE OF SERVICE

State of Colorado
______________ County of ______________ } ss.

I hereby certify that I served the within Notice to Quit on ______________________________ (date) by:

- ☐ delivering a true copy to ______________________________
  ☐ the tenant ☐ other person occupying such premises.
- ☐ leaving a true copy with ______________________________, a member of the tenant's family over the age of fifteen, residing on or in charge of the premises.
- ☐ posting a true copy in a conspicuous place on the premises, (describe) ______________________________
  ______________, at ______________________________,
  in the ______________ County of ______________________, Colorado.

* Insert "City and" where applicable.

____
Signature

No. 219R. Rev. 5-05. NOTICE TO QUIT (Repeat Violation of Covenant/Condition) ©
Bradford Publishing, 1743 Wazee St., Denver, CO 80202 — 303-292-2500 — www.bradfordpublishing.com

3. Filling Out the Notice to Quit (Repeat Violation of Covenant/ Condition)

A completed form of this Notice is provided in Exhibit O.

Blank 1: Insert the names of all the tenants named in the lease, as well as any parties that you believe are on the premises who are not named in the lease. If you believe there may be others occupying the premises or if you do not have the names of all of the parties, add the phrase "and any other parties occupying the premises" to the identified tenants.

Blank 2: Date on which the first Demand for Compliance or Possession was served.

Blank 3: Breach of condition or covenant that was set forth in first Demand for Compliance or Possession and subsequently violated.

Blank 4: Insert the date of the subsequent violation.

Blank 5: Insert the date when the tenancy shall terminate (three business days after delivery).

Blank 6: Insert the street address.

Blank 7: Insert the lot number of the property from legal description.

Blank 8: Insert the block number of the property from the legal description.

Blank 9: Insert which addition or subdivision is applicable from the legal description.

Blank 10: Insert the city or town where the premises are located; if the premises are in Denver or Broomfield, insert "City and."

Blank 11: Insert the county.

Blank 12: Date of service.

Blank 13: Signature(s) of all owner(s), or

Blank 14: Signature of the authorized attorney or agent.

Note: The bottom of form 219R is filled out and served in the same way as form 235PA. Read Chapter IV for these instructions.

EXHIBIT O

NOTICE TO QUIT
(Repeat Violation of Covenant/Condition)

TO: Temerity Tenant, [and any other parties occupying the premises commonly known as
13 Capitol Hill, Denver, Colorado 80210

Pursuant to Title 13-40-104(1)(e.5), Colorado Revised Statutes, you are notified by the undersigned owner that on March 1st, 2009, you were served with a Demand for Compliance or Possession by reason of a violation of a covenant or condition under the terms of the Lease, specifically:

Paragraph 15(e) of the Lease, providing that "Neither Tenant nor Tenant's licensees or invitees shall be a nuisance or act in any manner that would interfere with the quiet enjoyment by adjacent property owners or other tenants (or their invitees) of their premises. This prohibition includes, but is not limited to, loud noises, loud music, noxious or unpleasant odors, and disruptive behavior or actions."

You have subsequently violated the same covenant or condition on April 1st, 2009.

THEREFORE, your tenancy of the lands and premises described below is hereby terminated as of April 5th, 2009, and you are accordingly notified to quit said premises and surrender possession on or before said date.

Street Address 13 Capitol Hill, Denver, Colorado 80210
Lot(s) No. 7, Block No. 5, Addition/Subdivision Trout Falls
________, in the City and * County of Denver,
State of Colorado.

Dated this 2nd day of April, 2009.

/s/
Owner Liberal Landlord

By: ________
Agent

CERTIFICATE OF SERVICE

State of Colorado
________ County of ________ } ss.

I hereby certify that I served the within Notice to Quit on ________ (date) by:

☐ delivering a true copy to ________
☐ the tenant ☐ other person occupying such premises.
☐ leaving a true copy with ________, a member of the tenant's family over the age of fifteen, residing on or in charge of the premises.
☐ posting a true copy in a conspicuous place on the premises, (describe) ________
________, at ________,
in the ________ County of ________, Colorado.

* Insert "City and" where applicable.

____
Signature

No. 219R. Rev. 5-05. NOTICE TO QUIT (Repeat Violation of Covenant/Condition) ©
Bradford Publishing, 1743 Wazee St., Denver, CO 80202 — 303-292-2500 — www.bradfordpublishing.com

B. Substantial Violation of Lease

1. Notice to Quit (Substantial Violation) (Form No. 219S)

A second addition to the FED law has been special provisions that are applicable to tenants who have committed violent or criminal acts on or near the leased premises. In the event of such an occurrence, no Demand for Compliance or Possession is required. Rather, only a Three Day Notice to Quit, similar to that for repeat violations of covenant, is required.[131]

The law states that it is an implied term of every lease of real property that a tenant shall not commit a "substantial violation" while in possession of the premises. A substantial violation is defined in the statute as any act by the tenant, or by "any guest or invitee" of the tenant, which either:

1. occurs on or near the premises, and (i) endangers the person, or (ii) willfully and substantially endangers the property of the landlord, co-tenant, or any person living on or near the premises, or
2. occurs on or near the premises and is a violent or drug-related felony under certain provisions of the Criminal Code, or
3. occurs on the tenant's leased premises or the common areas, hallways, grounds, parking lot, or other area located in the same building or complex in which the tenant's leased premises are located and constitutes a criminal act in violation of federal or state law or local ordinance that:
   a. carries a potential sentence of incarceration of 180 days or more; and
   b. has been declared to be a public nuisance under state law or local ordinance based on a state statute.[132]

If a substantial violation occurs, a landlord may then terminate the tenancy by serving a Notice to Quit; this termination is effective three days after service.[133] **This Notice does not provide a right to cure.** If the tenant is served with this notice and the time period has elapsed, the landlord may proceed to an eviction action. If an eviction action is filed, the landlord has the burden of proving that a "substantial violation" has occurred by a preponderance of the evidence.[134]

Two defenses are provided to a claim of substantial violation:

1. The tenant is a victim of domestic violence, this fact has been documented as provided in § 13-40-104(4), C.R.S., and the domestic violence is the basis for the termination notice;[135] or

2. The tenant did not know of, and could not reasonably have known of or prevented the commission of, a substantial violation by a guest or invitee, but the tenant immediately notified a law enforcement officer of his or her knowledge of the substantial violation.[136]

CAUTION: This relatively new law was drafted to address "crack house" type situations in the Denver metropolitan area. Many cases are sure to follow interpreting this law. I suspect that this law will be attacked in the near future on a constitutional basis, and probably modified. Given the other remedies available to a landlord (i.e., other defaults and violations of the lease) and the substantial burden on the landlord to basically prove the commission of a crime, I would strongly suggest that the landlord use the other provisions of the FED laws, if possible, rather than the Criminal Violation provisions. If employing this method of eviction, it is strongly suggested that you contact an attorney.

This Notice to Quit is served in the same manner as the Demand for Compliance or Possession (see Chapter IV). The same conservative construction of the three days as discussed in the previous chapter is advisable.

2. Checklist for Notice to Quit (Substantial Violation) (Form 219S)

- [x] Must be in writing.
- [x] Must be addressed to the tenant or lessee.
- [x] Description of the premises.
- [x] Grounds for termination (nature of the substantial violation).
- [x] Statement that the lease will terminate.
- [x] Date when the termination will be effective.
- [x] Signed by the landlord or the landlord's agent or attorney.

Exhibit P is a form incorporating the statutorily required information.

EXHIBIT P

NOTICE TO QUIT
(Substantial Violation)

TO: ___❶___________________________________

Pursuant to Title 13-40-107.5, Colorado Revised Statutes, you are hereby notified by the undersigned owner that on ______❷______________, 20______, you, your guest(s) and/or invitee(s) committed an act, or series of acts, which, as defined by law, constitutes a substantial violation, specifically:

☐ ___❸___________________________________

____

____

which occurred on or near the premises and endangered the person or willfully and substantially endangered the property of the landlord, any co-tenant, or any person living on or near the premises; or

☐ ___❸___________________________________

____

____

which occurred on or near the premises and constitutes a violent or drug-related felony prohibited under article 3, 4, 6, 7, 9, 10, 12, or 18 of title 18, C.R.S.

☐ ___❸___________________________________

____

____

which occurred on the tenant's leased premises or the common areas, hallway, grounds, parking lot, or other area located in the same building or complex in which the tenant's leased premises are located, and constitutes a criminal act in violation of federal or state law or local ordinances that carries a potential sentence of incarceration of one hundred eighty days or more, and has been declared to be a public nuisance under state law or local ordinance based on a state statute.

THEREFORE, your tenancy of the lands and premises described below is hereby terminated as of _____❹______________, 20______, and you are accordingly notified to quit said premises and surrender possession on or before said date.

Street Address ____❺____________________________

Lot(s) No. ____❻__________, Block No. ____❼______, Addition/Subdivision ______❽___

____________________, in the ____❾______ * County of _____❿__________,

State of Colorado.

Dated this ________ day of ____⓫______________, 20______.

____⓬______________________
Owner

* Insert "City and" where applicable.

By: ____⓭______________________
Agent

Bradford Publishing, 1743 Wazee St., Denver, CO 80202 — 303-292-2500 — www.bradfordpublishing.com

3. Filling Out the Notice to Quit (Substantial Violation) (Form 219S)

Exhibit Q is a completed Notice to Quit (Substantial Violation).

Blank 1: Insert the names of all tenants named in the lease, as well as any parties that you believe are on the premises who are not named in the lease. In the event of a domestic violence incident, review Chapter XV for additional requirements. If you believe that others may be occupying the premises or if you do not have the names of all of the parties, add the phrase "and any other parties occupying the premises" to the identified tenants.

Blank 2: Insert the date when the substantial violation occurred.

Blank 3: Specify the type of substantial violation (e.g., "assaulted Capricious Co-Tenant").

Blank 4: Date when the tenancy will terminate (three business days after delivery).

Blank 5: Insert the street address.

Blank 6: Insert the lot number of the property from the legal description.

Blank 7: Insert the block number of the property from the legal description.

Blank 8: Insert which addition or subdivision is applicable from the legal description.

Blank 9: Insert the city or town where the premises are located. If the premises are in Denver or Broomfield insert "City and."

Blank 10: Insert the county.

Blank 11: Insert the date of service.

Blank 12: Insert all the owner's/owners' signature(s), or

Blank 13: Insert the signature of an authorized attorney or agent.

Note: The Proof of Service on the back of Form 219S is filled out and served the same as Form 235PA. Read Chapter IV for those instructions.

EXHIBIT Q

NOTICE TO QUIT
(Substantial Violation)

TO: **Transient Tenant, an individual, [and any other parties occupying the premises commonly known as 444 St. James Place, Lafayette, Colorado 80026**

Pursuant to Title 13-40-107.5, Colorado Revised Statutes, you are hereby notified by the undersigned owner that on **February 10th**, 20**09**, you, your guest(s) and/or invitee(s) committed an act, or series of acts, which, as defined by law, constitutes a substantial violation, specifically:

☐ ______

which occurred on or near the premises and endangered the person or willfully and substantially endangered the property of the landlord, any co-tenant, or any person living on or near the premises; or

☒ **Threatened Capricious Co-Tenant with a 9mm Luger, placing Capricious in fear of serious bodily injury, constituting menacing in violation of Section 18-3-206, C.R.S.**

which occurred on or near the premises and constitutes a violent or drug-related felony prohibited under article 3, 4, 6, 7, 9, 10, 12, or 18 of title 18, C.R.S.

☐ ______

which occurred on the tenant's leased premises or the common areas, hallway, grounds, parking lot, or other area located in the same building or complex in which the tenant's leased premises are located, and constitutes a criminal act in violation of federal or state law or local ordinances that carries a potential sentence of incarceration of one hundred eighty days or more, and has been declared to be a public nuisance under state law or local ordinance based on a state statute.

THEREFORE, your tenancy of the lands and premises described below is hereby terminated as of **February 16th**, 20**09**, and you are accordingly notified to quit said premises and surrender possession on or before said date.

Street Address **38 Special Street, Unit 2**

Lot(s) No. **1**, Block No. **2**, Addition/Subdivision **Presage**

______, in the **Lafayette** * County of **Boulder**, State of Colorado.

Dated this **11th** day of **February**, 20**09**.

/s/
Owner **Lenient Landlord, an individual**

By: ______
Agent

* Insert "City and" where applicable.

Chapter VI. Pre-litigation Notice: Termination of Tenancy/Notice to Vacate

A termination of tenancy is distinguished from a default by the fact that the tenant has done nothing "wrong." Rather, the landlord is, at a legally appropriate time, simply ending the tenant's occupancy of the premises. It is important to point out that this type of notice cannot be used to terminate a lease that has a specific commencement date and a specific termination date during its term. In fact, most parties, both landlords and tenants, enter into such leases so that they have assurance that they will have a predictable period of tenancy and rent, absent defaults discussed elsewhere in this book.

Example:

Three basic types of termination are most common:

☐ *End of Term Lease:* The tenant has a one-year written lease with the landlord. The lease term expired on June 30, 2009, for example, but the tenant has failed to move out, and the landlord wants the tenant out immediately.

☐ *Holdover Tenancy:* Same facts as the example above, except: On July 1, August 1 and September 1, 2009, the tenant pays and landlord accepts rental payments; the landlord then wants to get the tenant out.

☐ *Periodic Tenancy:* The landlord and tenant have an oral (or in rare cases, written) lease based on an agreed periodic tenancy (e.g., week to week; month to month; year to year); the landlord wants the tenant out at the end of a specific period.

A. Termination Procedures

Depending on the type of situation, different procedures and different time periods are applicable.

1. End of Term

This is the simplest type of termination. It is well-settled law that no pre-litigation notice (Notice to Vacate) is required to be given to a tenant at the end of a term certain.[137] The tenant is deemed a trespasser, and an eviction proceeding may be commenced immediately (see Chapter VII).

The landlord must be careful not to ignore the fact that tenant's term has expired. If the landlord handles the situation as if a tenancy still exists, for example, by collecting further rents, a court may deem a holdover tenancy to have been created. However, the simple fact that a landlord does not immediately undertake an eviction action does not, without more, create a holdover situation.

2. Holdover Tenancy

If a tenant remains on the leased premises after the expiration of a term certain and the landlord continues to treat the tenant as a tenant (i.e., continues to collect rent or undertake other affirmative conduct), a holdover tenancy has been created.[138] The period of the holdover tenancy depends on a number of factors, which are listed in order of importance:

1. *Lease*: If the lease specifies the period created by a holdover situation, the lease controls.[139]
2. *Term of Original Lease*: If the lease is silent as to the consequences of a holdover, then the term of the original lease is important. If the original lease is for one year or more, the period is a year-to-year tenancy. If the original lease is for less than one year, the period is equal to the lease term.[140]
3. *Rental Payment*: If no other information is available, the period is determined by when periodic rental payments are made (i.e., monthly, weekly, yearly).[141]

In a holdover situation, once it is determined which period is applicable, one must then proceed under the law governing periodic tenancy. It should be noted that there is some confusion on this point. Some cases seem to suggest that a holdover creates successive "terms certain," in which case no pre-litigation Notice to Quit would be necessary. Others suggest that it is a periodic tenancy and a Notice to Quit is a prerequisite to an eviction action.[142] The better and more prudent view would be to treat all holdovers as periodic tenancies and provide the requisite Notice.

3. Periodic Tenancy

Service of a Notice to Vacate[143] upon the tenant is required to effect a termination of a periodic tenancy. It is of utmost importance that this Notice to Vacate be properly timed. Timing of the notice depends on the period involved. The most typical tenancy periods and their respective notice requirements are listed below:

Year-to-Year:	Three months
Month-to-Month:	Ten days
Week-to-Week and Tenancy-at-Will:	Three days[144]

The law further requires that the notice must be served "not less than the respective period fixed *before the end of the applicable tenancy*."[145] In other words, the notice must be served so that its deadline for termination coincides with an end of the applicable period. If a lease contains a longer notice period (some typically provide for 30 days' notice on a month-to-month tenancy) then the longer period controls. The above requirement can best be explained through example.

> **Example:**
>
> Tenant Y has a month-to-month tenancy that began September 1, 2009. Landlord desires to terminate tenancy, and let the premises to new tenant X effective May 1, 2010. Landlord must give tenant Y a Notice to Vacate ten days before the end of the monthly rental period. Thus, the notice must be given on or before April 19, 2010 to terminate the tenancy effective April 30, 2010 (remember, the day it is served does not count). If the landlord is a couple of days late, and serves the tenant on April 21, 2010, the tenancy would not be terminated on April 30, 2010, *nor would it terminate on the next day*, May 1, 2010. The termination must coincide with the end of a period of the tenancy. Note that you can always give more time (e.g., 11 days, etc.,) but never less.

While a mistake by the landlord in the timing of notice in a month-to-month situation may only delay termination by one more period (i.e., one month), a miscalculation involving a year-to-year tenancy may be disastrous.

> **NOTE:** If the Notice to Vacate is being served in connection with a building being converted into a condominium, different time periods apply. See § 38-33-112, C.R.S. for more information.

B. Notice to Vacate

1. Contents of Notice to Vacate

The contents of a Notice to Vacate are specified by statute.[146] Unlike the Demand for Compliance or Possession, it does not give the tenant alternatives, but simply informs the tenant that the tenancy is terminated and that the premises must be vacated upon a date certain.

2. Checklist for Notice to Vacate (Form No. 219)

- [x] Must be in writing.
- [x] Must be addressed to the tenant or lessee.

- [x] Description of the premises (preferably, both the legal description and the street address).
- [x] Particular time when the tenancy shall terminate.
- [x] Signed by either: (i) all persons claiming possession (all owners), or (ii) an authorized agent or attorney.

Exhibit R is a sample form which, if completed properly, will meet all of the statutory requirements.

EXHIBIT R

NOTICE TO VACATE

TO: ___❶___________________________________

Pursuant to Title 13-40-107, Colorado Revised Statutes, you are hereby notified by the undersigned owner that your tenancy of the lands and premises described below is terminated as of the ___________ day of ______❷______, 20______, and you are accordingly notified to quit said premises and surrender possession thereof on or before said date.

Street Address ___❸___________________________

Lot(s) No. ___❹___________, Block No. ___❺___________, Addition/Subdivision ___❻___

_______________________, in the ___❼_______ * County of ___❽___________,

State of Colorado.

Dated this _________ day of ___❾_______________, 20______.

___❿___________________
Owner

By: ___⓫___________________
Agent

CERTIFICATE OF SERVICE

State of Colorado
_______________ County of ____________________ } ss.

I hereby certify that I served the within Notice to Vacate on ______________________ (date) by:

☐ delivering a true copy to ____

☐ the tenant ☐ other person occupying such premises.

☐ leaving a true copy with ______________________________, a member of the tenant's family over the age of fifteen, residing on or in charge of the premises.

☐ posting a true copy in a conspicuous place on the premises, (describe) ________________

____________________, at ____,

in the ______________ County of _________________________, Colorado.

____
Signature

* Insert "City and" where applicable.

No. 219. Rev. 5-05. NOTICE TO VACATE ©

Bradford Publishing, 1743 Wazee St., Denver, CO 80202 — 303-292-2590 — www.bradfordpublishing.com

3. Filling Out the Notice to Vacate (Form No. 219)

Exhibit S is a completed example of a Notice to Vacate form for a month-to-month tenancy that commenced on the first of the month. Exhibit T is a completed example of a Notice to Vacate for a year-to-year tenancy which commenced June 1, 2008.

Blank 1: Insert the name(s) of the tenant(s) and those known to occupy premises, along with the phrase "Any other parties occupying the premises commonly known as . . . " if there may be additional unidentified tenants.

Blank 2: Insert the date of termination (typically, the last day of the month). Remember this date must coincide with the last date of a tenancy period as well as comporting to the respective three-day, ten-day or three-month termination notice period.

Blank 3: Insert the street address.

Blank 4: Insert the lot number of the property from the legal description.

Blank 5: Insert the block number of the property from the legal description.

Blank 6: Insert which addition or subdivision is applicable from the legal description.

Blank 7: Leave this blank unless the premises are in Denver or Broomfield; if the premises are in Denver or Broomfield, insert "City and."

Blank 8: Insert the name of the county.

Blank 9: Insert the date of service.

Blank 10: Insert the signature(s) of all owners, or

Blank 11: Insert the signature of an authorized agent or attorney.

Note: The Proof of Service on the lower portion of form 219 is filled out and served the same as form 235PA. Read Chapter IV for those instructions.

Note: If the notice is being provided in conjunction with a lease clause requiring a longer notice provision, it is advisable to recite that clause in the notice as well.

EXHIBIT S

NOTICE TO VACATE

TO: Terrestrial Tenant, [and any other occupants of the premises commonly known as 1369 Gaia Avenue, Golden, Colorado 80403]

Pursuant to Title 13-40-107, Colorado Revised Statutes, you are hereby notified by the undersigned owner that your tenancy of the lands and premises described below is terminated as of the 30th day of April, 20 09, and you are accordingly notified to quit said premises and surrender possession thereof on or before said date.

Street Address 1369 Gaia Avenue, Golden, Colorado 80403

Lot(s) No. 9, Block No. 13, Addition/Subdivision Pangaea ______, in the ______ * County of Jefferson, State of Colorado.

Dated this 18th day of April, 20 09.

/s/
Owner Lama Landlord

By: ______
Agent

CERTIFICATE OF SERVICE

State of Colorado }
______ County of ______ } ss.

I hereby certify that I served the within Notice to Vacate on ______ (date) by:

☐ delivering a true copy to ______

☐ the tenant ☐ other person occupying such premises.

☐ leaving a true copy with ______, a member of the tenant's family over the age of fifteen, residing on or in charge of the premises.

☐ posting a true copy in a conspicuous place on the premises, (describe) ______ ______, at ______, in the ______ County of ______, Colorado.

______
Signature

* Insert "City and" where applicable.

Bradford Publishing, 1743 Wazee St., Denver, CO 80202 — 303-292-2590 — www.bradfordpublishing.com

EXHIBIT T

NOTICE TO VACATE

TO: Troubador Tenant, [and any other occupants of the premises commonly known as 669 Minstrel Way, Boulder, Colorado 80301]

Pursuant to Title 13-40-107, Colorado Revised Statutes, you are hereby notified by the undersigned owner that your tenancy of the lands and premises described below is terminated as of the 31st day of May, 20 09, and you are accordingly notified to quit said premises and surrender possession thereof on or before said date.

Street Address 669 Minstrel Way, Boulder, Colorado 80301

Lot(s) No. 10, Block No. 11, Addition/Subdivision Glenn Miller

_______________, in the City and * County of Boulder,

State of Colorado.

Dated this 27th day of February, 20 09.

/s/
Owner Lyrical Landlord

By: _______________
Agent

CERTIFICATE OF SERVICE

State of Colorado
_______________ County of _______________ } ss.

I hereby certify that I served the within Notice to Vacate on _______________ (date) by:

☐ delivering a true copy to _______________

☐ the tenant ☐ other person occupying such premises.

☐ leaving a true copy with _______________, a member of the tenant's family over the age of fifteen, residing on or in charge of the premises.

☐ posting a true copy in a conspicuous place on the premises, (describe) _______________

_______________, at _______________,

in the _______________ County of _______________, Colorado.

____
Signature

* Insert "City and" where applicable.

No. 219. Rev. 5-05. NOTICE TO VACATE ©

Bradford Publishing, 1743 Wazee St., Denver, CO 80202 — 303-292-2590 — www.bradfordpublishing.com

4. Service of Notice to Vacate

The requirements of service of a Notice to Vacate are identical to that of the Demand for Compliance or Possession (see Chapter IV). The same rules regarding timing of the Demand for Compliance or Possession apply to the Notice to Vacate with *one major exception*: in periods involving over seven days (e.g., 10-day notice), weekends and holidays do count towards the period.[147] However, if the last day of the period is a weekend day or legal holiday, the period is run until the end of the next day which is not a Saturday, Sunday, or legal holiday.

Chapter VII. Complaint

A. Contents of Complaint

If, after the landlord has complied with the applicable pre-litigation notice requirements, the appropriate time period has passed and the tenant has failed to comply with the request set forth in the demand or notice, a complaint may then be prepared, filed, and served on the tenant. The filing of a complaint officially commences an eviction proceeding. The law sets forth specific requirements regarding the contents of a complaint filed in an eviction case, as well as additional matters that may be included.[148]

1. Checklist for Complaint (Form No. 94)

- ☐ Caption: contains court, action number, and parties.[149]
- ☐ Statement as to jurisdiction (in county court, state that the claim is under $15,000, exclusive of costs and attorney fees.
- ☐ Description of the property with reasonable certainty (provide the legal description, street address, and the apartment or unit number).
- ☐ Name(s) of the person(s) in possession or occupancy.
- ☐ Include the basis of the tenancy (e.g., written lease).
- ☐ The grounds for recovery.
- ☐ Request for recovery of the premises (e.g., request to kick the tenants out).[150]
- ☐ Amount of rent/damages due.
- ☐ Request for recovery of damages due (including present and future damages, costs, and any other relief to which the plaintiff is entitled).[151]
- ☐ Statement referring to a Demand for Possession or Notice to Quit, if applicable.
- ☐ Notarized signature, address, and phone number of plaintiff[152] *or* the signature of the attorney, with requisite information.

Exhibit U is a sample form which, if completed properly, would meet all of the above requirements.

EXHIBIT U

☐ County Court ❶ ☐ District Court ❷ ________________ County, Colorado Court address: ❸	
Plaintiff(s): ❹ v. **Defendant(s):** ❺	▲ COURT USE ONLY ▲
Attorney or Party Without Attorney (Name and Address): ❻ Phone Number: FAX Number: E-mail: Atty. Reg. #:	Case Number: ❼ Division: ❽ Courtroom: ❽

COMPLAINT (UNLAWFUL DETAINER)

Plaintiff, named above, states and alleges as follows:

1. Plaintiff is the owner, or agent for the owner, of the premises in the County of ❾ ________________, State of Colorado, described as follows:
❿

2. Defendant leased and occupied the premises pursuant to a rental agreement [more specifically:
⓫ ☐ pursuant to a written lease, a copy of which is attached hereby as Exhibit A and incorporated herein by reference,
⓬ ☐ pursuant to a verbal month-to-month tenancy,
⓭ ☐ pursuant to a verbal tenancy at will,
⓮ ☐ other] at a monthly rental of $________________, payable (in advance*) on the _______ day of each month.

⓯ 3. ☐ Defendant failed to pay the monthly rental due on the following date(s) ⓐ ________________ ________________________________ and as of this filing is indebted to the Plaintiff for past due rent in the amount of $ⓑ________________, and for damages in the amount of $ⓒ________________, for a total of $ⓓ________________.

⓰ 4. ☐ Defendant has violated the terms and conditions of the rental agreement by failing to comply with the following covenants or conditions of said rental agreement:
ⓐ

* Strike as applicable.

Bradford Publishing, 1743 Wazee St., Denver, CO 80202 — 303-292-2590 — www.bradfordpublishing.com

17 5. Plaintiff properly served a written demand for compliance with the terms of the rental agreement and applicable law, (a copy of which is attached hereto as Exhibit B and incorporated herein by reference) pursuant to Section 13-40-104, C.R.S., on the ___18___ day of ________________, 20_____, but Defendant has failed or refused to comply with said demand or to give up possession.

6. The Defendant unlawfully, and wrongfully holds possession of the described premises without the consent of the Plaintiff. Rent will continue to accrue at the rate of $___19___________ per day until Plaintiff regains possession of the described premises.

20 7. ☐ This Complaint is filed in County Court and:
   - ☐ the amount demanded by Plaintiff (or the monthly rental value) does not exceed $15,000.00.
   - ☐ the amount demanded by Plaintiff (or the monthly rental value) exceeds $15,000.00, however the Plaintiff wishes to limit recovery to the jurisdiction of this Court.

   ☐ This Complaint is filed in District Court.

8. The Defendant is not engaged in the military service of the United States and is engaged in a civilian occupation.

9. (If applicable) The residential rental agreement attached as Exhibit A (if written) ☐ does ☐ does not contain a provision for the prevailing party to obtain attorney's fees pursuant to 13-40-123, C.R.S.

21 10. The Plaintiff ☐ does ☐ does not demand trial by jury (if demand is made a jury fee must be paid.

WARNING: ALL FEES ARE NON-REFUNDABLE. IN SOME CASES, A REQUEST FOR A JURY TRIAL MAY BE DENIED PURSUANT TO LAW EVEN THOUGH A JURY FEE HAS BEEN PAID.

WHEREFORE, Plaintiff requests judgment for recovery of possession of the premises, for the rent, if any, due or to become due, for present and future damages, together with proper interests, costs, attorney's fees, and any other items allocable by statute or specific agreement.

22 ________________________________
Plaintiff's/Attorney's Signature
(Type Plaintiff's name, address, and tele. no. below)

[Optional]

23 Subscribed and affirmed or sworn to before me on the _______ day of ________________, 20____, in the County of ________________________, State of ________________________.

My commission expires ________________.

24 ________________________________
Notary Public

No. 94. Rev. 9-08. COMPLAINT (UNLAWFUL DETAINER) (Page 2 of 2)

2. Filling Out the Complaint (Form No. 94)

Exhibit V is a sample complaint filled out in a non-payment of rent situation. Exhibit W is a sample complaint under a violation of covenant situation where the tenant is paid up on the rent. Exhibit X is a sample complaint pursuant to a termination of a periodic tenancy.

Blank 1: Check the box for the court, either "County" (damages under $15,000) or "District" (damages over $15,000).

Blank 2: Insert the name of the county.

Blank 3: Insert the address of the court. (www.courts.state.co.us contains a list of courts and addresses).

Blank 4: Insert the landlord's name or the landlord's agent's name. If there is more than one owner, insert all their names.). If the landlord is a business entity instead of a natural person, refer to section A5 at the end of this chapter.

Blank 5: Insert all the tenants' names, as well as the names of all others known to be occupying the property. If there are additional persons occupying the premises or you do not have the names of all of the parties, add the phrase "and any other parties occupying the premises commonly known as . . . ."

Blank 6: Insert the plaintiff's name and address and other contact information (or of the attorney preparing the form, if applicable).

Blank 7: Leave this blank. When the case is filed, the clerk will either stamp a case number on the complaint or tell you what number to fill in. This number is important and must be on all other papers filed in your case.

Blank 8: Leave this blank. The clerk will stamp or tell you the division and courtroom, if applicable.

Blank 9: Insert the name of the county.

Blank 10: Insert the street address and legal description, if available, including the apartment or unit number if applicable.

Box 11: If a written lease exists, check this box and attach a photocopy of the lease to all copies of the complaint. On the bottom of the first page of the lease, write or type "EXHIBIT A." If a written lease does not exist, cross out this line. Note that, while it is not explicitly required by law that the lease be attached as an exhibit to the complaint, this is provided for by the form designed by the Colorado Supreme Court and is quite helpful to the court in the event of any questions concerning the language of the lease.

Boxes 12 & 13: If a verbal month-to-month tenancy or tenancy-at-will exists, check the appropriate box.

Blank 14: Insert the monthly rental rate and the day it was payable (usually, the first of the month). Typically, rents are paid in advance; thus the "in advance" language should remain unless rent was paid in arrears, which is rare.

Box 15: This box should be checked if there was a default for nonpayment of rent.

a) Insert the date when the rent was due (e.g., June 1, 2009); if more than one time, insert additional dates.

b) Insert the amount of rent due as of the filing date. Note that the calculation of this amount is subject to some controversy. Almost all leases provide that the rent is payable monthly, in advance. Thus, after the first of the month the entire month's rent is due for that month or any portion of that month. It is thus appropriate to state that the amount past due is the full monthly rent which has not been paid. Despite the language of leases, courts have been less than open to claims for full rent if the landlord is seeking to dispossess a tenant prior to the end of that period.

c) If any other damages are claimed, such as destruction of the premises, a claim for same may be inserted here or a separate page may be incorporated by reference.

d) Insert the total sum claimed to be currently due and owing,

Box 16: This box should be checked if the tenant defaulted by violating a covenant or condition of the tenancy.

a) Insert the specific provision of the lease that was violated, and quote specific language from lease (see Exhibit V). If any other damages are claimed, they may be inserted here or a separate page may be incorporated by reference.

Note: If the tenant is in breach of both the rent provisions and other covenants, check and complete both boxes 15 and 16.

Line 17: If (as in most cases) a pre-litigation demand was required (Form 235PA), attach a photocopy and label it "EXHIBIT B." However, if this is a termination of tenancy pursuant to a Notice to Vacate (Form 219), it should be attached as Exhibit B and the alteration as set forth in Exhibit X should be included. If pre-litigation notice was a Notice to Quit (Substantial Violation) make the appropriate alteration and attach a copy of the Notice as Exhibit B. If a Notice to Quit (Repeat Violation) was used, attach both the first Demand for Compliance and the Notice to Quit as "Group Exhibit B."

Blank 18: Insert the date that the Notice was served on the tenant.

Blank 19: Insert the rent accruing.

Box 20: In most situations, the amount of damages will be under $15,000 and the case will be in County Court. If so, check the first box. If the amount of damages is over $15,000 and you desire to remain in county court, check the second box. You will be limited to $15,000 in recovery (exclusive of costs and attorney fees). If it is over $15,000 and you do not wish to limit your claim, then the claim must be brought in the district court.

Box 21: Check the appropriate box with respect to a jury demand.

Line 22: Signature of plaintiff or attorney.

Line 23: If this verification is desired, it is to be filled out by a notary public or the court clerk. Note that a verification is no longer required by law.[153]

Line 24: Notary or clerk signature and seal, if applicable.

3. Exhibits to Complaint

Although not legally required, it is highly advisable to attach a copy of the written lease (if one exists), as well as a copy of all pre-litigation notices served on the tenant as exhibits to the complaint.

4. Jury Demand

Landlords are almost always better off with a "bench trial" than a jury trial. A bench trial is one in which the trial proceeds in front of a judge, without a jury, and the judge makes the final decision. A jury trial is available for eviction actions,[154] if desired. Keep in mind that requesting a jury may delay the trial. If a jury is requested, check the appropriate box. An additional fee will be charged.[155]

5. Landlord is "Non-natural" Person

All examples in this text assume that the landlord is a natural person or persons. If the landlord is a different type of entity (e.g., corporation, limited liability company, limited or general partnership), depending on the specific facts, representation by an attorney may be required.[156] There is an exception for officers of close (small) entities which have three owners or less in controversies involving $10,000 or less,[157] and a general partnership may arguably represent themselves.[158] If the officer represents the entity, the court must be provided with evidence of authority to represent the entity. The law further provides that a resolution may be deemed appropriate evidence and that certain officers are presumed to have authority upon providing evidence of the person's position. However, if the landlord is not a natural person, consultation with an attorney is strongly suggested.

EXHIBIT V

☒ County Court ☐ District Court Denver County, Colorado Court address: 1515 Cleveland Place, 4th Floor Denver, Colorado 80202	
Plaintiff(s): Laconic Landlord, an individual v. **Defendant(s):** Transpersonal Tenant [and any other parties occupying the premises commonly known as 620 West Surf, Apartment 5, Denver, Colorado]	▲ COURT USE ONLY ▲
Attorney or Party Without Attorney (Name and Address): Laconic Landlord 1245 Main Street Littleton, Colorado 80123 Phone Number: 303-555-1212 FAX Number: N/A E-mail: LLandlord@gmail.com Atty. Reg. #: N/A	Case Number: Division: Courtroom:

COMPLAINT (UNLAWFUL DETAINER)

Plaintiff, named above, states and alleges as follows:

1. Plaintiff is the owner, or agent for the owner, of the premises in the County of Denver, State of Colorado, described as follows: **620 West Surf, Apartment 5, Denver, Colorado 80218, legally described as a portion of Lot 1, Block 6, Salmon Run Addition, 3rd Filing, County of Denver, State of Colorado.**

2. Defendant leased and occupied the premises pursuant to a rental agreement [more specifically: ☒ pursuant to a written lease, a copy of which is attached hereby as Exhibit A and incorporated herein by reference, ☐ pursuant to a verbal month-to-month tenancy, ☐ pursuant to a verbal tenancy at will, ☐ other] at a monthly rental of $___750.00___, payable (in advance*) on the __1st__ day of each month.

3. ☒ Defendant failed to pay the monthly rental due on the following date(s) February 1, 2009 ________________ and as of this filing is indebted to the Plaintiff for past due rent in the amount of $___750.00___, and for damages in the amount of $___N/A___, for a total of $___750.00___.

4. ☐ Defendant has violated the terms and conditions of the rental agreement by failing to comply with the following covenants or conditions of said rental agreement:

* Strike as applicable.

5. Plaintiff properly served a written demand for compliance with the terms of the rental agreement and applicable law, (a copy of which is attached hereto as Exhibit B and incorporated herein by reference) pursuant to Section 13-40-104, C.R.S., on the __**10th**__ day of __**February**__, 20__**09**__, but Defendant has failed or refused to comply with said demand or to give up possession.

6. The Defendant unlawfully, and wrongfully holds possession of the described premises without the consent of the Plaintiff. Rent will continue to accrue at the rate of $________________ per day until Plaintiff regains possession of the described premises.

7. ☒ This Complaint is filed in County Court and:
   - ☒ the amount demanded by Plaintiff (or the monthly rental value) does not exceed $15,000.00.
   - ☐ the amount demanded by Plaintiff (or the monthly rental value) exceeds $15,000.00, however the Plaintiff wishes to limit recovery to the jurisdiction of this Court.

   ☐ This Complaint is filed in District Court.

8. The Defendant is not engaged in the military service of the United States and is engaged in a civilian occupation.

9. (If applicable) The residential rental agreement attached as Exhibit A (if written) ☒ does ☐ does not contain a provision for the prevailing party to obtain attorney's fees pursuant to 13-40-123, C.R.S.

10. The Plaintiff ☐ does ☒ does not demand trial by jury (if demand is made a jury fee must be paid.

WARNING: ALL FEES ARE NON-REFUNDABLE. IN SOME CASES, A REQUEST FOR A JURY TRIAL MAY BE DENIED PURSUANT TO LAW EVEN THOUGH A JURY FEE HAS BEEN PAID.

WHEREFORE, Plaintiff requests judgment for recovery of possession of the premises, for the rent, if any, due or to become due, for present and future damages, together with proper interests, costs, attorney's fees, and any other items allocable by statute or specific agreement.

__**/s/**________________________________
Plaintiff's/Attorney's Signature
(Type Plaintiff's name, address, and tele. no. below)
Laconic Landlord
1245 Main Street
Littleton, Colorado 80123
303-555-1212

[Optional]
Subscribed and affirmed or sworn to before me on the ________ day of __________________, 20____, in the County of ___________________________, State of ___________________________.

My commission expires __________________.

____
Notary Public

No. 94. Rev. 9-08. COMPLAINT (UNLAWFUL DETAINER) (Page 2 of 2)

EXHIBIT W

☒ County Court ☐ District Court Denver County, Colorado Court address: 1515 Cleveland Place, 4th Floor Denver, Colorado 80202	
Plaintiff(s): Liberal Landlord, an individual v. **Defendant(s):** Temerity Tenant, [and any other parties occupying the premises commonly known as 13 Capitol Hill, Denver, Colorado 80210]	▲ COURT USE ONLY ▲
Attorney or Party Without Attorney (Name and Address): Liberal Landlord 999 Park Avenue Boulder, Colorado 80309 Phone Number: 303-555-1212 FAX Number: N/A E-mail: LLandlord@gmail.com Atty. Reg. #: N/A	Case Number: Division: Courtroom:

COMPLAINT (UNLAWFUL DETAINER)

Plaintiff, named above, states and alleges as follows:

1. Plaintiff is the owner, or agent for the owner, of the premises in the County of Denver, State of Colorado, described as follows: 13 Capitol Hill, Denver, Colorado 80210, legally described as Lot 7, Block 5, Trout Falls Subdivision, City and County of Denver, State of Colorado

2. Defendant leased and occupied the premises pursuant to a rental agreement [more specifically: ☒ pursuant to a written lease, a copy of which is attached hereby as Exhibit A and incorporated herein by reference, ☐ pursuant to a verbal month-to-month tenancy, ☐ pursuant to a verbal tenancy at will, ☐ other] at a monthly rental of $ 1,000.00, payable (in advance*) on the 1st day of each month.

3. ☐ Defendant failed to pay the monthly rental due on the following date(s) ______________ and as of this filing is indebted to the Plaintiff for past due rent in the amount of $__________, and for damages in the amount of $__________, for a total of $__________.

4. ☒ Defendant has violated the terms and conditions of the rental agreement by failing to comply with the following covenants or conditions of said rental agreement: Paragraph 15(e) of the Lease, providing that "Neither Tenant nor Tenant's licensees or invitees shall be a nuisance or act in any manner that would interfere with the quiet enjoyment by adjacent property owners or other tenants (or their invitees) of their premises. <u>This prohibition includes, but is not limited to, loud noises, loud music, noxious or unpleasant odors, and disruptive behavior or actions</u>."
Defendant's punk rock band, the "Moody Miners," could be heard playing from 10:00 p.m. to 4:00 a.m. on March 1st, 2009. A Demand was provided as set forth in Paragraph 15(e) and pursuant to Paragraph 28 of the Lease. The band again caused a disturbance on April 1st, 2009. A Notice to Quit (Repeat Violation) was then served upon Defendant on April 2nd, 2009 (a copy of which is attached hereto and incorporated herein as Exhibit C).

* Strike as applicable.

Bradford Publishing, 1743 Wazee St., Denver, CO 80202 — 303-292-2590 — www.bradfordpublishing.com

5. Plaintiff properly served a written demand for compliance with the terms of the rental agreement and applicable law, (a copy of which is attached hereto as Exhibit B and incorporated herein by reference) pursuant to Section 13-40-104, C.R.S., on the **1st** day of **March**, 20**09**, but Defendant has failed or refused to comply with said demand or to give up possession.

6. The Defendant unlawfully, and wrongfully holds possession of the described premises without the consent of the Plaintiff. Rent will continue to accrue at the rate of $**32.26** per day until Plaintiff regains possession of the described premises.

7. ☒ This Complaint is filed in County Court and:
   - ☒ the amount demanded by Plaintiff (or the monthly rental value) does not exceed $15,000.00.
   - ☐ the amount demanded by Plaintiff (or the monthly rental value) exceeds $15,000.00, however the Plaintiff wishes to limit recovery to the jurisdiction of this Court.

   ☐ This Complaint is filed in District Court.

8. The Defendant is not engaged in the military service of the United States and is engaged in a civilian occupation.

9. (If applicable) The residential rental agreement attached as Exhibit A (if written) ☐ does ☐ does not contain a provision for the prevailing party to obtain attorney's fees pursuant to 13-40-123, C.R.S.

10. The Plaintiff ☐ does ☒ does not demand trial by jury (if demand is made a jury fee must be paid.

WARNING: ALL FEES ARE NON-REFUNDABLE. IN SOME CASES, A REQUEST FOR A JURY TRIAL MAY BE DENIED PURSUANT TO LAW EVEN THOUGH A JURY FEE HAS BEEN PAID.

WHEREFORE, Plaintiff requests judgment for recovery of possession of the premises, for the rent, if any, due or to become due, for present and future damages, together with proper interests, costs, attorney's fees, and any other items allocable by statute or specific agreement.

/s/ ______________________
Plaintiff's/Attorney's Signature
(Type Plaintiff's name, address, and tele. no. below)
Liberal Landlord
999 Park Avenue
Boulder, Colorado 80309
303-555-1212

[Optional]
Subscribed and affirmed or sworn to before me on the ________ day of ________________, 20____, in the County of __________________________, State of __________________________.

My commission expires _________________.

____
Notary Public

No. 94. Rev. 9-08. COMPLAINT (UNLAWFUL DETAINER) (Page 2 of 2)

EXHIBIT X

☒ County Court ☐ District Court Jefferson County, Colorado Court address: Jefferson County Court & Administrative Facility 100 Jefferson County Parkway Golden, Colorado 80401	
Plaintiff(s): Lama Landlord, an individual v. **Defendant(s):** Terrestrial Tenant, [and any other parties occupying the premises commonly known as 1369 Gaia Avenue, Golden, Colorado 80403]	▲ COURT USE ONLY ▲
Attorney or Party Without Attorney (Name and Address): Lama Landlord 16 Pearl Street Boulder, Colorado 80302 Phone Number: 303-867-5309 FAX Number: N/A E-mail: LLandlord@gmail.com Atty. Reg. #: N/A	Case Number: Division: Courtroom:
COMPLAINT (UNLAWFUL DETAINER)	

Plaintiff, named above, states and alleges as follows:

1. Plaintiff is the owner, or agent for the owner, of the premises in the County of Jefferson, State of Colorado, described as follows: **1369 Gaia Avenue, Golden, Colorado 80403, legally described as Lot 9, Block 13, Pangaea Subdivision, County of Jefferson, State of Colorado.**

2. Defendant leased and occupied the premises pursuant to a rental agreement [more specifically: ☐ pursuant to a written lease, a copy of which is attached hereby as Exhibit A and incorporated herein by reference, ☒ pursuant to a verbal month-to-month tenancy, ☐ pursuant to a verbal tenancy at will, ☐ other] at a monthly rental of $ 1,000.00, payable (in advance*) on the 1st day of each month.

3. ☐ Defendant failed to pay the monthly rental due on the following date(s) ________________ ________________ and as of this filing is indebted to the Plaintiff for past due rent in the amount of $________________, and for damages in the amount of $________________, for a total of $________________.

4. ☒ Defendant has violated the terms and conditions of the rental agreement by failing to comply with the following covenants or conditions of said rental agreement:

   Defendant occupied the premises as a month-to-month tenant and has failed to vacate the premises after being served with the appropriate Notice to Vacate per Section 13-40-107, C.R.S., on the 18th day of April, 2009.

* Strike as applicable.

5. Plaintiff properly served a written demand for compliance with the terms of the rental agreement and applicable law, (a copy of which is attached hereto as Exhibit B and incorporated herein by reference) pursuant to Section 13-40-104, C.R.S., on the **18th** day of **April**, 20**09**, but Defendant has failed or refused to comply with said demand or to give up possession.

6. The Defendant unlawfully, and wrongfully holds possession of the described premises without the consent of the Plaintiff. Rent will continue to accrue at the rate of $**24.19** per day until Plaintiff regains possession of the described premises.

7. ☒ This Complaint is filed in County Court and:
   - ☒ the amount demanded by Plaintiff (or the monthly rental value) does not exceed $15,000.00.
   - ☐ the amount demanded by Plaintiff (or the monthly rental value) exceeds $15,000.00, however the Plaintiff wishes to limit recovery to the jurisdiction of this Court.

   ☐ This Complaint is filed in District Court.

8. The Defendant is not engaged in the military service of the United States and is engaged in a civilian occupation.

9. (If applicable) The residential rental agreement attached as Exhibit A (if written) ☒ does ☐ does not contain a provision for the prevailing party to obtain attorney's fees pursuant to 13-40-123, C.R.S.

10. The Plaintiff ☐ does ☒ does not demand trial by jury (if demand is made a jury fee must be paid.

WARNING: ALL FEES ARE NON-REFUNDABLE. IN SOME CASES, A REQUEST FOR A JURY TRIAL MAY BE DENIED PURSUANT TO LAW EVEN THOUGH A JURY FEE HAS BEEN PAID.

WHEREFORE, Plaintiff requests judgment for recovery of possession of the premises, for the rent, if any, due or to become due, for present and future damages, together with proper interests, costs, attorney's fees, and any other items allocable by statute or specific agreement.

/s/
Plaintiff's/Attorney's Signature
(Type Plaintiff's name, address, and tele. no. below)
Lama Landlord
16 Pearl Street
Boulder, Colorado 80302
303-867-5309

[Optional]
Subscribed and affirmed or sworn to before me on the ________ day of ________________, 20____, in the County of __________________________, State of __________________________.

My commission expires _________________.

____
Notary Public

Chapter VIII. Summons

A. Contents of Summons

A summons is a document informing an individual that he or she is a defendant in a legal action. Further, it informs the defendant of the time and place the defendant must file an answer and when to appear in court (the "Return Date"). The summons must be prepared at the same time as the complaint. Technically, service of the summons brings the defendant under jurisdiction of the court. Once served, the court may enter judgment(s) against the defendant without further notice.[159]

Note that the summons form used in Forcible Entry and Unlawful Detainer cases is different from the summons for a *conventional* county court case.

> **Example:**
>
> The county courts have a specific form for summons in Forcible Entry and Unlawful Detainer (County Court Form 1A). Note that this is a different form than that which is used for other civil matters in county court. Under C.R.C.P. 310, use of this form is mandatory in County Court.

If the claim exceeds $15,000, the action must be filed in district court. Another summons (Form No. 83D) is designed for use in district court, but not shown in this book. Both summons forms are available at Bradford Publishing Company.

CAUTION: Make sure you have the appropriate summons form.

A plaintiff in an eviction action is responsible for causing the defendant to be served with the summons, as well as a copy of the complaint and answer form (if in County Court), before any further proceedings may occur in the court case.[160]

1. Checklist for Summons in Forcible Entry and Unlawful Detainer (Form No. 83)

- ☐ Caption: contains court, action number, and parties.
- ☐ Contains a command to the defendant to appear before court.[161]
- ☐ Specify the time and place where the defendant is to appear.
- ☐ Include the following statutory statement:

> "If you fail to file with the court, at or before the time for appearance specified in the summons, an answer to the complaint setting forth the grounds upon which you base your claim for possession and denying or admitting all of the material allegations of the complaint, judgment by default may be taken against you for the possession of the property described in the complaint, for the rent, if any, due or to become due, for present and future damages and costs, and for any other relief to which the plaintiff is entitled. If you are claiming that the landlord's failure to repair the residential premises is a defense to the landlord's allegation of nonpayment of rent, the court will require you to pay into the registry of the court, at the time of filing your answer, the rent due less any expenses you have incurred based upon the landlord's failure to repair the residential premises."[162]

- ☑ Date.[163]
- ☑ Issued by the clerk of court or the attorney.[164]
- ☑ Copy of the complaint (with exhibits) and a blank answer form (in County Court).

Exhibit Y is a sample form which, if completed properly, would meet all of the above requirements.

> **NOTE:** Remember to include the complaint and a blank answer form with the summons. This is required by C.R.C.P. 304(b).

EXHIBIT Y

<table>
<tr><td>County Court, ❶ __________________ County, Colorado
Court address:
❷</td><td rowspan="3">

▲ COURT USE ONLY ▲</td></tr>
<tr><td>Plaintiff(s):
❸
v.
Defendant(s):
❹</td></tr>
<tr><td rowspan="2">Attorney or Party Without Attorney (Name and Address):
❺

Phone Number:
FAX Number:
E-mail:
Atty. Reg. #:</td></tr>
<tr><td>Case Number: ❻

Division: Courtroom: ❻</td></tr>
<tr><td colspan="2">SUMMONS IN FORCIBLE ENTRY AND UNLAWFUL DETAINER</td></tr>
</table>

To the above named Defendant(s): Take notice that

1. On ❼ ______________________________, 20______ at __________ o'clock _____. M., in the ❽ ________________ County Court, ❾ ______________________, Colorado, the Court may be asked to enter judgment against you as set forth in the complaint.

2. A copy of the complaint against you and an answer form which you must use if you file an answer are attached.

3. If you do not agree with the complaint, then you must either:

a. Go to the Court, located at ❷ ____, ______________________________, Colorado, at the above date and time and file an answer stating any legal reason you have why judgment should not be entered against you, **OR**

b. File the answer with the Court before that date and time.

4. When you file your answer, you must pay a filing fee to the Clerk of the Court.

5. If you file an answer, you must personally serve or mail a copy to the Plaintiff(s) or the attorney who signed the complaint.

6. If you do not file with the Court, at or before the time for appearance specified in this summons, an answer to the complaint setting forth the grounds upon which you base your claim for possession and denying or admitting all of the material allegations of the complaint, judgment by default may be taken against you for the possession of the property described in the complaint, for the rent, if any, due or to become due, for present and future damages and costs, and for any other relief to which the Plaintiff(s) is (are) entitled.

7. If you are claiming that the landlord's failure to repair the residential premises is a defense to the landlord's allegation of nonpayment of rent, the court will require you to pay into the registry of the court, at the time of filing your answer, the rent due less any expenses you have incurred based upon the landlord's failure to repair the residential premises. In addition to filing an answer, you are required to complete an Affidavit (JDF 109) to support the amount you will need to pay into the registry of the Court.

8. If you want a jury trial, you must ask for one in the answer and pay a jury fee in addition to the filing fee.

9. If you want to file an answer or request a jury trial and you are indigent, you must appear at the above date and time, fill out a financial affidavit, and ask the Court to waive the fee.

Dated at ❿______________________, Colorado, this _______ day of ⓫________________, 20____.

By ⓬________________________________
Deputy Clerk

⓭________________________________
Attorney for Plaintiff(s) (if applicable)

⓮________________________________
Address(es) of Plaintiff(s)

⓯________________________________
Telephone Number(s) of Plaintiff(s)

⓰

This Summons is issued pursuant to §13-40-111, C.R.S. A copy of the Complaint together with a blank answer form must be served with this Summons. This form should be used only for actions filed under Colorado's Forcible Entry and Detainer Act.

To the clerk: If this Summons is issued by the Clerk of the Court, the signature block for the clerk or deputy should be provided by stamp, or typewriter, in the space to the left of the attorney's name.

WARNING: ALL FEES ARE NONREFUNDABLE. IN SOME CASES, A REQUEST FOR A JURY TRIAL MAY BE DENIED PURSUANT TO LAW EVEN THOUGH A JURY FEE HAS BEEN PAID.

____________________ v. ____________________ Case No. __________

RETURN OF SERVICE

I declare under oath that:

1. I served this Summons, a copy of the Complaint in this case, and a copy of the Answer form on ____________________ on ____________________ (date), at __________ (time), in the County of ____________________, State of ____________________, at the following location: ____

   ____.

2. I served the above documents in the following manner (check one):
   - ☐ by handing them to a person identified to me as the Defendant.
   - ☐ by identifying the documents and offering to leave them with a person who I know, or have reason to identify, as the person being served, who refused service; and then by leaving them in a conspicuous place.
   - ☐ by leaving them at the Defendant's usual place of abode with ____________________, who is 18 years of age or older and a member of the Defendant's family.
   - ☐ by leaving them at the Defendant's usual workplace with ____________________, who is the Defendant's ____________________ (secretary, administrative assistant, bookkeeper, managing agent).
   - ☐ by leaving them with ______________________________, who as ____________________ (title), is authorized by appointment or law to receive service of process for the Defendant.
   - ☐ I have made diligent efforts but have been unable to make personal service on the Defendant and I have made service by posting the documents in a conspicuous place on the premises described herein.
   - ☐ by substituted service on ______________________________, in accordance with C.R.C.P. 304(e), and by then mailing the documents to the following address: ____
   - ☐ by serving them as follows (other service permitted by C.R.C.P. 304): ____________________ ____

3. ☐ I attempted to serve the Defendant on ________ occasions but have not been able to locate the Defendant. Return to the Plaintiff is made on ____________________ (date).
4. ☐ I am 18 years of age or older and am not a party to this case.
5. ☐ My fee for serving the above documents was $_______________.

____
Signature

☐ Private Process Server
☐ Sheriff, ____________________ County

Subscribed and affirmed or sworn to before me this ________ day of ____________________, 20____, in the County of ____________________, State of ____________________.

My commission expires: ____________________

____
Notary Public/Clerk

______________________________ v. ______________________________ Case No. __________

CERTIFICATE OF MAILING

I/we, the undersigned Plaintiff(s) (or agent for Plaintiff(s)), certify that on ______________________ (date), the date on which the Summons, Complaint, and Answer were filed, I/we mailed a copy of the Summons/Alias Summons, a copy of the Complaint, and Answer form by postage prepaid, first class mail, to ____, the Defendant(s) at the following address(es):

____
Plaintiff(s)/Agent for Plaintiff(s)

Section 13-40-111 Colorado Revised Statutes, as amended.

13-40-111. Issuance and return of summons.

(1) Upon filing the complaint as provided in §13-40-110, C.R.S., the clerk of the court or the attorney for the plaintiff shall issue a summons. The summons shall command the Defendant to appear before the court at a place named in such summons and at a time and on a day which shall be not less than five business days nor more than ten calendar days from the day of issuing the same to answer the complaint of Plaintiff. The summons shall also contain a statement addressed to the Defendant stating: "If you fail to file with the court, at or before the time for appearance specified in the summons, an answer to the complaint setting forth the grounds upon which you base your claim or possession and denying or admitting all of the material allegations of the complaint, judgment by default may be taken against you for the possession of the property described in the complaint, for the rent, if any, due or to become due, for present and future damages and costs, and for any other relief to which the Plaintiff is entitled". If you are claiming that the landlord's failure to repair the residential premises is a defense to the landlord's allegation of nonpayment of rent, the Court will require you to pay into the registry of the Court, at the time of filing your answer, the rent due less any expenses you have incurred based upon the landlordís failure to repair the residential premises.

(2) For purposes of this section, "business days" means any calendar day excluding Saturdays, Sundays, and legal holidays.

13-40-112. Service.

(1) Such summons may be served by personal service as in any civil action. A copy of the complaint must be served with the summons.

(2) If personal service cannot be had upon the Defendant by a person qualified under the Colorado Rules of Civil Procedure to serve process, after having made diligent effort to make such personal service, such person may make service by posting a copy of the summons and the complaint in some conspicuous place upon the premises. In addition thereto, the Plaintiff shall mail, no later than the next day following the day on which he/she files the complaint, a copy of the summons, or, in the event that an alias summons is issued, a copy of the alias summons, and a copy of the complaint to the Defendant at the premises by postage prepaid, first class mail.

(3) Personal service or service by posting shall be made at least five days before the day for appearance specified in such summons, and the time and manner of such service shall be endorsed upon such summons by the person making service thereof.

(4) For purposes of this section, "business days" means any calendar day excluding Saturdays, Sundays, and legal holidays.

2. Filling Out the Summons (Form No. 83)

Exhibit Z is a completed sample summons.

Blank 1: Insert the name of the county.

Blank 2: Insert the address of the court and its common name (e.g., "Boulder County Justice Center, 1777 6th Street, Boulder, Colorado, 80302").

Blank 3: Insert the names of all plaintiffs.

Blank 4: Insert the names of all defendants.

Blank 5: Insert the plaintiff's name and address (or of the attorney preparing the form, if applicable).

Blank 6: Insert the civil action number and courtroom number, if available (obtain this from the clerk).

Blank 7: Insert the date and time (obtain this from the clerk).

Blank 8: Insert the name of the county.

Blank 9: Insert the name of the city.

Blank 10: Insert the name of the city or town in which you are filing this.

Blank 11: Leave this blank. The clerk issuing the summons will fill this in; if this is not filled in, insert the date the summons was issued.

Blank 12: Leave this blank (the clerk will fill this in).

Blank 13: If an attorney is issuing the summons, the attorney must sign and insert the information listed below.

Blank 14: Insert the plaintiff's address.

Blank 15: Insert the plaintiff's telephone number.

Blank 16: Insert information to aid in service of the summons (e.g., "Sheriff please serve Defendant at: 1276 Second Street, 3rd Floor, Nederland, Colorado before 8:00 a.m. or after 5:00 p.m.").

EXHIBIT Z

<table>
<tr><td>County Court, Denver County, Colorado
Court address: 1515 Cleveland Place, 4th Floor
Denver, Colorado 80202</td><td rowspan="3">▲ COURT USE ONLY ▲</td></tr>
<tr><td>Plaintiff(s): Liberal Landlord, an individual

v.
Defendant(s): Temerity Tenant, [and any other parties occupying the premises commonly known as 13 Capitol Hill, Denver, Colorado 80210]</td></tr>
<tr><td rowspan="2">Attorney or Party Without Attorney (Name and Address):
Liberal Landlord
999 Park Avenue
Boulder, Colorado 80309

Phone Number: 303-555-1212
FAX Number: N/A
E-mail: Llandlord@gmail.com
Atty. Reg. #: N/A</td></tr>
<tr><td>Case Number: 09CV1236

Division: Courtroom:</td></tr>
<tr><td colspan="2">SUMMONS IN FORCIBLE ENTRY AND UNLAWFUL DETAINER</td></tr>
</table>

To the above named Defendant(s): Take notice that

1. On **April 17th**, 20**09** at **9:00** o'clock **A**. M., in the **Denver** County Court, **Denver**, Colorado, the Court may be asked to enter judgment against you as set forth in the complaint.

2. A copy of the complaint against you and an answer form which you must use if you file an answer are attached.

3. If you do not agree with the complaint, then you must either:

   a. Go to the Court, located at **1515 Cleveland Place, 4th Floor, Denver, Colorado 80202**, __________, Colorado, at the above date and time and file an answer stating any legal reason you have why judgment should not be entered against you, **OR**

   b. File the answer with the Court before that date and time.

4. When you file your answer, you must pay a filing fee to the Clerk of the Court.

5. If you file an answer, you must personally serve or mail a copy to the Plaintiff(s) or the attorney who signed the complaint.

6. If you do not file with the Court, at or before the time for appearance specified in this summons, an answer to the complaint setting forth the grounds upon which you base your claim for possession and denying or admitting all of the material allegations of the complaint, judgment by default may be taken against you for the possession of the property described in the complaint, for the rent, if any, due or to become due, for present and future damages and costs, and for any other relief to which the Plaintiff(s) is (are) entitled.

7. If you are claiming that the landlord's failure to repair the residential premises is a defense to the landlord's allegation of nonpayment of rent, the court will require you to pay into the registry of the court, at the time of filing your answer, the rent due less any expenses you have incurred based upon the landlord's failure

No. 83. Rev. 3-09. SUMMONS IN FORCIBLE ENTRY AND UNLAWFUL DETAINER (C.R.C.P. Form 1A) (Page 1 of 4)

Bradford Publishing, 1743 Wazee St., Denver, CO 80202 — (303) 292-2590 — www.bradfordpublishing.com

to repair the residential premises. In addition to filing an answer, you are required to complete an Affidavit (JDF 109) to support the amount you will need to pay into the registry of the Court.

8. If you want a jury trial, you must ask for one in the answer and pay a jury fee in addition to the filing fee.

9. If you want to file an answer or request a jury trial and you are indigent, you must appear at the above date and time, fill out a financial affidavit, and ask the Court to waive the fee.

Dated at **Denver**, Colorado, this **3rd** day of **April**, 20**09**.

By ______________________
Deputy Clerk

/s/
Attorney for Plaintiff(s) (if applicable)
Liberal Landlord

999 Park Avenue, Boulder, Colorado 80302
Address(es) of Plaintiff(s)

303-555-1212
Telephone Number(s) of Plaintiff(s)

Sheriff, please serve defendant at:
13 Capitol Hill
Denver, Colorado 80210
before 8:00 a.m. or after 5:00 p.m.

This Summons is issued pursuant to §13-40-111, C.R.S. A copy of the Complaint together with a blank answer form must be served with this Summons. This form should be used only for actions filed under Colorado's Forcible Entry and Detainer Act.

To the clerk: If this Summons is issued by the Clerk of the Court, the signature block for the clerk or deputy should be provided by stamp, or typewriter, in the space to the left of the attorney's name.

WARNING: ALL FEES ARE NONREFUNDABLE. IN SOME CASES, A REQUEST FOR A JURY TRIAL MAY BE DENIED PURSUANT TO LAW EVEN THOUGH A JURY FEE HAS BEEN PAID.

No. 83. Rev. 3-09. SUMMONS IN FORCIBLE ENTRY AND UNLAWFUL DETAINER (C.R.C.P. Form 1A) (Page 2 of 4)

B. Filing of Complaint and Issuance of Summons

Once the complaint, summons, and exhibits are prepared, they are ready to be filed, issued and, served. Be sure to make several photocopies of all these documents. A good rule is to make four copies of each document plus one for each additional defendant.

Take all documents to the respective clerk of court. The clerk will collect your filing fees, assign your case a civil action number, file your original complaint, file stamp all of your copies, and issue your summons. An attorney handling the case is also empowered to issue a summons.[165] The clerk will also give you the information regarding the return date, time, and place; this must be inserted into the appropriate blanks on the summons. Note that many jurisdictions now require attorneys to electronically file (E-File) all court documents, including County Court FED actions. Check in each jurisdiction for current rules and policies, since these are changing rapidly. Note that if you are not an attorney you are not required (and as of this writing are not able) to effect E-filings. This may change in the near future.

C. Where to File

The eviction action must be filed in the county where the property is located. As discussed previously, if the amount sought is over $15,000, the case must be filed with the district court. If the amount sought is under $15,000, the case should be filed with the county court.[166]

D. Service of Process

Each defendant named in the case must be served with his or her own individual copy of the summons and complaint. This is known as "service of process" or simply "service." This is essential because if a defendant is not served, he or she is not subject to the court's orders. Improper service will hold up a case while the problem is being resolved, and may result in dismissal, so it is better to get good service the first time around. The rules regarding proper service upon a party are set forth in § 13-40-112, C.R.S. and C.R.C.P. 4 and 304. These laws are reprinted in Appendix C. You are strongly encouraged to review these laws and obtain an understanding of them.

E. Authorized Process Servers

Process can either be served by either: (a) the sheriff of the county where service is made; or (b) any person over the age of 18 not a party to the action.

The service must be made by a disinterested person (i.e., not a relative, employee, agent, etc.). Typically, this is a private process server. For pro se litigants, it is suggested that the sheriff be used because: (a) it lends an air of authority to the proceeding; (b) the sheriff is relatively inexpensive and cost-effective; and (c) if there is a dispute as to service, the sheriff makes a very credible witness. Alternatively, you may also hire a private detective or other qualified courier to serve process. Check the Yellow Pages under "private detective" or "process servers."

Bring copies of the complaint, the original summons, and a blank answer form to the sheriff or process server. Be prepared to pay a service fee (plus mileage) to the sheriff and leave sufficient copies with the sheriff. The sheriff may also request that a separate form setting forth information relevant to service be filled out. Practices vary by county.

F. Method of Service

Like other civil cases, the service of process in an eviction case may be by personal service.[167] Personal service is preferable because it will give the court jurisdiction to enter an order for both possession *and monetary judgments*. Service may also be achieved by posting and mail.

1. Requirements for Personal Service

Personal service may be effected on an individual defendant (not a defendant who is a business entity) by any of the following methods:

- Delivery of process to the defendant personally.
- Leaving a copy of process at the defendant's place of abode with some member of the defendant's family over the age of 18.
- Leaving a copy of process at the defendant's usual workplace with the defendant's "secretary, administrative assistant, bookkeeper, or managing agent."
- Delivering a copy of process to an agent authorized by law to receive process.[168]

2. Requirements for Service by Posting and Mail

Unlike other civil cases, process may also be served by "posting" and mail.[169] This method of service is also known as "constructive service" and more informally as "nail and mail." This must be accomplished by a person authorized to serve process and may only be carried out after the server has made a "diligent effort to make . . . personal service."[170] Service by posting is only adequate to bestow the court with jurisdiction over the property, i.e., an order for possession may be entered, but not for monetary damages.

For proper service by posting and mail, the following steps must be accomplished:

1. Before service by posting and mail, the landlord must make a diligent effort to serve the tenant through personal service.
2. A copy of the summons and complaint, along with a blank answer form, must be posted in a conspicuous place on the premises.
3. Mail a copy of the summons to the defendant no later than the next business day after the day on which the complaint was filed, by first class mail.[171]

Clarify with your process server who will mail the copy of the summons and complaint. Depending on who you use and the jurisdiction you are in, either you or the process server may mail the summons and complaint.

It is advisable to always mail a copy of the documents, in compliance with the above steps, even if you hope to get personal service. Because of the short time period, you will not know what type of service has been effected until after the deadline for mailing has passed; thus for the price of a first class stamp, you have covered all contingencies.

G. Timing of Service

The law requires that the return date on the summons shall not be less than five business days, nor more than ten calendar days from the date of issuance. Service of summons, whether by posting or personal service, must be made on the defendant at least five business days before the return date. Therefore, there is only a small window of one to five days in which to serve the defendant. As previously stated, if it is anticipated that the defendant might have to be served by posting a copy of the summons, it should be mailed to the defendant immediately after issuing it and filing the complaint.[172] If service is by posting, the court will not consider any claim for money damages and is only empowered to consider the issue of possession of the premises.[173] Business days do not include Saturdays, Sundays, or legal holidays.[174]

H. Return of Service

The return of service portion on the back of the summons (Form No. 83) must be completed by the process server and filed with the court.[175] The court will not take any action on a case without a return of service in the file. It is the responsibility of the landlord to establish with the process server who will be filing the return of service and to make sure it is filed before the return date. Sometimes the sheriff or private process server will prepare their own form of proof of service. Verify this when placing papers for service.

CAUTION: If the process server does not use the return of service on the back of Form No. 83 for proof of service, be sure that the statement made by the server includes a statement that the summons, complaint and an answer form were served. This relatively new requirement of including the answer form could be overlooked.

Although the return of service is prepared by the sheriff or private process server with respect to personal service or posting, examples of both are provided as Exhibits Z-1 and Z-2, respectively. Furthermore, recall that if service is made by posting, a proof of mailing will also be required (see certificate of mailing on Exhibit Z-2). Finally, if a separate return of service form is used by the process server, you may prepare a separate certificate of mailing (see Exhibit Z-3).

EXHIBIT Z-1

Liberal Landlord v. Temerity Tenant Case No. 09CV1236

RETURN OF SERVICE

I declare under oath that:

1. I served this Summons, a copy of the Complaint in this case, and a copy of the Answer form on Temerity Tenant on April 6th, 2009 (date), at 7:30 a.m. (time), in the County of Denver, State of Colorado, at the following location: 13 Capitol Hill, Denver, Colorado 80210 _____.
2. I served the above documents in the following manner (check one):
   - ☒ by handing them to a person identified to me as the Defendant.
   - ☐ by identifying the documents and offering to leave them with a person who I know, or have reason to identify, as the person being served, who refused service; and then by leaving them in a conspicuous place.
   - ☐ by leaving them at the Defendant's usual place of abode with _____, who is 18 years of age or older and a member of the Defendant's family.
   - ☐ by leaving them at the Defendant's usual workplace with _____, who is the Defendant's _____ (secretary, administrative assistant, bookkeeper, managing agent).
   - ☐ by leaving them with _____, who as _____ (title), is authorized by appointment or law to receive service of process for the Defendant.
   - ☐ I have made diligent efforts but have been unable to make personal service on the Defendant and I have made service by posting the documents in a conspicuous place on the premises described herein.
   - ☐ by substituted service on _____, in accordance with C.R.C.P. 304(e), and by then mailing the documents to the following address: _____
   - ☐ by serving them as follows (other service permitted by C.R.C.P. 304): _____
3. ☐ I attempted to serve the Defendant on _____ occasions but have not been able to locate the Defendant. Return to the Plaintiff is made on _____ (date).
4. ☐ I am 18 years of age or older and am not a party to this case.
5. ☐ My fee for serving the above documents was $_____.

/s/
Signature **Persistent Process Server**

☒ Private Process Server
☐ Sheriff, _____ County

Subscribed and affirmed or sworn to before me this 7th day of April, 20 09, in the County of Denver, State of Colorado.

My commission expires: April 15, 2011

/s/
Notary Public/Clerk **Notable Notary**

EXHIBIT Z-2

Liberal Landlord v. **Temerity Tenant** Case No. **09CV1236**

RETURN OF SERVICE

I declare under oath that:

1. I served this Summons, a copy of the Complaint in this case, and a copy of the Answer form on **Temerity Tenant** on ______________ (date), at ________ (time), in the County of ______________, State of ______________, at the following location: ______________________________.
2. I served the above documents in the following manner (check one):
   - ☐ by handing them to a person identified to me as the Defendant.
   - ☐ by identifying the documents and offering to leave them with a person who I know, or have reason to identify, as the person being served, who refused service; and then by leaving them in a conspicuous place.
   - ☐ by leaving them at the Defendant's usual place of abode with ______________, who is 18 years of age or older and a member of the Defendant's family.
   - ☐ by leaving them at the Defendant's usual workplace with ______________, who is the Defendant's ______________ (secretary, administrative assistant, bookkeeper, managing agent).
   - ☐ by leaving them with ______________, who as ______________ (title), is authorized by appointment or law to receive service of process for the Defendant.
   - ☐ I have made diligent efforts but have been unable to make personal service on the Defendant and I have made service by posting the documents in a conspicuous place on the premises described herein.
   - ☐ by substituted service on ______________, in accordance with C.R.C.P. 304(e), and by then mailing the documents to the following address: ______________
   - ☐ by serving them as follows (other service permitted by C.R.C.P. 304): ______________
3. ☒ I attempted to serve the Defendant on **four (4)** occasions but have not been able to locate the Defendant. Return to the Plaintiff is made on **April 13th, 2009** (date).
4. ☐ I am 18 years of age or older and am not a party to this case.
5. ☐ My fee for serving the above documents was $________.

/s/
Signature **Persistent Process Server**

☒ Private Process Server
☐ Sheriff, ______________ County

Subscribed and affirmed or sworn to before me this **7th** day of **April**, 20**09**, in the County of **Denver**, State of **Colorado**.

My commission expires: **April 15, 2011**

/s/
Notary Public/Clerk **Notable Notary**

EXHIBIT Z-3

Liberal Landlord v. **Temerity Tenant** Case No. **09CV1236**

CERTIFICATE OF MAILING

I/we, the undersigned Plaintiff(s) (or agent for Plaintiff(s)), certify that on **April 3rd, 2009** (date), the date on which the Summons, Complaint, and Answer were filed, I/we mailed a copy of the Summons/Alias Summons, a copy of the Complaint, and Answer form by postage prepaid, first class mail, to **Temerity Tenant**, the Defendant(s) at the following address(es):

13 Capitol Hill
Denver, Colorado 80210

/s/
Plaintiff(s)/Agent for Plaintiff(s) **Liberal Landlord**

Section 13-40-111 Colorado Revised Statutes, as amended.

13-40-111. Issuance and return of summons.

(1) Upon filing the complaint as provided in §13-40-110, C.R.S., the clerk of the court or the attorney for the plaintiff shall issue a summons. The summons shall command the Defendant to appear before the court at a place named in such summons and at a time and on a day which shall be not less than five business days nor more than ten calendar days from the day of issuing the same to answer the complaint of Plaintiff. The summons shall also contain a statement addressed to the Defendant stating: "If you fail to file with the court, at or before the time for appearance specified in the summons, an answer to the complaint setting forth the grounds upon which you base your claim or possession and denying or admitting all of the material allegations of the complaint, judgment by default may be taken against you for the possession of the property described in the complaint, for the rent, if any, due or to become due, for present and future damages and costs, and for any other relief to which the Plaintiff is entitled". If you are claiming that the landlord's failure to repair the residential premises is a defense to the landlord's allegation of nonpayment of rent, the Court will require you to pay into the registry of the Court, at the time of filing your answer, the rent due less any expenses you have incurred based upon the landlordís failure to repair the residential premises.

(2) For purposes of this section, "business days" means any calendar day excluding Saturdays, Sundays, and legal holidays.

13-40-112. Service.

(1) Such summons may be served by personal service as in any civil action. A copy of the complaint must be served with the summons.

(2) If personal service cannot be had upon the Defendant by a person qualified under the Colorado Rules of Civil Procedure to serve process, after having made diligent effort to make such personal service, such person may make service by posting a copy of the summons and the complaint in some conspicuous place upon the premises. In addition thereto, the Plaintiff shall mail, no later than the next day following the day on which he/she files the complaint, a copy of the summons, or, in the event that an alias summons is issued, a copy of the alias summons, and a copy of the complaint to the Defendant at the premises by postage prepaid, first class mail.

(3) Personal service or service by posting shall be made at least five days before the day for appearance specified in such summons, and the time and manner of such service shall be endorsed upon such summons by the person making service thereof.

(4) For purposes of this section, "business days" means any calendar day excluding Saturdays, Sundays, and legal holidays.

No. 83. Rev. 3-09. SUMMONS IN FORCIBLE ENTRY AND UNLAWFUL DETAINER (C.R.C.P. Form 1A) (Page 4 of 4)

Chapter IX. Tenant's Pre-trial Procedure

A tenant facing eviction proceedings must keep in mind that the single most important thing a tenant can do is to pay attention to the situation. Do not ignore phone calls, pre-trial notices, or process. Communication is of the utmost importance because a failure to communicate could have drastic consequences.

A. Early Letters and Phone Calls

At least 75% of the time before a landlord even considers pursuing legal action, the landlord will attempt to contact the tenant by phone or letter regarding an actual or perceived problem. A large portion of problems are resolved with early communication.

Tenants should respond promptly to phone calls or letters from the landlord. There is nothing that will force the onset of litigation more rapidly than a stonewalling tenant. If a problem exists regarding such things as the timely payment of rent or a barking dog, the tenant should be aware of the interests and concerns of the landlord.

> **Example:**
>
> Although a five-day delay in the payment of rent may seem minimal to a tenant, for a landlord who relies on this sum to pay the monthly mortgage, a delay in payment can be significant—it can literally put the landlord in default of the mortgage and place the building in jeopardy of foreclosure.

The tenant should explain to the landlord any problems or special circumstances that brought about the problem and suggest resolution of the matter. Written correspondence is recommended. Send letters confirming the contents of any telephone conversations. In your communications, do not offer to undertake any payments or other obligations which you know you will not be able to honor.

If a resolution or compromise is reached, the agreement should be memorialized in writing. This agreement need not be fancy or formal, but should contain the information set forth in the following checklist.

1. Checklist for Agreement

- ☐ Date of the agreement.
- ☐ Name, address, and phone number of the parties (landlord and tenant).

- [x] Statement of obligations.
- [x] Property description.
- [x] Recitation as to what the original agreement/lease required (i.e., the bargain of each party: "Tenant agreed to give X, Landlord agreed to accept X.").
- [x] Recitation of the new agreement, including modified terms such as reduced payments, different timing, etc.(e.g., "Tenant agrees to pay Y; Landlord agrees to accept Y.")
- [x] Dates when the new agreement begins and ends.
- [x] A description of what happens if parties fail to comply with agreement.
- [x] Signatures of the parties.

An example of an agreement is included as Exhibit AA.

There is a certain controversy as to whether a rent modification agreement is really a legally enforceable contract if the landlord does not get something other than what he or she already has (e.g., the rent). This is legally known as "lack of consideration." It is advisable to make sure that each side gets something new, for instance the tenant gets more time, and the landlord gets interest payments on late rental amounts (which is in addition to what the landlord is entitled to under the lease).

EXHIBIT AA

THIS AGREEMENT is entered into this 1st day of June, 2008 by and between LASCIVIOUS LANDBARON (Landlord) and TRANSITORY TENANT (Tenant) in consideration of the respective undertakings herein contained and other good and valuable consideration.

1. Landlord and Tenant entered into an Apartment Lease for Apartment No. 5, 1983 Rosehill Drive, Boulder, Colorado on February 1st, 2008 (Lease) wherein Tenant is required to pay the Landlord a monthly rental payment of Six Hundred and no/100 Dollars ($600.00) due on the first of every month.
2. On April 20th, 2008, Tenant lost his job as a Pizza Delivery Clown at Pizza Circus.
3. Tenant failed to pay his May rental payment, which constitutes a breach of the Lease. However, Landlord is willing to waive such breach pursuant to the conditions and obligations contained in this Agreement.
4. Tenant now has a full-time job as a parrot psychologist at Petco.
5. Landlord agrees to accept and Tenant agrees to pay the May rent plus interest of Fifteen and no/100 Dollars ($15.00) on or before June 15th, 2008, along with the regular June 1st, 2008 rental payment.
6. All remaining terms and conditions of the Lease are in full force and effect. Subsequent defaults shall not be deemed waived by this Agreement.

______________________________ ______________________________

LASCIVIOUS LANDBARON TRANSITORY TENANT

B. Receipt of Pre-Litigation Notice

As discussed in Chapters IV, V and VI, prior to almost all eviction proceedings, the tenant is entitled to a pre-litigation notice. Typically this is either a Demand for Compliance or Possession, a Notice to Vacate or Notice to Quit. A tenant's possible action depends on what type of notice is sent.

1. Demand for Compliance or Possession

The first thing a tenant should do after receiving a Demand for Compliance or Possession is check the lease to see if a longer period or additional notices are required. If a period longer than three days is required by the lease, the tenant should inform the landlord of that provision. The tenant should be sure to document this communication.

If nothing else is required by the lease, the next step is to double-check the time period with regard to the notice. This is particularly important if you were served by posting.[176] If served by posting, it is possible that the notice was posted some time ago and the cure period has already expired. As long as the landlord has complied with the statutory requirements of posting, there is no requirement that the tenant actually see the Notice within the three-day period. In other words, a tenant can be on a two-week vacation and be legally served with a Three Day Notice which expires before the tenant returns.

Next, evaluate the demand contained in the notice. Is the demand correct? Is there a default? If so, you must decide whether to comply with the demand (pay past due rent, or comply with covenants or conditions) or vacate the premises.

CAUTION: If you vacate the premises, you may still be liable for subsequent rental payments through the term of your lease![177]

If you decide to cure the default, contact the landlord and inform the landlord of your intentions immediately. Make arrangements to cure the default before the three-day period has expired. The payment or cure must be timely and for the full amount. Do not make a partial payment unless the landlord expressly agrees to one.[178] A letter should accompany payment. Exhibit BB is an example of such a letter.

CAUTION: Because the period allowed by the statute is only three days from receipt of the notice, time is of the essence. A tenant responding to a notice should make sure the letter is received by the landlord within the appropriate time. Suggested methods include personal delivery or overnight messenger service.

EXHIBIT BB

TRANSITORY TENANT
1222 Enlightenment Avenue
Boulder, Colorado

December 5, 2008

Mr. Lascivious Landbaron
1545 Millionaire Drive
Aspen, Colorado

VIA OVERNIGHT DELIVERY

Dear Mr. Landbaron:

I am in receipt of your Demand for Compliance or Possession dated and received by me on December 4, 2008. Please be advised that the alleged violation of the condition set forth on page 21, paragraph 15 of the lease prohibiting "Pets or birds of over 6 feet tall on the premises" has been cured as of this date. For your information, Otto, my former pet ostrich, was sold to Billy Bob's Boot Factory today. If there are any further problems regarding this issue, please contact me.

Happy Festivus

Transitory Tenant
Phone: (303) 555-BOOT

2. Notice to Vacate/Notice to Quit

Unlike a Demand for Compliance or Possession, a Notice to Vacate or Notice to Quit gives no alternatives and simply states the tenancy is terminated and requires that the premises be vacated by a specific date. Upon receipt of a Notice to Vacate, the tenant should examine the time periods involved and required (see Chapter VI). If there is a defect in the timing or method of service, a defense may exist. A Notice to Quit may also be defective and serve as a basis for a defense if it contains factual flaws or is improperly used (e.g., no prior Demand is sent in conjunction with "Repeat Violation Notice to Quit;" no substantial violation existed in conjunction with a "Substantial Violation Notice to Quit"). Otherwise, the landlord is entitled to terminate the tenancy and dispossess the tenant of the property as provided in the notice.

C. Receipt of Process

If no cure or vacation of the premises has occurred after the requisite pre-litigation notice period has passed, the sheriff or private process server will serve the tenant with process (see Chapter VIII). The summons will specify the return date which serves both as: (a) the deadline for the tenant to file the answer, and (b) the date and time that the tenant must appear to set trial upon the case.[179]

If the tenant agrees with everything in the complaint and does not dispute any of its facts, has no defenses and no counterclaims (claims against the landlord), there is not much more the tenant can do except to show up at the return date, watch the judge enter a judgment and be ready to get dispossessed by the sheriff within approximately two to fourteen days. However, it is rare that a tenant agrees with everything that a landlord alleges, or does not claim a defense. It is essential that the tenant prepare and file an answer in the proper timeframe.

D. Answer

The answer is a document that the defendant files with the court and serves on the plaintiff. The answer must be filed "at or before the time specified for [the defendant's] appearance," i.e., the return date.[180] The statute mandates the contents of the answer and gives a suggested form.[181] Because a large majority of eviction cases are brought in county court, all answer forms presented in this book are for county court. A written answer must be filed by every defendant wishing to contest an eviction action. If an answer is not filed, it is conclusively presumed that the defendant admits all of the allegations contained in the complaint.[182] Any answer that fails to specifically admit or deny the allegations of the complaint will be deemed to have admitted the allegations.[183]

The answer (or a separate written motion) must contain each and every defense which the defendant intends to rely on.[184] As discussed extensively in Chapter II, if the tenant is asserting a breach of the Warranty of Habitability, this defense must be asserted here (in the event of monetary defaults). Once again, please be aware that a court may be likely to request a tenant to deposit into the court registry the amounts past due as claimed under the action. Therefore, caution should be exercised to assert a provable, valid defense concerning breach of the Warranty of Habitability. Finally, if you plan to argue that the timing and or form of the service of process was improper, this must be done through a special appearance addressing this matter first; if you generally appear (file an answer addressing the substantive issues) the court will likely rule that your appearance cures any defective summons and service.[185] If this type of defense is contemplated, consult with an attorney before you file anything with the court.

I. Defenses to Eviction

The following is not an exhaustive list of defenses to evictions, but only some of the most common and most recognized by the courts.[186]

a. No Default

Obviously, if no default exists under the lease, an eviction will not be successful. Typically, a defense under this category would involve alleging facts showing that:

- the rent at issue was timely and fully paid or tendered,[187] or
- the covenants claimed to have been violated were cured in a timely manner or had, in fact, never occurred.[188]

b. Waiver and Estoppel

A waiver is a situation where a default did in fact occur but the landlord, either by word or conduct, explicitly or implicitly, assented to it or "let it go."[189] A waiver may be demonstrated by a written agreement,[190] verbal statements,[191] or by conduct.[192]

Estoppel is a related concept by which a landlord caused a tenant to believe that strict adherence to the lease terms was not required.[193] If a waiver is established, this will serve as a defense to an eviction action based on the alleged default.

Example:

The following situation demonstrates a possible waiver defense:

The lease requires that rent be paid on the first of the month. The tenant has consistently paid the rent to the landlord on the tenth of the month. The landlord never complained, and in fact on several occasions the landlord said, "I know the rent is late, just get it to me when you can." The landlord then brings a lawsuit against the tenant on the fifth of the month, claiming breach of the lease. The tenant may assert a defense of waiver.

c. *Defective Notice; Defective Service of Process*

Pre-litigation notice is not required before serving a summons and complaint if the term of the lease has ended. However, any other type of termination requires proper pre-litigation notice[194] and in those situations failure to provide pre-litigation notice renders the notice defective. Notice may be defective for several other reasons, as discussed previously:

- Improper time period.[195]
- Improper party or parties were named or served.[196]
- Improper method of service.[197]
- Improper contents.[198]
- Improper type of notice.

A tenant who seeks to assert a defense of defective notice should review the statutory requirements for notice and allege all defects that the facts give rise to (see Chapters IV, V and VI). A successful allegation of defective pre-litigation notice may cause the eviction action to be thrown out and will require the landlord to comply with the notice requirements and re-file the action.

Example:

Not all defects in pre-litigation notices will amount to a valid defense. For example, cases have held that a demand in the notice for more rent than is actually due will not invalidate the notice, provided that some rent is in fact due and owing. In another case, a tenant argued that a notice which was set forth on two separate pages did not comply with the statutory notice requirements. The court rejected this argument.[199]

Defective service of process will also constitute a defense. It must be underscored that an objection based on improper service of process is a jurisdictional issue. A court must be informed of the improper service issue prior to any other defenses or arguments on the merits of the case. If a defendant appears in court and responds to merits, the defendant waives the defense of improper service. Because of the potential damages of losing an important defense, consultation with an attorney is suggested if a service problem is suspected.

d. Constructive Eviction

A constructive eviction situation arises when a tenant is denied the full use and enjoyment of the leased premises, or when the premises are rendered unfit for occupancy as a result of an action or omission by the landlord, and such action or omission causes the tenant to abandon the leased premises. The defense of constructive eviction would come into play in a situation where a landlord sues a tenant for rent or other damages after a tenant has moved out of the premises because of its condition.[200] Two major requirements must be satisfied before a court will find constructive eviction: (1) denial of the use of the premises (the premises were rendered unfit for occupancy);[201] and (2) abandonment of premises by the tenant within a reasonable time.[202]

The landlord should always be notified in writing at the earliest possible time of a perceived constructive eviction problem. A constructive eviction defense imposed as an afterthought, subsequent to receiving a notice or process, will almost surely fail.

> **Example:**
>
> This pitfall is best illustrated by the following demonstration:
>
> *Example 1:* The tenant takes possession of the premises on May 1. The tenant pays May rent and June rent. On June 15, the tenant sends a letter to the landlord informing the landlord that the premises are uninhabitable because of a malfunctioning heating system which keeps the premises at a constant temperature of 115° fahrenheit and that the tenant intends to abandon the premises. The tenant vacates the property and fails to pay July rent. The landlord then institutes an action. A constructive eviction defense will probably succeed.
>
> *Example 2:* The same as Example 1 above, except the tenant sends the letter to landlord, and continues to occupy the premises after the landlord has instituted an eviction action. Constructive eviction will probably fail.

e. *Breach of Covenant of Quiet Enjoyment*

This defense is very similar to constructive eviction, but an actual abandonment is not necessary.[203] A breach of this covenant may be found in leases that do not contain an agreement to the contrary.[204] The requirement for breach would be: "A disturbance of a lessee's possession by the lessor which renders the premises unfit for occupancy for the purposes for which they were leased."

> **Example:**
>
> Cases finding a breach of the implied covenant of quiet enjoyment include: flooding from pipes in an architectural studio, rodent infestation and structural problems, heating and plumbing problems in combination with a collapsed ceiling.

The constructive eviction and quiet enjoyment defenses are some of the most rapidly evolving areas of landlord/tenant law. They are also some of the most complex. Even judges and experienced lawyers tend to confuse the two issues. Therefore, if a constructive eviction or quiet enjoyment defense is anticipated, it is important to consult an experienced real estate attorney.

Finally, there is some confusion in case law as to whether these concepts may be employed as defenses or only as counterclaims to evictions. This relates to whether the lease covenants were deemed to be independent or dependent.[205] Once again, this issue is quite complex and beyond the scope of this book.

f. *Implied Warranty of Habitability*

Colorado has recently enacted a new law, the Warranty of Habitability Law, which provides a tenant with assurances and standards for suitable housing. An extensive and thorough discussion of this new law is set forth in Chapter II. Therefore, when raising this defense, please first refer to Chapter II for a full explanation and understanding of this law. Note that this defense may only be raised if the default was nonpayment of rent; it is not available for other defaults.[206] The tenant should also be aware that if this defense is employed, then "upon the filing of the tenant's answer the court shall order the tenant to pay into the registry of the court all or part of the rent accrued after due consideration of expenses already incurred by the tenant based upon the landlord's breach the warranty of habitability."[207]

g. *Failure to Mitigate*

A tenant may be responsible for subsequent rent after default and dispossession of the premises if the lease so provides.[208] However, a landlord is under a duty to take reasonable steps to mitigate the possible damages.[209]

Mitigation means cutting your losses. A landlord cannot simply sit idle and watch the damages add up—landlords have a "duty to mitigate." This means a landlord must take reasonable actions (such as attempting to relet the premises for the balance of the term of the lease) in an effort to minimize the damages from the tenant's default.

While the defense of failure to mitigate may not serve to help the tenant retain possession, it may serve to reduce damages claimed due and owing by the landlord. Recent cases have found a failure to mitigate where the landlord refused to accept a sublessee or assignee for an invalid or arbitrary reason,[210] or accepted an entry premium from a subsequent tenant and failed to apply the amount to the former tenant's account.[211] However, it must be kept in mind that the duty to mitigate, like all other duties of the landlord and tenant, may be modified (though not eliminated) by the language in the lease.

> **Example:**
>
> A typical clause modifying a landlord's duty to mitigate would read as follows:
>
> "If the tenant shall fail to pay rent and the landlord re-enters the premises, the landlord may then re-let the premises at the current commercial rental rate, and upon such other terms and conditions as the landlord, in its sole discretion, may deem advisable."

2. Counterclaims

A "counterclaim" is any claim that a defendant (tenant) has against the plaintiff (landlord). A counterclaim must be filed when the Answer is filed.[212] The filing of a counterclaim by a tenant will not preclude the landlord from obtaining possession of the premises. However, a successful counterclaim may serve to reduce or eliminate money judgments for rent and, in some circumstances, the amount of damages awarded to the tenant may even exceed the damages claimed by the landlord.

a. *Breach of Quiet Enjoyment and Constructive Eviction*

The same theories discussed under the defenses section—including breach of quiet enjoyment and constructive eviction—may be brought as counterclaims. The measure of damages in a breach of quiet enjoyment claim is the difference between original rent and the fair rental value of the premises after the breach.[213] The measure of damages on a constructive eviction claim is the rental value of the unexpired term of the lease, less the rent reserved, plus other losses resulting from wrongful eviction.[214] Because the issues are quite complicated, it is suggested that you consult with an attorney experienced in these matters.

b. Unjust Enrichment, Conversion, and Outrageous Conduct

Typically, a written lease will state that all improvements a tenant makes upon the premises accrue to the benefit of the landlord and the tenant is not entitled to reimbursement for them. However, if the lease is silent as to this aspect, there is at least one case which holds that a tenant can recover money from the landlord equal to the value of the tenant's improvements to the property .[215] Such a situation might occur if a tenant installed ceiling fans in an apartment and was then evicted. The tenant might then claim the value of the fans in a counterclaim. Another possible counterclaim might be for conversion. This claim would arise for damage or loss to the tenant's personal property which occurred by virtue of landlord's affirmative actions or omission with regard to the premises. Other counterclaims may include intentional infliction of emotional distress or outrageous conduct.[216]

c. Implied Warranty of Habitability

The law explicitly allows for such a claim to be asserted as a counterclaim.[217] Furthermore, unlike the provision governing the assertion of defenses, a counterclaim under the Act may be asserted by any tenant, not just by a tenant defending against a nonpayment of rent claim. Finally, in such a claim the tenant may seek the "damages directly arising from a breach of the warranty of habitability, which may include, but are not limited to, any reduction in the fair rental value of the dwelling unit . . . ."[218]

Counterclaims could be of several varieties:

- A tenant's personal property is removed from the leased premises by the landlord, without authority of law. The landlord throws the property on the curbside. The property is stolen or damaged.
- A tenant's personal property is legally within the leased premises. The landlord, intentionally or with reckless disregard, damages the tenant's personal property.
- An intentional infliction of emotional distress counterclaim could arise in situations where the landlord repeatedly makes harassing telephone calls and visits, demanding the rent at all hours of the day and evening. The landlord threatens to have thugs kick the tenant out in the middle of the night. The landlord's actions cause the tenant to suffer verifiable mental or physical ailments.

- A breach of the warranty of habitability claim could involve a situation where the landlord, despite the tenant's statutory notices, fails to fix a leaking pipe and the leak causes discomfort and damage to the tenant. The tenant may seek to recover the difference in value between the premises with the defect and without it, as well as remuneration for any personal property damaged by the defect.

This list is not exhaustive. Counterclaims and defenses are very fact-oriented. For example, some other counterclaims that have recently been raised include:

- Violation of the Federal Fair Housing Act (42 U.S.C. §§ 3601 *et seq.*) and/or the Colorado Fair Housing Act (§ 24-34-502.2, C.R.S.) — *Boulder Meadows v. Saville*, 2 P.3d 131 (Colo. App. 2000).
- Violation of the Fair Debt Collection Practices Act (15 U.S.C. § 1692) — *Romea v. Heiberger & Assocs.*, 163 F.3d 111 (2nd Cir. 1998).
- Retaliatory eviction — *W.W.G. Corp. v. Hughes*, 960 P.2d 720 (Colo. App. 1998).

If some sort of wrong or damage is done to a tenant by a landlord there is probably a cause of action and remedy. The best resource for this type of claim would be relevant case law or consultation with an attorney experienced in these matters.

3. Checklist for Answer (Form No. 63)

☐ Must be in writing.

☐ Caption: contains court, action number, and parties.

☐ Set forth grounds on which the claim for possession is based.

☐ Admission or denial of all the material allegations of the complaint.

☐ Presentation of every defense.

☐ Counterclaim (if applicable); cross-claim (if applicable).

☐ Jury demand (if applicable).

☐ Signature of the tenant (or signature of the tenant's attorney).[219]

☐ Address and telephone number of the tenant (or telephone number of the tenant's attorney).[220]

C.R.C.P. 304 provides that, except in certain cases of service by publication, a blank copy of the answer form must be provided to the tenant when the summons and complaint are served. C.R.C.P. 308 provides that the form and content are no longer suggested but are instead mandatory.

Exhibit CC is a sample form which, if filled in correctly, would comply with the statutory requirements.

EXHIBIT CC

<table>
<tr><td>County Court, ❶ ______________ County, Colorado
Court address:
❷</td><td rowspan="3">

▲ COURT USE ONLY ▲</td></tr>
<tr><td>Plaintiff(s):
❸
v.
Defendant(s):
❹</td></tr>
<tr><td rowspan="2">Attorney or Party Without Attorney (Name and Address):
❺

Phone Number:
FAX Number:
E-mail:
Atty. Reg. #:</td></tr>
<tr><td>Case Number: ❻

Division: Courtroom:</td></tr>
<tr><td colspan="2">ANSWER UNDER SIMPLIFIED CIVIL PROCEDURE
(Including Counterclaim(s) and Cross Claim(s))</td></tr>
</table>

The Defendant(s), ❼ ______________________________ answer(s) the Complaint as follows:

1. The amount of damages claimed to be due to the Plaintiff(s) by the Complaint in this action is not due and owing for the following reasons:

❽

OR the Plaintiff(s) is/are not entitled to possession of the property and Defendant(s) is/are entitled to retain possession for the following reasons:

❾

OR the injunctive relief requested by the Plaintiff(s) should not be allowed for the following reasons:

❿ 2. (If applicable) the Defendant(s), ______________________, assert(s) the following counterclaim(s) or setoff(s) against the Plaintiff(s), ______________________:

⓫

12 3. (If applicable) the Defendant(s), ______________________________,
assert(s) the following cross claim(s) against ______________________________,
named Defendant(s) (you are limited to the jurisdiction of the Court):

13

14 4. If a counterclaim is asserted above, you must check one of the following statements:

a ☐ The amount of the counterclaim does not exceed the jurisdiction of the Court (County Court filing fee required).

b ☐ The amount of the counterclaim exceeds the jurisdiction of the Court, but I wish to limit my recovery to the jurisdiction of the Court (County Court filing fee required).

c ☐ The amount of the counterclaim exceeds the jurisdiction of the Court, and I wish the case transferred to the District Court (District Court filing fee required).

5. (If applicable) The residential rental agreement between the parties ☐ does ☐ does not contain a provision for the prevailing party to obtain attorney fees pursuant to 13-40-123, C.R.S.

15 6. The Defendant(s) ☐ does (do) ☐ does (do) not demand trial by jury (if demand is made a jury fee must be paid).

WARNING: ALL FEES ARE NON-REFUNDABLE. IN SOME CASES, A REQUEST FOR A JURY TRIAL MAY BE DENIED PURSUANT TO LAW EVEN THOUGH A JURY FEE HAS BEEN PAID.

Note: All Defendants filing this Answer must sign unless the Answer is signed by an attorney.

16 ______________________________	18 ______________________________
Signature(s) of Defendant(s)	Signature of Attorney for Defendant(s) (if applicable)
17 ______________________________	19 ______________________________
Address(es) of Defendant(s)	Telephone number(s) of Defendant(s)

CERTIFICATE OF MAILING

I certify that on ____________________ (date), a copy of the Answer was mailed, postage prepaid, to ______________________________ (Plaintiff(s) or Plaintiff's attorney), addressed as follows:

____
Defendant(s) or Attorney for Defendant(s)

No. 63. Rev. 9-08. ANSWER UNDER SIMPLIFIED CIVIL PROCEDURE (Including Counterclaim(s) and Cross Claim(s)) (Page 2 of 2)

4. Filling Out the Answer (Form No. 63)

Unfortunately, the required answer form makes it quite difficult to include the statutorily required information on the form itself. It is essential for an answering party to insert all of the requisite information because the law states that any allegations of material facts not denied in the answer are deemed admitted.[221] If more space is needed, additional information can be typed on 8 1/2 x 11 paper and referenced on the answer form as an attachment. Exhibit DD is a filled-in sample form having a defense of tender of payment and a counterclaim for breach of warranty of quiet enjoyment.

Blank 1: Insert the name of the county.

Blank 2: Insert the address of the court and its common name (e.g., "Boulder County Justice Center, 1777 6th Street, Boulder, Colorado 80302").

Blank 3: Insert the names of all plaintiffs (see complaint).

Blank 4: Insert the names of all defendants (see complaint).

Blank 5: Insert the plaintiff's name and address (or the name and address of the attorney preparing the form, if applicable)

Blank 6: Insert the case number (see complaint caption).

Blank 7: Insert the names of defendant(s) filing this answer.

Blank 8:

- Important: Insert admissions or denials to each material allegation contained in the complaint. The best way to do this is to read each paragraph of the complaint and either admit or deny it. Note: You may admit parts of paragraphs and deny others. E.g., "Defendant admits Paragraphs 1, 7 and 8 of the complaint and denies the remaining allegation of complaint except Defendant admits that a verbal month-to-month tenancy was entered into."
- Insert additional facts that support your argument that the amount claimed is not due to the plaintiff.
- State that you are attaching any documents that support your argument (if applicable).

Blank 9:

- Insert additional facts that support the argument that the premises should not be turned over (e.g., no default under lease, defective Notice to Vacate, defective Demand for Compliance or Possession, waiver by plaintiff, etc.).

Note: In most cases you should strike the next line "OR the injunctive relief requested by the Plaintiff, etc." See C.R.C.P. 365 for an explanation as to when injunctive relief is available in county court.

Blank 10: Insert the defendant's name and the plaintiff's name.

Blank 11: Insert any facts supporting counterclaims or set-offs.

Blank 12: Insert the defendant's name and the plaintiff's name.

Blank 13: If you have any cross-claims against co-defendants, insert those cross-claims here.

Blank 14: If you assert any counterclaims, check:

a) If the claim is worth less than $15,000.

b) If the claim is over $15,000, but you wish to keep the case in county court and limit any recovery to $15,000 or less.

c) If the claim is over $15,000, and you wish to have the case transferred to district court

Blank 15: Check the first box if a jury is desired; check the second box if a jury is not desired. (See the discussion on jury demands at the end of this chapter for more information.)

Blank 16: Insert your signature.

Blank 17: Insert your address.

Blank 18: Attorney's signature, if applicable.

Blank 19: Insert your phone number.

Note: If you mail the answer form, fill out the certificate of mailing and keep a copy for your records. This verifies that you mailed it to the plaintiff or the plaintiff's attorney.

EXHIBIT DD

County Court, **Denver** County, Colorado Court address: **1515 Cleveland Place, 4th Floor** **Denver, Colorado 80202**	
Plaintiff(s): **Laconic Landlord, an individual** v. **Defendant(s):** **Transpersonal Tenant [and any other parties occupying the premises commonly known as 620 West Surf, Apartment 5, Denver, Colorado]**	
Attorney or Party Without Attorney (Name and Address): **Laconic Landlord** **1245 Main Street** **Littleton, Colorado 80123**	▲ COURT USE ONLY ▲
Phone Number: **303-555-1212** FAX Number: **N/A** E-mail: **Llandlord@gmail.com** Atty. Reg. #: **N/A**	Case Number: **09CV999** Division: Courtroom:

ANSWER UNDER SIMPLIFIED CIVIL PROCEDURE
(Including Counterclaim(s) and Cross Claim(s))

The Defendant(s), **Transpersonal Tenant** answer(s) the Complaint as follows:

1. The amount of damages claimed to be due to the Plaintiff(s) by the Complaint in this action is not due and owing for the following reasons: **Tenant admits Paragraphs 1, 7 and 8 of the Complaint and denies the remaining allegations of the Complaint. Tenant further states that the monthly rental was reduced to $500 per month on January 1st, 2009, as per attached Exhibit A. Rental payment for February, 2009 was tendered by Tenant but rejected by the Landlord. No additional amounts are due and owing.**

OR the Plaintiff(s) is/are not entitled to possession of the property and Defendant(s) is/are entitled to retain possession for the following reasons: **(a) No default existed under the lease, all rents due were tendered on a timely basis but not accepted by Landlord; (b) Landlord's 3 Day Notice was defective. Notice was served upon my daughter on February 10th, 2009 and this action was commenced on February 11th, 2009; (c) 3 Day Notice was improperly served: daughter receiving service was five (5) years of age (in violation of § 13-40-106, C.R.S.).**

~~**OR** the injunctive relief requested by the Plaintiff(s) should not be allowed for the following reasons:~~

2. (If applicable) the Defendant(s), **Transpersonal Tenant**, assert(s) the following counterclaim(s) ~~or setoff(s)~~ against the Plaintiff(s), **Laconic Landlord: (a) Landlord has breached the Warranty of Quiet Enjoyment by virtue of constant construction in the basement from the beginning of the tenancy. Damaged suffered: $5,000.00 (Five Thousand and no/100 Dollars).**

~~3. (If applicable) the Defendant(s), ______,~~
~~assert(s) the following cross-claim(s) against ______,~~
~~named Defendant(s) (you are limited to the jurisdiction of th~~e Court):

4. If a counterclaim is asserted above, you must check one of the following statements:
   ☒ The amount of the counterclaim does not exceed the jurisdiction of the Court (County Court filing fee required).
   ☐ The amount of the counterclaim exceeds the jurisdiction of the Court, but I wish to limit my recovery to the jurisdiction of the Court (County Court filing fee required).
   ☐ The amount of the counterclaim exceeds the jurisdiction of the Court, and I wish the case transferred to the District Court (District Court filing fee required).

5. (If applicable) The residential rental agreement between the parties ☐ does ☐ does not contain a provision for the prevailing party to obtain attorney fees pursuant to 13-40-123, C.R.S.

6. The Defendant(s) ☒ does (do) ☐ does (do) not demand trial by jury (if demand is made a jury fee must be paid).

WARNING: ALL FEES ARE NON-REFUNDABLE. IN SOME CASES, A REQUEST FOR A JURY TRIAL MAY BE DENIED PURSUANT TO LAW EVEN THOUGH A JURY FEE HAS BEEN PAID.

Note: All Defendants filing this Answer must sign unless the Answer is signed by an attorney.

/s/	
Signature(s) of Defendant(s) **Transpersonal Tenant**	Signature of Attorney for Defendant(s) (if applicable)
620 West Surf, Apartment 5, Denver, Colorado	**(303) 555-1111**
Address(es) of Defendant(s)	Telephone number(s) of Defendant(s)

CERTIFICATE OF MAILING

I certify that on **February 20th, 2009** (date), a copy of the Answer was mailed, postage prepaid, to **Laconic Landlord** (Plaintiff(s) or Plaintiff's attorney), addressed as follows:

1245 Main Street
Littleton, Colorado 80123

/s/
Defendant(s) or Attorney for Defendant(s)
Transpersonal Tenant

No. 63. Rev. 9-08. ANSWER UNDER SIMPLIFIED CIVIL PROCEDURE (Including Counterclaim(s) and Cross Claim(s)) (Page 2 of 2)

5. Filing the Answer

a. When to File and Where to File

The answer must be filed with the clerk of the court on or before the return date listed on the summons.[222] It is suggested that the answer be filed at least the day before the return date so that if the clerk's office is crowded on the return date, you will not be rushed. An answer fee must be paid when the answer is filed. As of this time, the fee in county court is $75; if a counterclaim or cross-claim is filed, the cost is $79. This is subject to change. If you cannot afford the fee, tell the clerk. You will then need to file a Motion to File without Payment and a Supporting Financial Affidavit and submit it to the court. The court will then decide if you need to pay the filing fee.[223] Remember to make several photocopies of the answer. Present the original answer to the clerk and have the clerk file-stamp your copies. A copy of the answer must be served on the plaintiff prior to filing or within 48 hours after filing.[224]

If you are filing the answer the day before your appearance date or on the date of your appearance, then you can simply hand a copy of your answer to the plaintiff in court. Service for this section means hand delivery or first class mail. If you mail the answer, fill out the certificate of mailing on the back of the form.

b. Jury Demand

The landlord and/or tenant are entitled to request a jury trial if they so desire. An additional jury fee must be paid when the demand is filed. Presently, the jury fee is $98 in county court. In district court, the rules allow a jury demand to be filed "not later than ten days after the service of the last pleading."[225] Because of the conflicting time periods in an eviction proceeding, such timing may not be possible.[226] In county court, the jury demand must be endorsed on the answer or complaint. It may also be made orally at the time of the initial appearance. In district court, it may either appear on the pleadings or in a separate document. Once a jury is demanded, the other party must either pay the requisite jury fee or file a Notice of Waiver of the Right to Trial by Jury.[227]

Chapter X. Return Date Procedure

A. Return Date/Setting of Trial

1. Return Date

On the return date, the parties must appear at the time and place designated on the summons. If a sufficient answer has been filed, the case is deemed at issue and the case will be set for trial. If no answer has been filed, and all other requirements have been complied with, the court will enter a default judgment against the tenant.

2. Setting of Trial

Unlike other types of cases, eviction actions were intended by the legislature to provide a summary proceeding to determine possession. Thus, an accelerated trial date is contemplated under the statute and is proper.[228] When setting the trial date, the court will probably give the parties a date one to five days from the return date.[229] The trial date may be the date of the return if both parties and the court are ready. It is advisable to be ready for trial on the return date just in case this occurs. A party may be required to post a bond or other security if he or she requests a delay in trial for longer than five days. The amount of security must be equal to the amount that a non-moving party would be damaged. This bond requirement is at the discretion of the court and only good cause must be shown.[230]

B. Default

If the defendant fails to file a written answer on or before the return date, a default judgment in favor of the plaintiff may be obtained. The judgment may be for possession of the premises and the amount due, including interest, costs, and other items provided by statute or contract.[231]

The procedure involved in asking for a default judgment is known as a "motion." Motions may be either oral or written. In county court, written motions are not permitted without the permission of the court.[232] On the other hand, in district court, motions are almost always written. Because a majority of all evictions are pursued in county court, this book focuses on county court procedures.[233]

1. Oral Motion for Default Judgment

At the court hearing on the return date, the plaintiff should approach the judge when the case is called. Report to the judge that no answer is on file and the defendant is not present in court, and then request that a default judgment be entered against the defendant. The judge will determine if procedures were followed properly and all requirements met before entering a default judgment. The plaintiff must be prepared to provide the following specific information and proof on the return date when asking for a default judgment:

a. Notice; Personal Jurisdiction

The judge must be provided with proof that the defendant has been adequately notified and is under the jurisdiction of the court. Two different proofs are required: (1) pre-litigation notice, and (2) service of process.

Pre-litigation notice may be proven by presenting a copy of the Demand, Notice to Vacate, or Notice to Quit with the proof of service portion completed by the party who effected service on the tenant.

Service of process will be proven by the return of service that has been filed either by the sheriff or private process server. The plaintiff should check the file before the return date to make sure it is in the file. If it is not in the file, the respective server should be notified and a duplicate return of service should be obtained. Remember that if service was only by posting, the court will only have jurisdiction to enter an order for possession and not for monetary damages.[234] If service is by posting, then proof of compliance with the mailing element is also required. This is known as a Certificate of Mailing. (See Exhibit Z-3.)

b. Venue

The law specifically requires that the judge ascertain that proper venue exists before a default judgment is entered.[235] "Venue" means the place (county) of the trial. In all cases affecting real property, such as an eviction, venue is proper in the county where the property is located. Therefore, simply inform the judge of the location of the property and the fact that it is located in that county.

c. Damages

If monetary damages are sought in addition to possession, additional documentation may be required. The lease, setting forth the monthly rent, preferably with original signatures, should be made available for the court's review. Any further documentation such as a rent register should also be made available. Finally, a party with personal knowledge of the amounts claimed should attend. In the alternative, an affidavit detailing the claimed damages signed by an individual with personal knowledge is recommended. This requirement is especially important if the complaint filed was signed by an attorney and was not verified by the plaintiff.

Although courts vary as to what they require in a default situation, a plaintiff armed with the above information and a verified complaint will be well prepared to satisfy a judge's inquiries before entry of a default order.[236] Remember, if personal service has not been effected, then the court may only enter an order for possession and not for a monetary judgment.

Chapter XI. Trial

A complete discussion of civil trial procedure is well beyond the scope of this book. However, this book will attempt to list and describe some of the most important trial preparations and procedures. These are the procedures that tend to take most non-attorneys by surprise, no matter how many episodes of *Boston Legal* or *Law and Order* a person has seen. Therefore, reading this chapter should not be viewed as a substitute for professional legal representation. This chapter deals only with bench trials and not jury trials. "Bench trials" are trials in which the judge is the finder of fact and no jury is present. If a jury trial is contemplated, representation by an experienced attorney is highly recommended.

A. Chronology of Trial

Although many of the parties to an eviction appear *pro se* (on behalf of themselves), the judge is still required to adhere to the rules of civil procedure and evidence that govern the conduct of a trial. Additionally, many courtroom practices are governed by custom and are not written in the law.[237] Some judges may relax evidentiary or procedural requirements in *pro se* situations; however, this depends almost entirely on the judge. If a *pro se* party is litigating against an attorney, it is very likely that the judge will feel more pressure to enforce the procedural and evidentiary rules.

There is no rule or statute setting forth the order of trial in Colorado. However, the courts almost universally stick to the following order:

1. Opening statement of plaintiff.
2. Opening statement of defendant.
3. Presentation of plaintiff's direct evidence.
4. Presentation of defendant's direct evidence (in defense to plaintiff's claim and presentation of counterclaim, if any).
5. Presentation of plaintiff's rebuttal evidence.
6. Closing argument by plaintiff.
7. Closing argument by defendant.[238]

NOTE: Parties are also entitled to cross-examination during their adversary's case-in-chief. In other words, the parties are allowed to ask questions of their opponent's witnesses.

B. Opening Statement

This is an opportunity for the parties to tell the court what they intend to prove in their cases. The statements are not for the purpose of introducing evidence in the case, but rather serve as a guide to what will be presented. The opening statement should preview the witnesses and exhibits that will be presented, the evidence which they will elicit, and the theory of the claim or defense.[239]

C. Direct Evidence

Basically, all evidence that the court considers must come through either testimony of a witness or exhibits that are admitted into evidence. The parties therefore must review the elements to be proven (or rebutted) in their respective cases and plan which document or witness will satisfy the respective requirements.

1. Landlord's Direct Evidence

In a typical eviction, the landlord must prove each of the following elements:

- Ownership of the property, the existence and terms of the tenancy (e.g., month-to-month oral agreement; written lease).
- Default of the tenancy by the tenant, or termination by the landlord or tenant.
- Proper notification was given to the tenant (Demand for Compliance or Possession).
- Tenant's failure to cure the default.
- Damages (the amount of rent owing).

The sources of evidence a landlord would normally employ include:

- Written lease (original) (and authenticating evidence).[240]
- Copy of the Demand or Notice.
- Proof of Service of Demand or Notice (original).
- Testimony of the party who served the Demand or Notice.
- Testimony of a party with personal knowledge as to the defaults, failure to cure, and damages.

2. Tenant's Direct Evidence

In a typical eviction action, the tenant must attempt to rebut the elements listed immediately above. Additionally, if a defense or counterclaim is possible, the tenant must learn the elements required by the respective defense or counterclaim and prove those.

D. Rebuttal Evidence

Rebuttal evidence is presented in reaction and in opposition to the direct evidence. When giving rebuttal evidence, do not present evidence as to issues which were not raised in the direct case the evidence is rebutting. Rebuttal may be accomplished by presenting new witnesses or recalling witnesses who were called in the case-in-chief. An example of a case when a rebuttal is proper follows.

> **Example:**
>
> Tenant, in its case-in-chief, asserted the waiver defense and offered evidence demonstrating that the landlord told the tenant, "Don't worry about paying your rent for the next year – you're my best buddy."
>
> After the tenant's case-in-chief has concluded, the landlord may present rebuttal evidence disputing this waiver defense. For example, the tenant had slipped the tea-totaling landlord a pint of grain alcohol in the landlord's non-alcoholic beer immediately before the landlord made this statement. Upon recovering from a massive hangover, the next day the landlord wrote the tenant a letter specifically disavowing "any word coming out of my mouth" the night the alleged waiver was uttered.

E. Rules of Evidence

A party *must* be familiar with the rules of evidence that govern what the court will and will not consider as evidence.[241] A discussion of the rules of evidence is far beyond the scope of this book, but three very oversimplified evidentiary rules of thumb are:

- The evidence must be relevant (relate to the subject at issue).[242]
- The testimonial evidence must be based on personal knowledge;[243] documentary evidence must be an original or a duplicate document.[244]
- Physical evidence (documents, photographs, objects) must be authenticated (proven to be what they are purported to be).[245]

Most eviction actions involve a lease as evidence. This may be authenticated either through testimony of a witness who has personal knowledge that a document is what it is being claimed to be, or through identification of handwriting by a non-expert if this party is familiar with the handwriting and it was not acquired for the purpose of litigation. Typically, the party who signed the document is called to identify it. Parties may also stipulate (agree) to authentication issues. This stipulation may be made in writing before trial, or made orally at the time of trial.

There are numerous exceptions and modifications of these rules as well as many other equally important rules. By no means should these rules of thumb be viewed as an alternative to familiarity with the Colorado Rules of Evidence.[246] A party preparing a case must keep these rules in mind. A party appearing at a hearing should also keep these rules in mind when objecting to testimony that does not comport with these requirements.

F. Closing Arguments

The purpose of the closing argument is to comment on the evidence that has been admitted and to present reasonable inferences that may be drawn from the evidence. The parties should point out the strengths in their case, and point out the weakness of their opponent's case. The elements of the respective claims and defenses should be recapped with reference to the specific evidence (or lack of specific evidence) presented on the particular points.

G. Motion to Dismiss

After the close of the plaintiff's direct evidence, the defendant may move for a dismissal of the case. A dismissal in favor of the defendant is appropriate if "upon the facts and the law the plaintiff has shown no right to relief."[247] Typically, a defendant will make this motion if the plaintiff failed to establish a crucial element of his or her case (e.g., no evidence presented regarding required pre-litigation notice; no evidence presented regarding alleged default). The court will then rule on this motion. If the court renders a judgment in favor of the defendant, the case is over and there is no need to go forward with any further evidence. If, however, the judge denies the motion, the defendant will then be entitled to present his or her case-in-chief.[248]

H. Judgment

After all evidence has been received by the court, the court will enter a judgment on all claims, defenses, and counterclaims. The rules specifically require that at the conclusion of a case, the court must "orally announce its decision, including findings of fact and conclusions of law, and direct the entry of the appropriate judgment."[249] No written findings are required.

1. Damages

The law provides that the prevailing party in an eviction action is entitled to damages that may include the following:

- ☐ Damages "on account of the unlawful detention of the property by the defendant" (i.e., past due rent).[250]
- ☐ Damages "on account of injuries to the property" (i.e., destruction of the premises, legally known as "waste").[251]
- ☐ Court costs (i.e., clerk and sheriff fees).[252]
- ☐ Reasonable attorney fees,[253] but only if the residential rental agreement between the parties contains a provision for either party to obtain attorney fees.[254]

NOTE: The damage total may not exceed the jurisdictional limit of the court ($15,000 for county courts).[255]

2. Possession

At the time of judgment, a court may enter an order for immediate possession by the landlord. However, the execution on the writ of restitution is stayed for 48 hours after judgment is entered.[256]

Chapter XII. Writ of Restitution Procedure

The Writ of Restitution is the written document issued by the court to the sheriff, directing the sheriff to physically remove the tenant and the tenant's personal property from the premises. A landlord should have this issued if the tenant has not voluntarily vacated the premises within 48 hours after the judgment has been entered.

A. When Writ Issued

A Writ of Restitution may not be issued until "after the expiration of forty-eight hours from the time of the entry of such judgment."[257] Nonetheless, the plaintiff should have the writ form completed and available for the court's review at the time of the judgment.

B. Who Issues Writ

Depending on the jurisdiction, either the court will issue the writ or will authorize the clerk to issue it after the 48-hour period has passed. The specific mechanics of obtaining the writ vary by county. The general practice is to wait 48 hours and then request the issuance of a writ of restitution form from the clerk if the tenant has not vacated. In some jurisdictions, the court will issue the writ and postdate it by 48 hours. If you are uncertain about the local procedure, you may ask the judge or clerk.

C. Writ of Restitution Form (Form No. 538)

The law does not set forth specific requirements for the contents of this document. However, Colorado appears to have accepted the form available from Bradford Publishing Company as the unofficial standard. Exhibit EE is an example of this form.

EXHIBIT EE

☐ County Court ❶ ☐ District Court ❷ ______________ County, Colorado Court address: ❸	
Plaintiff(s): ❹ v. **Defendant(s):** ❺	▲ COURT USE ONLY ▲
	Case Number: ❻ Division: ❼ Courtroom: ❼
WRIT OF RESTITUTION	

The People of the State of Colorado, to the Sheriff of the above County:

WHEREAS Plaintiff(s) obtained a judgment on ❽ ______________ (date), against Defendant(s), pursuant to the Colorado Forcible Entry and Detainer (FED) statutes, § 13-40-101, *et seq.*, C.R.S., ordering possession of the premises located at:

❾

YOU ARE HEREBY ORDERED, pursuant to § 13-40-122, C.R.S., to remove the Defendant(s) and their property from the premises and restore the Plaintiff(s) to the possession of the premises stated above, and to make proper return according to law.

Dated: ❿ ______________

⓫ ______________
Judge/Magistrate

By: ⓬ ______________

Bradford Publishing, 1743 Wazee St., Denver, CO 80202 — 303-292-2590 — www.bradfordpublishing.com

D. Filling Out the Writ of Restitution (Form No. 538)

A completed Writ of Restitution form is included as Exhibit FF.

Blank 1: Check the box for County or District court.

Blank 2: Insert the name of the county.

Blank 3: Insert the court's address.

Blank 4: Insert the plaintiff's name(s).

Blank 5: Insert the defendant's name(s).

Blank 6: Insert the case number.

Blank 7: Insert the court or division.

Line 8: Insert the date of the order of possession (usually occurring on the return date or at trial).

Blank 9: Insert the legal description and street address, including the unit or apartment number, if applicable.

Blank 10: Date issued. This will be inserted by the clerk or judge.

Blank 11: Signature/seal of the clerk or judge.

Blank 12: Signature/seal of the clerk or judge.

EXHIBIT FF

☒ County Court ☐ District Court Denver County, Colorado Court address: 1515 Cleveland Place, 4th Floor Denver, CO 80202	
Plaintiff(s): Laconic Landlord, an individual v. **Defendant(s):** Transpersonal Tenant [and any other parties occupying the premises commonly known as 620 West Surf, Apartment 5, Denver, Colorado]	▲ COURT USE ONLY ▲ Case Number: 09CV999 Division: Courtroom:

WRIT OF RESTITUTION

The People of the State of Colorado, to the Sheriff of the above County:

WHEREAS Plaintiff(s) obtained a judgment on March 1st, 2009 (date), against Defendant(s), pursuant to the Colorado Forcible Entry and Detainer (FED) statutes, § 13-40-101, *et seq.*, C.R.S., ordering possession of the premises located at:

620 West Surf, Apartment 5, Denver, Colorado

YOU ARE HEREBY ORDERED, pursuant to § 13-40-122, C.R.S., to remove the Defendant(s) and their property from the premises and restore the Plaintiff(s) to the possession of the premises stated above, and to make proper return according to law.

Dated: March 4th, 2009

/s/
Judge/Magistrate Judge A. Justice

By: ______________________

E. Service of Writ

Only the sheriff, undersheriff, or deputy is authorized to serve the writ. It may only be served "in the daytime and between sunrise and sunset."[258] The sheriff will charge an additional fee for service of the writ. The law permits both on and off-duty officials to serve the writ. The statute does not set forth the specific procedures which the sheriff must follow in acting on the writ. Depending on the county, some sheriffs will call or send a postcard prior to serving the writ. Finally, in some counties, the sheriff will serve the writ, wait for a period, and then return to physically dispossess the tenant if the tenant has not moved out. The sheriff of your county should be contacted to ascertain the specific procedures.

F. Execution of Writ

The sheriff, undersheriff, or deputy executing (carrying out) a writ technically is obliged to remove not only the tenant but also "to remove the tenant's personal property and effects from the premises." [259] A landlord should be available at the time of the execution of the writ to allow access to the premises. However, beyond letting the authorities in, unless otherwise directed, the landlord should do nothing. Do not remove the property. Do not make efforts to store the property. If the landlord follows this directive, he or she will not be liable for damages for the manner in which a sheriff executes the writ in the course of lawful eviction or removal of the tenant's property. Despite the technical language of the law, it is becoming much more common in various Colorado jurisdictions for the sheriff to only supervise the execution while the landlord's agents (usually movers) conduct the actual physical removal of the personal property.

> **NOTE:** Counties handle the responsibility for actual removal of the property differently. Inquire as to the proper procedure. This may include the hiring of a third party moving company. In any event, follow the county's procedure precisely. Make sure the sheriff is supervising the actual removal.

An officer executing a writ is held only to a minimum standard of care. The officer must remove the tenant's property "without damaging them more than is necessary to execute the writ, consistent with the natural consequences of removal." Additionally, after removal, the officer has no duty to safeguard the tenant's possessions "even though he knows the tenant's belongings might be taken if they are left unattended."[260]

The legislature has codified certain common law immunities which apply to the duties concerning a sheriff executing a Writ of Restitution. The law also sets forth certain guidelines and immunities concerning landlords who remove and/or store personal property of a tenant following the execution of a Writ of Restitution. These provisions appear in § 13-40-122, C.R.S. which reads as follows:

> 13-40-122. Writ of restitution after judgment.
>
> (1) No writ of restitution shall issue upon any judgment entered in any action under the provisions of this article out of any court until after the expiration of forty-eight hours from the time of the entry of such judgment; and such writs shall be executed by the officer having the same only in the daytime and between sunrise and sunset. Any writ of restitution governed by this section may be executed by the county sheriff's office in which the property is located by a sheriff, undersheriff, or deputy sheriff, as described in section 16-2.5-103(1) or (2), C.R.S., while off duty or on duty at rates charged by the employing sheriff's office in accordance with section 30-1-104(1)(gg), C.R.S.
>
> (2) The officer that executes a writ of restitution under subsection (1) of this section and the law enforcement agency that employs such officer shall be immune from civil liability for any damage to a tenant's personal property that was removed from the premises during the execution of the writ. A landlord who complies with the lawful directions of the officer executing a writ of restitution shall be immune from civil and criminal liability for any act or omission related to a tenant's personal property that was removed from the premises during or after the execution of a writ of restitution.
>
> (3) A landlord has no duty to store or maintain a tenant's personal property that is removed from the premises during or after the execution of a writ of restitution. Regardless of whether a landlord elects to store or maintain the personal property so removed, the landlord shall have no duty to inventory the personal property or to determine ownership of or the condition of the personal property. Such storage shall not create either an implied or express bailment of the personal property, and the landlord shall be immune from liability for any loss or damage to the personal property.
>
> (4) A landlord who elects to store a tenant's personal property that was removed from the premises during or after the execution of a writ of restitution may charge the tenant the reasonable costs of storing the personal property. To recover such costs, the landlord may either dispose of the personal property under any lien rights the landlord has under part 1 of article 20 of title 38, C.R.S., or the landlord may allow the tenant to recover the

personal property after paying the reasonable storage charges incurred by the landlord.

Remember, the above immunities only apply if the property has been removed pursuant to a Writ of Restitution and under proper directions of the sheriff. This provides no protection to a landlord exercising a "self-help" remedy.

Chapter XIII. Appeals

An eviction case tried in the county court may be appealed to the district court. The appeal may stay (stop) all further proceedings, including an action on the writ of restitution, while the appeal is pending. If an appeal is contemplated, an attorney familiar with the appeal process should be consulted at once. There are many requirements regarding deadlines, bonds, and other undertakings that must be complied with or the case will be thrown out.[261] The first of these deadlines is fifteen days from the date of the judgment. Therefore, timing and fast action are critical if an appeal is pursued. In addition to the regular appeal bond, a defendant appealing an eviction action must also deposit with the court the amount of money that was found due and owing as rent, plus additional rental payments as they become due during the pendency of the appeal.[262] Finally, the court may order an additional bond at the request of the appellee (non-appealing party) after a hearing.[263]

Chapter XIV. Security Deposit Issues

A constant source of confusion between landlords and tenants is the status of security deposits. This chapter addresses the parties' respective rights and responsibilities with regard to security deposits.

A. Law on Wrongful Withholding of Security Deposits

The statute relating to the return of residential security deposits is definitely one of the most pro-tenant provisions in the Colorado statutes. This statute sets forth requirements as to how a landlord must return security deposits to tenants and imposes severe penalties for failure to comply. This statute cannot be waived by oral or written agreement (e.g., the lease).[264] The statute, § 38-12-103(1), C.R.S., is reprinted in Appendix D. Note that this law applies only to residential and not to commercial tenancies.

B. Return of Deposit

Within one month after the termination of a lease or surrender of the premises, the landlord is obliged to return to the tenant the security deposit. The lease may specify a longer period, but this period may not exceed sixty days.[265] The law requires that the deposit be returned to the tenant's "last known address."

C. Written Statement Required for Retention of Security Deposit

If the landlord retains any portion of a security deposit, a written statement setting forth the exact reasons for the retention of that portion is required. This statement must be accompanied by a return of the balance of the deposit. Exhibit GG is an example of a written statement. It is important that these items be provided prior to the expiration of the initial time provided under the law.

EXHIBIT GG
SECURITY DEPOSIT REFUND STATEMENT

TO:	Transitional Tenant	Date:	April 15, 2009
	511 Grant Place	Commencement Date:	April 1, 2008
	Basement Unit	Security Deposit:	$500.00
	Empire, Colorado	Termination Date:	March 31, 2009

This statement is furnished to you pursuant to Section 38-12-103 of the *Colorado Revised Statutes*, which governs the return of security deposits for residential premises. Enclosed is a check representing your security deposit minus deductions.

<u>Credits</u>:

Security Deposit: $500.00

<u>Deductions</u>:

Replacement of broken mirror: ($125.00)

1. Vanity mirror in bathroom

Mirror:	$75.00 at Milo's Mirror Mall
Labor:	$50.00; 2 hours @ $25.00/hour by Hank's Handymen

Replacement of kitchen knobs: ($10.00)

2. Missing kitchen cabinet knobs; replacement

Knobs:	$10.00; 10 @ $1.00/each
Labor:	NO CHARGE

3. Unpaid March, 2005 rent: <u>($250.00)</u>

LESS TOTAL of ABOVE ITEMIZED REPAIRS/RENT: <u>$385.00</u>

TOTAL REFUND: $115.00

1. What May Be Deducted From Security Deposit

Absent a contrary provision in the lease, portions of the security deposit may be retained for:

- Nonpayment of rent.
- Abandonment of the premises.
- Nonpayment of utility charges.
- Repair work.
- Cleaning.[266]

Colorado statutes prohibit landlords from deducting money from a security deposit for "normal wear and tear" of the premises.[267] "Normal wear and tear" is defined as "deterioration which occurs based upon the use for which the rental unit is intended, without negligence, carelessness, accident, or abuse of the premises or equipment or chattels by the tenant or members of his household, or their invitees or guests."[268]

2. Delivery of Written Statement and/or Refund

The landlord is deemed to comply with the requirements of the statute if the landlord mails a written statement and any required payment to the tenant at the tenant's last known address.

3. Effect of Failure to Deliver Written Statement

If landlord fails to comply with the above requirements and does not deliver a written statement and/or refund within the required time, the landlord forfeits all of the landlord's rights to withhold any portion of the security deposit. If the retention is "in willful violation," the landlord may be liable to the tenant for treble (three times) the amount of the security deposit wrongfully withheld plus attorney fees and court costs.

D. Tenant Action to Recover Security Deposit

If a landlord is willfully retaining a security deposit, a tenant has the right to institute legal proceedings to recover it. A successful tenant may recover treble (three times) the amount of that portion of the security deposit wrongfully withheld, as well as costs and attorney fees. If a tenant contemplates an action against the landlord, it is imperative that the tenant comply with statutory requirements of a pre-litigation notice and further that the tenant be aware of the law as it relates to "wrongful withholding."

I. Pre-Litigation Notice

Before a tenant can file a legal action against the landlord for the return of a security deposit, the tenant must notify the landlord of his or her intention to file a legal proceeding. This notice must be given at least seven days before filing the action. It is suggested that this notice be sent via regular first class mail, as well as certified mail, return receipt requested, so there is proof that the landlord received the notice and that seven days have passed before the action is filed. An example of a pre-litigation notice appears in Exhibit HH.

CAUTION: Landlords must be aware that once the initial period has passed, if the Landlord has not accounted for amounts withheld, it is too late to withhold any portion of the security deposit and the landlord must return the entire amount to the tenant. As the Colorado Supreme Court has recently stated, "The purpose of the seven-day notice provision in subsection (3)(a) is to give landlords one last week to avoid treble damages by returning the security deposit. It does not give landlords a second chance to account for the deposit."[269]

EXHIBIT HH

TO: Laird Landlord
2147 West Ohio Street
Boulder, Colorado 80301

VIA FIRST CLASS MAIL AND CERTIFIED MAIL
RETURN RECEIPT REQUESTED
DELIVERY RESTRICTED TO ADDRESSEE ONLY

Date: March 15, 2008

NOTICE OF INTENT TO SUE

YOU ARE HEREBY NOTIFIED, pursuant to Colorado Revised Statutes Section 38-12-103(3)(a), that I, TRANSPERSONAL TENANT, intend to file legal proceedings to recover the security deposit in the sum of Five Hundred and no/100 Dollars ($500.00) which is wrongfully withheld by you. The deposit was given to you in connection with my tenancy of the premises commonly known as 1330 Dearborn Street, Longmont, Colorado. This tenancy terminated on December 31, 2007. No written statement and/or refund has been received as of this date. Under applicable law you have forfeited the right to retain any portion of the deposit. I request that the deposit be returned immediately.

YOU ARE FURTHER NOTIFIED that said action will be filed on or after seven days from the date which you receive this Notice. This action will seek TREBLE THE AMOUNT OF THE DEPOSIT WHICH YOU CURRENTLY RETAIN, PLUS COSTS AND ATTORNEY FEES.

Signed,

Transpersonal Tenant

2. Suit to Recover

Once the seven-day period has expired, the tenant may file a lawsuit. Because attorney fees are recoverable, a tenant may consider consulting with an attorney and having the attorney file the case in county court.[270] However, if a tenant chooses to pursue the matter *pro se*, the small claims division of the county court is a simple and expeditious alternative.[271] Small claims courts have a jurisdictional limit of $7,500.[272] This amount is subject to change and should be checked before filing. Generally, no attorneys may appear in small claims court to represent litigants. An attorney may appear to represent himself or herself, however, and if an attorney appears, the opposing party also may be represented by an attorney.[273] By law, the clerks for small claims court are required to help people understand the court's procedures and provide all necessary forms; however, they cannot engage in the "practice of law."[274] Service of process may be made by certified mail or personal service. A filing fee is also required. The return date set in small claims court will also be the trial date.

3. Willful and Wrongful Withholding

For a tenant to prevail against a landlord for treble damages, the court must find that the landlord's retention of the security deposit was both "willful" and "wrongful."[275]

a. Willful

"Willful retention" has been defined by the courts as "deliberate retention." If a landlord deliberately fails to return a security deposit within the required seven-day notice period, the retention is "logically willful under the act." A recent case has further determined that if the landlord fails to return or account for the deposit during the initial period, the landlord must return the entire security deposit to tenant within the seven-day period; otherwise, the landlord will be considered to be willfully withholding the deposit.[276]

b. Wrongful

The landlord bears the burden of proof that withholding of the security deposit was not wrongful. "Wrongful" has been defined as acting in bad faith. One indication of a landlord's good faith is conformance with the written statement requirement when retaining a security deposit. On the other hand, if the landlord retains the security deposit and fails to provide the written statement, the withholding is presumed wrongful.[277]

4. Damages

A successful tenant in a willful and wrongful security deposit retention action may recover treble (three times) damages. The calculation is based on the amount willfully and wrongfully retained, and not the entire amount of the security deposit. The tenant may also recover reasonable attorney fees and costs of the suit. The costs of suit include filing fees and service of process fees.

In 2005, the Colorado Supreme Court in a case entitled *Mishkin v. Young*, 107 P.3d 393 (Colo. 2005), laid down some further guidelines on security deposit retention:

- A landlord must provide an accounting and/or return of security deposit within the initial 30 (or up to 60) days after the termination of the lease. If landlord fails to do so: (i) the landlord forfeits all rights to retain any portion of the security deposit; and (ii) retention by the landlord is considered "wrongful" as a matter of law.
- In the event of a wrongful retention, upon receipt of a statutory "7 day demand," the landlord must return the entire amount of the security deposit wrongfully retained within this period. The landlord may not provide an accounting at this late stage. If the landlord returns the security deposit within this time, treble damages do not accrue upon the portion so returned.
- If the landlord fails to return the entire amount wrongfully retained within the seven-day period, the retention is deemed "willful" as a matter of law.
- A tenant is thus entitled to recover treble damages upon that portion of the security deposit which was both wrongfully and willfully retained by the landlord.

E. Special Provision: Gas Appliances

The legislature has enacted guidelines in regard to hazardous conditions of gas appliances.[278] If a gas company service person informs a tenant that there is a hazardous condition, the tenant must immediately notify the landlord in writing. The landlord then has 72 hours to have the hazardous condition repaired. If the landlord fails to have the condition repaired, the tenant may vacate the premises and the lease becomes null and void. The tenant may then make a demand upon the landlord for immediate return of the security deposit. The landlord then has 72 hours in which to return the security deposit and/or written statement regarding any deposit retained and any rent abatement due. If this is not received by the tenant within the 72-hour period, the retention is deemed willful and wrongful, and the tenant is entitled to *twice* the amount of the deposit, plus attorney fees.[279] This 72-hour period excludes Saturdays, Sundays, and holidays.

F. Inspection Report

The execution of pre-occupancy and post-occupancy checklists signed by both parties is one way in which the parties to a lease may document the relative condition of the property. If a dispute subsequently arises, this checklist will serve as objective evidence as to the property's condition at a certain time. A checklist, Form 1133 Inspection Report, is available from Bradford Publishing.

Chapter XV. Domestic Violence Issues

The legislature has enacted certain laws that are intended to aid victims of domestic violence and/or abuse[280] with landlord/tenant matters. These laws can be categorized in four parts: (1) protection of domestic victims from evictions; (2) termination of leases by domestic violence victims; (3) non-waiver provisions in leases; and (4) protections with respect to warranty of habitability matters.

A. Protection of Victims From Evictions

The FED law has been revised so that a landlord may not effect an eviction against a victim of domestic violence or abuse if the violence or abuse was essentially the cause of the eviction to begin with.[281] The law further requires documentation for such defense to be in the form of a police report or a civil or emergency protection order.[282] While the law essentially provides an affirmative defense to a victim, it also explicitly states that the landlord is not prevented from seeking judgment for possession against the tenant who perpetrated the violence or abuse.[283]

B. Termination of Lease by Victims

If a documented victim of domestic violence "seeks to vacate the premises due to fear of imminent danger for self or children because of domestic violence or domestic abuse," the victim is entitled to terminate the lease by providing written notice to the landlord and documentation of the abuse or violence.[284] Upon vacation of the premises, the victim's liability to the landlord is limited to one month's rent. The law also provides additional details with regard to return of the security deposit and documentation of the landlord's costs and damages.[285]

C. Non-Waiver Provisions

The law provides that a lease may not contain waivers of the domestic abuse and violence protections discussed above.[286] Further, a lease may not include a provision permitting the landlord to terminate the lease or impose any other penalty by reason of the tenant's calls made to the police or other emergency assistance because of domestic violence, nor waive the right of the tenant to call for police or emergency assistance.[287]

D. Warranty of Habitability Provisions

The Act provides for an exception to the tenant's misconduct in events of domestic violence. In cases where the tenant is either a victim of domestic violence or abuse, and the uninhabitable condition is a result of that abuse or violence, it shall not be deemed to be a result of tenant misconduct and thus not an available defense for the landlord.[288]

Chapter XVI. Conclusion

Participating in an eviction, whether as a landlord, tenant or neophyte attorney, can be an emotional, anxiety-provoking, and mysterious experience. No matter how professionally the parties conduct themselves, emotions will always be present because litigation is, by its very nature, unpredictable. Throughout this book, we have attempted to give readers a better idea of what to expect, and we hope this knowledge will serve to alleviate at least some of the mystery and anxiety during the eviction process.

Table of Appendices

APPENDIX A

Printed and electronic Eviction forms and Leases available from Bradford Publishing.

Form No.	Title	Exhibit in this Guide
1000	Residential Lease	A & B
992	Notice of Uninhabitable Condition	C & D
993	Notice to Remedy Breach and Notice of Termination for Breach of Warranty of Habitability	E & F
994	Agreement Concerning Maintenance or Repair of Residential Premises by Tenant	G & H
235PA	Demand for Compliance or Possession (also known as "Three Day Notice")	I – M
219R	Notice to Quit (Repeat Violation of Covenant)	N & O
219S	Notice to Quit (Substantial Violation)	P & Q
219	Notice to Vacate (also known as "Ten Day Notice"/ "Notice to Quit")	R – T
94	Complaint (FED)	U – X
83	Summons (FED)	Y – Z-3
63	Answer	CC & DD
538	Writ of Restitution	EE & FF

APPENDIX B

Colorado Revised Statutes

13-40-101. Forcible entry and detainer defined. (1) If any person enters upon or into any lands, tenements, mining claims, or other possessions with force or strong hand or multitude of people, whether any person is actually upon or in the same at the time of such entry, or if any person by threats of violence or injury to the party in possession or by such words or actions as have a natural tendency to excite fear or apprehension of danger gains possession of any lands, tenements, mining claims, or other possessions and detains and holds the same, such person so offending is guilty of a forcible entry and detainer within the meaning of this article.

(2) If any person enters peaceably upon any lands, tenements, mining claims, or other possessions, whether any person is actually in or upon the same at the time of such entry and by force turns the party in possession out or, by threats or by words or actions which have a natural tendency to excite fear or apprehension of danger, frightens the party out of possession and detains and holds the same, such person so offending is guilty of a forcible detainer within the meaning of this article.

(3) If any person enters upon or into any lands, tenements, mining claims, or other possessions by force or by threats of violence, or words or actions which have a natural tendency to excite fear or apprehension of danger, and intimidates the party entitled to possession from returning upon or possessing the same, such person so offending is guilty of a forcible entry within the meaning of this article.

13-40-102. Forcible entry prohibited. No person shall enter into or upon any real property, except in cases where entry is allowed by law, and in such cases not with strong hand or with a multitude of people, but only in a peaceable manner.

13-40-103. Forcible detention prohibited. No person, having peaceably entered into or upon any real property without right to the possession thereof, shall forcibly hold or detain the same as against the person who has a lawful right to such possession.

13-40-104. Unlawful detention defined. (1) Any person is guilty of an unlawful detention of real property in the following cases:

(a) When entry is made, without right or title, into any vacant or unoccupied lands or tenements;

(b) When entry is made, wrongfully, into any public lands, tenements, mining claims, or other possessions which are claimed or held by a person who may have located, entered, or settled upon the same in conformity with the laws, rules, and regulations of the United States, or of this state, in relation thereto;

(c) When any lessee or tenant at will, or by sufferance, or for any part of a year, or for one or more years, of any real property, including a specific or undivided portion of a building or dwelling, holds over and continues in possession of the demised premises, or any portion thereof, after the expiration of the term for which the same were leased, or after such tenancy, at will or sufferance, has been terminated by either party;

(d) When such tenant or lessee holds over without permission of his landlord after any default in the payment of rent pursuant to the agreement under which he holds, and three days' notice in writing has been duly served upon the tenant or lessee holding over, requiring in the alternative the payment of the rent or the possession of the premises. No such agreement shall contain a waiver by the tenant of the three days' notice requirement of this paragraph (d). It shall not be necessary, in order to work a forfeiture of such agreement, for nonpayment of rent, to make a demand for such rent on the day on which the same becomes due; but a failure to pay such rent upon demand, when made, works a forfeiture.

(d.5) When such tenant or lessee holds over, without the permission of the landlord, contrary to any condition or covenant the violation of which is defined as a substantial violation in section 13-40-107.5, and notice in writing has been duly served upon such tenant or lessee in accordance with section 13-40-107.5;

(e) When such tenant or lessee holds over, without such permission, contrary to any other condition or covenant of the agreement under which such tenant or lessee holds, and three days' notice in writing has been duly served upon such tenant or lessee requiring in the alternative the compliance with such condition or covenant or the delivery of the possession of the premises so held;

(e.5) (I) When a tenant or lessee has previously been served with the notice described in paragraph (e) of this subsection (1) requiring compliance with a condition or covenant of the agreement, and subsequent to that notice holds over, without permission of the tenant or lessee's landlord, contrary to the same condition or covenant.

(II) A tenancy may be terminated at any time pursuant to this paragraph (e.5) on the basis of a subsequent violation. The termination shall be effective three days after service of written notice to quit.

(f) When the property has been duly sold under any power of sale, contained in any mortgage or trust deed that was executed by such person, or any person under whom such person claims by title subsequent to date of the recording of such mortgage or trust deed, and the title under such sale has been duly perfected and the purchaser at such sale, or his or her assigns, has duly demanded the possession thereof;

(g) When the property has been duly sold under the judgment or decree of any court of competent jurisdiction and the party or privies to such judgment or decree, after the expiration of the time of redemption when redemption is allowed by law, refuses or neglects to surrender possession thereof after demand therefor has been duly made by the purchaser at such sale, or his or her assigns;

(h) When an heir or devisee continues in possession of any premises sold and conveyed by any personal representative with authority to sell, after demand therefor is duly made;

(i) When a vendee having obtained possession under an agreement to purchase lands or tenements, and having failed to comply with his agreement, withholds possession thereof from his vendor, or assigns, after demand therefor is duly made.

(2) and (3) Repealed.

(4) (a) It shall not constitute an unlawful detention of real property as described in paragraph (d.5), (e), or (e.5) of subsection (1) of this section if the tenant or lessee is the victim of domestic violence, as that term is defined in section 18-6-800.3, C.R.S., or of domestic abuse, as that term is defined in section 13-14-101 (2), which domestic violence or domestic abuse was the cause of or resulted in the alleged unlawful detention and which domestic violence or domestic abuse has been documented by the following:

(I) A police report; or

(II) A valid civil or emergency protection order.

(b) A person is not guilty of an unlawful detention of real property pursuant to paragraph (a) of this subsection (4) if the alleged violation of the rental or lease agreement is a result of domestic violence or domestic abuse against the tenant or lessee.

(c) A rental, lease, or other such agreement shall not contain a waiver by the tenant or lessee of the protections provided in this subsection (4).

(d) Nothing in this subsection (4) shall prevent the landlord from seeking judgment for possession against the tenant or lessee of the premises who perpetuated the violence or abuse that was the cause of or resulted in the alleged unlawful detention.

13-40-105. Crops of possessor. In all cases arising under section 13-40-104 (1) (c) to (1) (i), the person in possession is entitled to cultivate and gather the crops, if any, planted or sown by him previous to the service of the demand to deliver up possession, and then grown or growing on the premises, and shall have the right to enter such premises for the purpose of cultivating or removing such crops, first paying or tendering to the party entitled to the possession of said premises a reasonable compensation for the use of the land before removing such crops.

13-40-106. Written demand. The demand required by section 13-40-104 shall be made in writing, specifying the grounds of the demandant's right to the possession of such premises, describing the same, and the time when the same shall be delivered up, and shall be signed by the person claiming such possession, his agent, or his attorney.

13-40-107. Notice to quit. (1) A tenancy may be terminated by notice in writing, served not less than the respective period fixed before the end of the applicable tenancy, as follows:

(a) A tenancy for one year or longer, three months;

(b) A tenancy of six months or longer but less than a year, one month;

(c) A tenancy of one month or longer but less than six months, ten days;

(d) A tenancy of one week or longer but less than one month, or a tenancy at will, three days;

(e) A tenancy for less than one week, one day.

(2) Such notice shall describe the property and the particular time when the tenancy will terminate and shall be signed by the landlord or tenant, the party giving such notice or his agent or attorney.

(3) Any person in possession of real property with the assent of the owner is presumed to be a tenant at will until the contrary is shown.

(4) No notice to quit shall be necessary from or to a tenant whose term is, by agreement, to end at a time certain.

(5) Except as otherwise provided in section 38-33-112, C.R.S., the provisions of subsections (1) and (4) of this section shall not apply to the termination of a residential tenancy during the ninety-day period provided for in said section.

13-40-107.5. Termination of tenancy for substantial violation - definition - legislative declaration. (1) The general assembly finds and declares that:

(a) Violent and antisocial criminal acts are increasingly committed by persons who base their operations in rented homes, apartments, and commercial properties;

(b) Such persons often lease such property from owners who are unaware of the dangerous nature of such persons until after the persons have taken possession of the property;

(c) Under traditional landlord and tenant law, such persons may have established the technical, legal right to occupy the premises for a fixed term which continues long after they have demonstrated themselves unfit to coexist with their neighbors and co-tenants; furthermore, such persons often resist eviction as long as possible;

(d) In certain cases it is necessary to curtail the technical, legal right of occupancy of such persons in order to protect the equal or greater rights of neighbors and co-tenants, the interests of property owners, the values of trust and community within neighborhoods, and the health, safety, and welfare of all the people of this state.

(2) It is declared to be an implied term of every lease of real property in this state that the tenant shall not commit a substantial violation while in possession of the premises.

(3) As used in this section, "substantial violation" means any act or series of acts by the tenant or any guest or invitee of the tenant that, when considered together:

(a) Occurs on or near the premises and endangers the person or willfully and substantially endangers the property of the landlord, any co-tenant, or any person living on or near the premises; or

(b) Occurs on or near the premises and constitutes a violent or drug-related felony prohibited under article 3, 4, 6, 7, 9, 10, 12, or 18 of title 18, C.R.S.; or

(c) Occurs on the tenant's leased premises or the common areas, hallway, grounds, parking lot, or other area located in the same building or complex in which the tenant's leased premises are located and constitutes a criminal act in violation of federal or state law or local ordinance that:

(I) Carries a potential sentence of incarceration of one hundred eighty days or more; and

(II) Has been declared to be a public nuisance under state law or local ordinance based on a state statute.

(4) (a) A tenancy may be terminated at any time on the basis of a substantial violation. The termination shall be effective three days after service of written notice to quit.

(b) The notice to quit shall describe the property, the particular time when the tenancy will terminate, and the grounds for termination. The notice shall be signed by the landlord or by the landlord's agent or attorney.

(5) (a) In any action for possession under this section, the landlord has the burden of proving the occurrence of a substantial violation by a preponderance of the evidence.

(b) In any action for possession under this section, it shall be a defense that:

(I) (Deleted by amendment, L. 2005, p. 402, § 2, effective July 1, 2005.)

(II) The tenant did not know of, and could not reasonably have known of or prevented, the commission of a substantial violation by a guest or invitee but immediately notified a law enforcement officer of his or her knowledge of the substantial violation.

(c) (I) The landlord shall not have a basis for possession under this section if the tenant or lessee is the victim of domestic violence, as that term is defined in section 18-6-800.3, C.R.S., or of domestic abuse, as that term is defined in section 13-14-101 (2), which domestic violence or domestic abuse was the cause of or resulted in the alleged substantial violation and which domestic violence or domestic abuse has been documented pursuant to the provisions set forth in section 13-40-104 (4).

(II) Nothing in this paragraph (c) shall prevent the landlord from seeking possession against a tenant or lessee of the premises who perpetuated the violence or abuse that was the cause of or resulted in the alleged substantial violation.

13-40-108. Service of notice to quit. A notice to quit or demand for possession of real property may be served by delivering a copy thereof to the tenant or other person occupying such premises, or by leaving such copy with some person, a member of the tenant's family above the age of fifteen years, residing on or in charge of the premises, or, in case no one is on the premises at the time service is attempted, by posting such copy in some conspicuous place on the premises.

13-40-109. Jurisdiction of courts. The district courts in their respective districts and county courts in their respective counties have jurisdiction of all cases of forcible entry, forcible detainer, or unlawful detainer arising under this article, and the person entitled to the possession of any premises may recover possession thereof by action brought in any of said courts in the manner provided in this article. On and after January 1, 1991, in all actions brought before county courts under section 13-40-104 (1) (f) to (1) (i), where the allegations of the complaint are put in issue by a verified answer and in actions in which the verified answer alleges a monthly rental value of the property in excess of fifteen thousand dollars, the county court, upon the filing of said answer, shall suspend all proceedings therein and certify said cause and transmit the papers therein to the district court of the same county. Causes so certified by the county court shall be proceeded within the courts to which they have been so certified in all respects as if originally begun in the court to which they have been certified. On and after January 1, 1991, the jurisdiction of the county court to enter judgment for rent, or damages, or both and to render judgment on a counterclaim in forcible entry and detainer shall be limited to a total of fifteen thousand dollars in favor of either party, exclusive of costs and attorney fees.

13-40-110. Action - how commenced. (1) An action under this article is commenced by filing with the court a complaint in writing describing the property with reasonable certainty, the grounds for the recovery thereof, the name of the person in possession or occupancy, and a prayer for recovery of possession. The complaint may also set forth the amount of rent due, the rate at which it is accruing, the amount of damages due, and the rate at which they are accruing and may include a prayer for rent due or to become due, present and future damages, costs, and any other relief to which plaintiff is entitled.

(2) In an action for termination of a tenancy in a mobile home park, the complaint, in addition to the requirements of subsection (1) of this section, shall specify the particular reasons for termination as such reasons are stated in section 38-12-203, C.R.S. Such complaint shall specify the approximate time, place, and manner in which the tenant allegedly committed the acts giving rise to the complaint. If the action is based on the mobile home or mobile home lot being out of compliance with the rules and regulations adopted pursuant to section 38-12-203 (1) (c), C.R.S., the complaint shall specify that the home owner was given thirty days from the date of service or posting of the notice to quit to cure the noncompliance and that thirty days have passed and the noncompliance has not been cured.

13-40-111. Issuance and return of summons. (1) Upon filing the complaint as provided in section 13-40-110, the clerk of the court or the attorney for the plaintiff shall issue a summons. The summons shall command the defendant to appear before the court at a place named in such summons and at a time and on a day which shall be not less than five business days nor more than ten calendar days from the day of issuing the same to answer the complaint of plaintiff. The summons shall also contain a statement addressed to the defendant stating: "If you fail to file with the court, at or before the time for appearance specified in the summons, an answer to the complaint setting forth the grounds upon which you base your claim for possession and denying or admitting all of the material allegations of the complaint, judgment by default may be taken against you for the possession of the property described in the complaint, for the rent, if any, due or to become due, for present and future damages and costs, and for any other relief to which the plaintiff is entitled. If you are claiming that the landlord's failure to repair the residential premises is a defense to the landlord's allegation of nonpayment of rent, the court will require you to pay into the registry of the court, at the time of filing your answer, the rent due less any expenses you have incurred based upon the landlord's failure to repair the residential premises."

(2) For purposes of this section, "business days" means any calendar day excluding Saturdays, Sundays, and legal holidays.

(3) For actions commenced pursuant to section 13-40-104 (1) (f) and (1) (g) only, if no answer to the complaint is filed as provided in subsection (1) of this section, the court shall examine the complaint, and, if satisfied that venue is proper and the plaintiff is entitled to possession of the premises, the court shall dispense with appearances by the plaintiff or a hearing and shall forthwith enter a judgment for possession, present or future damages, and costs.

13-40-112. Service. (1) Such summons may be served by personal service as in any civil action. A copy of the complaint must be served with the summons.

(2) If personal service cannot be had upon the defendant by a person qualified under the Colorado rules of civil procedure to serve process, after having made diligent effort to make such personal service, such person may make service by posting a copy of the summons and the complaint in some conspicuous place upon the premises. In addition thereto, the plaintiff shall mail, no later than the next business day following the day on which he or she files the complaint, a copy of the summons, or, in the event that an alias summons is issued, a copy of the alias summons, and a copy of the complaint to the defendant at the premises by postage prepaid, first-class mail.

(3) Personal service or service by posting shall be made at least five business days before the day for appearance specified in such summons, and the time and manner of such service shall be endorsed upon such summons by the person making service thereof.

(4) For purposes of this section, "business days" means any calendar day excluding Saturdays, Sundays, and legal holidays.

13-40-113. Answer of defendant - additional and amended pleadings. (1) The defendant shall file with the court, at or before the time specified for his appearance in the summons, an answer in writing setting forth the grounds on which he bases his claim for possession and admitting or denying all of the material allegations of the complaint and presenting every defense which then exists and upon which he intends to rely, either by including the same in his answer or by filing simultaneously therewith motions setting forth every such defense.

(2) The court for good cause may permit the filing of additional and amended pleadings where such will not result in delay prejudicial to the defendant.

13-40-114. Delay in trial - undertaking. If either party requests a delay in trial longer than five days, the court in its discretion may, upon good cause shown, require either of the parties to give bond or other security approved and fixed by the court in an amount for the payment to the opposite party of such sum as he may be damaged due to the delay.

13-40-115. Judgment - writ of restitution. (1) Upon the trial of any action under this article if service was had only by posting in accordance with section 13-40-112 (2) and if the court finds that the defendant has committed an unlawful detainer, the court shall enter judgment for the plaintiff to have restitution of the premises and shall issue a writ of restitution. The court may also continue the case for further hearing from time to time and may issue alias and pluries summonses until personal service upon the defendant is had.

(2) Upon such trial or further hearing under this article after personal service is had upon the defendant in accordance with section 13-40-112 (1), if the court or jury has not already tried the issue of unlawful detainer, it may do so, and, if it finds that the defendant has committed an unlawful detainer, the court shall enter judgment for the plaintiff to have restitution of the premises and shall issue a writ of restitution. In addition to such judgment for restitution, the court or jury shall further find the amount of rent, if any, due to the plaintiff from the defendant at the time of trial, the amount of damages, if any, sustained by the plaintiff to the time of the trial on account of the unlawful detention of the property by the defendant, and damages sustained by the plaintiff to the time of trial on account of injuries to the property, and judgment shall enter for such amounts, together with reasonable attorney's fees and costs, upon which judgment execution shall issue as in other civil actions. Nothing in this section shall be construed to permit the entry of judgment in excess of the jurisdictional limit of the court.

(3) A writ of restitution that is issued by the court pursuant subsection (1) or (2) of this section shall remain in effect for forty-five days after issuance and shall automatically expire thereafter.

13-40-116. Dismissal. If the plaintiff's action brought for any of the causes mentioned in this article, upon the trial thereon, is dismissed or the action fails to prove the plaintiff's right to the possession of the premises described in the complaint, the defendant shall have judgment and execution for his costs.

13-40-117. Appeals. (1) If either party feels aggrieved by the judgment rendered in such action before the county court, he may appeal to the district court, as in other cases tried before the county court, with the additional requirements provided in this article.

(2) Upon the court's taking such appeal, all further proceedings in the case shall be stayed, and the appellate court shall thereafter issue all needful writs and process to carry out any judgment which may be rendered thereon in the appellate court.

(3) If the appellee believes that he may suffer serious economic harm during the pendency of the appeal, he may petition the court taking the appeal to order that an additional undertaking be required of the appellant to cover the anticipated harm. The court shall order such undertaking only after a hearing and upon a finding that the appellee has shown a substantial likelihood of suffering such economic harm during the pendency of the appeal and that he will not adequately be protected under the appeals bond and the other requirements for appeal pursuant to sections 13-40-118, 13-40-120, and 13-40-123.

13-40-118. Deposit of rent. In all appeals from the judgment of a county court, in an action founded upon section 13-40-104 (1) (d), the defendant, at the time of the filing thereof, shall deposit with the court the amount of rent found due and specified in such judgment. Unless such deposit is made, the appeal is not perfected, and proceedings upon such judgment shall thereupon be had accordingly. If the appeal is perfected, the court shall transmit such deposit to the clerk of the appellate court, with the papers in such case; and the appellant thereafter, at the time when the rents become due as specified in the judgment appealed from and as often as the same become due, shall deposit the amount thereof with the clerk of such appellate court. In case the appellant, at any time during the pendency of such appeal and before final judgment therein, neglects or fails to make any deposit of rent, falling due at the time specified in the judgment appealed from, the court in which such appeal is pending, upon such fact being made to appear and upon motion of the appellee, shall affirm the judgment appealed from with costs; and proceedings thereupon shall be had as in like cases determined upon the merits.

13-40-119. Rules of practice. In all actions brought under any provision of this article in any court, the proceedings shall be governed by the rules of practice and the provisions of law concerning civil actions in such court, except as may be otherwise provided in this article.

13-40-120. Appellate review. Appellate review of the judgment of the district courts of this state, in proceedings under this article, is allowed as provided by law and the Colorado appellate rules. In cases of appeal from judgments founded upon causes of action embraced in section 13-40-104 (1) (d), the deposit of rent money during pendency of appeal shall be made, or judgment of affirmance shall be entered, in the manner provided in section 13-40-118.

13-40-121. When deposit of rent is paid. The rent money deposited, as provided for in this article, shall be paid to the landlord entitled thereto, upon the order of the court wherein the same is deposited and at such time and in such manner as the court determines necessary to protect the rights of the parties.

13-40-122. Writ of restitution after judgment. (1) No writ of restitution shall issue upon any judgment entered in any action under the provisions of this article out of any court until after the expiration of forty-eight hours from the time of the entry of such judgment; and such writs shall be executed by the officer having the same only in the daytime and between sunrise and sunset. Any writ of restitution governed by this section may be executed by the county sheriff's office in which the property is located by a sheriff, undersheriff, or deputy sheriff, as described in section 16-2.5-103 (1) or (2), C.R.S., while off duty or on duty at rates charged by the employing sheriff's office in accordance with section 30-1-104 (1) (gg), C.R.S.

(2) The officer that executes a writ of restitution under subsection (1) of this section and the law enforcement agency that employs such officer shall be immune from civil liability for any damage to a tenant's personal property that was removed from the premises during the execution of the writ. A landlord who complies with the lawful directions of the officer executing a writ of restitution shall be immune from civil and criminal liability for any act or omission related to a tenant's personal property that was removed from the premises during or after the execution of a writ of restitution.

(3) A landlord has no duty to store or maintain a tenant's personal property that is removed from the premises during or after the execution of a writ of restitution.

Regardless of whether a landlord elects to store or maintain the personal property so removed, the landlord shall have no duty to inventory the personal property or to determine ownership of or the condition of the personal property. Such storage shall not create either an implied or express bailment of the personal property, and the landlord shall be immune from liability for any loss or damage to the personal property.

(4) A landlord who elects to store a tenant's personal property that was removed from the premises during or after the execution of a writ of restitution may charge the tenant the reasonable costs of storing the personal property. To recover such costs, the landlord may either dispose of the personal property under any lien rights the landlord has under part 1 of article 20 of title 38, C.R.S., or the landlord may allow the tenant to recover the personal property after paying the reasonable storage charges incurred by the landlord.

13-40-123. Damages. The prevailing party in any action brought under the provisions of this article is entitled to recover damages, reasonable attorney fees, and costs of suit; except that a residential landlord or tenant who is a prevailing party shall not be entitled to recover reasonable attorney fees unless the residential rental agreement between the parties contains a provision for either party to obtain attorney fees. Nothing in this section shall be construed to permit the entry of judgments in any single proceeding in excess of the jurisdictional limit of said court.

APPENDIX C

Colorado Revised Statutes

38-12-101. Legislative declaration. The provisions of this part 1 shall be liberally construed to implement the intent of the general assembly to insure the proper administration of security deposits and protect the interests of tenants and landlords.

38-12-102. Definitions. As used in this part 1, unless the context otherwise requires:

(1) "Normal wear and tear" means that deterioration which occurs, based upon the use for which the rental unit is intended, without negligence, carelessness, accident, or abuse of the premises or equipment or chattels by the tenant or members of his household, or their invitees or guests.

(2) "Security deposit" means any advance or deposit of money, regardless of its denomination, the primary function of which is to secure the performance of a rental agreement for residential premises or any part thereof.

38-12-103. Return of security deposit. (1) A landlord shall, within one month after the termination of a lease or surrender and acceptance of the premises, whichever occurs last, return to the tenant the full security deposit deposited with the landlord by the tenant, unless the lease agreement specifies a longer period of time, but not to exceed sixty days. No security deposit shall be retained to cover normal wear and tear. In the event that actual cause exists for retaining any portion of the security deposit, the landlord shall provide the tenant with a written statement listing the exact reasons for the retention of any portion of the security deposit. When the statement is delivered, it shall be accompanied by payment of the difference between any sum deposited and the amount retained. The landlord is deemed to have complied with this section by mailing said statement and any payment required to the last known address of the tenant. Nothing in this section shall preclude the landlord from retaining the security deposit for nonpayment of rent, abandonment of the premises, or nonpayment of utility charges, repair work, or cleaning contracted for by the tenant.

(2) The failure of a landlord to provide a written statement within the required time specified in subsection (1) of this section shall work a forfeiture of all his rights to withhold any portion of the security deposit under this section.

(3) (a) The willful retention of a security deposit in violation of this section shall render a landlord liable for treble the amount of that portion of the security deposit wrongfully withheld from the tenant, together with reasonable attorneys' fees and court costs; except that the tenant has the obligation to give notice to the landlord of his intention to file legal proceedings a minimum of seven days prior to filing said action.

(b) In any court action brought by a tenant under this section, the landlord shall bear the burden of proving that his withholding of the security deposit or any portion of it was not wrongful.

(4) Upon cessation of his interest in the dwelling unit, whether by sale, assignment, death, appointment of a receiver, or otherwise, the person in possession of the security deposit, including but not limited to the landlord, his agent, or his executor, shall, within a reasonable time:

(a) Transfer the funds, or any remainder after lawful deductions under subsection (1) of this section, to the landlord's successor in interest and notify the tenant by mail of such transfer and of the transferee's name and address; or

(b) Return the funds, or any remainder after lawful deductions under subsection (1) of this section, to the tenant.

(5) Upon compliance with subsection (4) of this section, the person in possession of the security deposit shall be relieved of further liability.

(6) Upon receipt of transferred funds under subsection (4) (a) of this section, the transferee, in relation to such funds, shall be deemed to have all of the rights and obligations of a landlord holding the funds as a security deposit.

(7) Any provision, whether oral or written, in or pertaining to a rental agreement whereby any provision of this section for the benefit of a tenant or members of his household is waived shall be deemed to be against public policy and shall be void.

38-12-104. Return of security deposit - hazardous condition - gas appliance. (1) Anytime service personnel from any organization providing gas service to a residential building become aware of any hazardous condition of a gas appliance, piping, or other gas equipment, such personnel shall inform the customer of record at the affected address in writing of the hazardous condition and take any further action provided for by the policies of such personnel's employer. Such written notification shall state the potential nature of the hazard as a fire hazard or a hazard to life, health, property, or public welfare and shall explain the possible cause of the hazard.

(2) If the resident of the residential building is a tenant, such tenant shall immediately inform the landlord of the property or the landlord's agent in writing of the existence of the hazard.

(3) The landlord shall then have seventy-two hours excluding a Saturday, Sunday, or a legal holiday after the actual receipt of the written notice of the hazardous condition to have the hazardous condition repaired by a professional. "Professional" for the purposes of this section means a person authorized by the state of Colorado or by a county or municipal government through license or certificate where such government authorization is required. Where no person with such government authorization is available, and where there are no local requirements for government authorization, a person who is otherwise qualified and who possesses insurance with a minimum of one hundred thousand dollars public liability and property damage coverage shall be deemed a professional for purposes of this section. Proof of such repairs shall be forwarded to the landlord or the landlord's agent. Such proof may also be used as an affirmative defense in any action to recover the security deposit, as provided for in this section.

(4) If the landlord does not have the repairs made within seventy-two hours excluding a Saturday, Sunday, or a legal holiday, and the condition of the building remains

hazardous, the tenant may opt to vacate the premises. After the tenant vacates the premises, the lease or other rental agreement between the landlord and tenant becomes null and void, all rights and future obligations between the landlord and tenant pursuant to the lease or other rental agreement terminate, and the tenant may demand the immediate return of all or any portion of the security deposit held by the landlord to which the tenant is entitled. The landlord shall have seventy-two hours following the tenant's vacation of the premises to deliver to the tenant all of, or the appropriate portion of, the security deposit plus any rent rebate owed to the tenant for rent paid by the tenant for the period of time after the tenant has vacated. If the seventy-second hour falls on a Saturday, Sunday, or legal holiday, the security deposit must be delivered by noon on the next day that is not a Saturday, Sunday, or legal holiday. The tenant shall provide the landlord with a correct forwarding address. No security deposit shall be retained to cover normal wear and tear. In the event that actual cause exists for retaining any portion of the security deposit, the landlord shall provide the tenant with a written statement listing the exact reasons for the retention of any portion of the security deposit. When the statement is delivered, it shall be accompanied by payment of the difference between any sum deposited and the amount retained. The landlord is deemed to have complied with this section by mailing said statement and any payments required by this section to the forwarding address of the tenant. Nothing in this section shall preclude the landlord from withholding the security deposit for nonpayment of rent or for nonpayment of utility charges, repair work, or cleaning contracted for by the tenant. If the tenant does not receive the entire security deposit or a portion of the security deposit together with a written statement listing the exact reasons for the retention of any portion of the security deposit within the time period provided for in this section, the retention of the security deposit shall be deemed willful and wrongful and, notwithstanding the provisions of section 38-12-103 (3), shall entitle the tenant to twice the amount of the security deposit and to reasonable attorney fees.

38-12-401. Definitions. As used in this part 4, unless the context otherwise requires:

(1) "Domestic abuse" shall have the same meaning as provided in section 13-14-101 (2), C.R.S.

(2) "Domestic violence" shall have the same meaning as provided in section 18-6-800.3 (1), C.R.S.

38-12-402. Protection for victims of domestic violence. (1) A landlord shall not include in a residential rental agreement or lease agreement for housing a provision authorizing the landlord to terminate the agreement or to impose a penalty on a residential tenant for calls made by the residential tenant for peace officer assistance or other emergency assistance in response to a domestic violence or domestic abuse situation. A residential tenant may not waive the residential tenant's right to call for police or other emergency assistance.

(2) (a) If a tenant to a residential rental agreement or lease agreement notifies the landlord in writing that he or she is the victim of domestic violence or domestic abuse

and provides to the landlord evidence of domestic violence or domestic abuse in the form of a police report written within the prior sixty days or a valid protection order and the residential tenant seeks to vacate the premises due to fear of imminent danger for self or children because of the domestic violence or domestic abuse, then the residential tenant may terminate the residential rental agreement or lease agreement and vacate the premises without further obligation except as otherwise provided in paragraph (b) of this subsection (2).

(b) If a tenant to a residential rental agreement or lease agreement terminates the residential rental agreement or lease agreement and vacates the premises pursuant to paragraph (a) of this subsection (2), then the tenant shall be responsible for one month's rent following vacation of the premises, which amount shall be due and payable to the landlord within ninety days after the tenant vacates the premises. The landlord shall not be obligated to refund the security deposit to the tenant until such time as the tenant has paid the one month's rent pursuant to this section. Notwithstanding the provisions of section 38-12-103, the landlord and the tenant to a residential rental agreement or lease agreement may use any amounts owed to the other to offset costs for the one month's rent or the security deposit. The provisions of this paragraph (b) shall apply only if the landlord has experienced and documented damages equal to at least one month's rent as a result of the tenant's early termination of the agreement.

(3) Nothing in this part 4 authorizes the termination of tenancy and eviction of a residential tenant solely because the residential tenant is the victim of domestic violence or domestic abuse.

RULE 4, C.R.C.P. PROCESS

(a) To What Applicable. This Rule applies to all process except as otherwise provided by these rules.

(b) Issuance of Summons by Attorney or Clerk. The summons may be signed and issued by the clerk, under the seal of the court, or it may be signed and issued by the attorney for the plaintiff. Separate additional or amended summons may issue against any defendant at any time. All other process shall be issued by the clerk, except as otherwise provided in these rules.

(c) Contents of Summons. The summons shall contain the name of the court, the county in which the action is brought, the names or designation of the parties, shall be directed to the defendant, shall state the time within which the defendant is required to appear and defend against the claims of the complaint, and shall notify the defendant that in case of the defendant's failure to do so, judgment by default may be rendered against the defendant. If the summons is served by publication, the summons shall briefly state the sum of money or other relief demanded. The summons shall contain the name, address, and registration number of the plaintiff's attorney, if any, and if none, the address of the plaintiff. Except in case of service by publication under Rule 4(g) or when otherwise ordered by the court, the complaint shall be served with the summons. In any case, where by special order personal service of summons is allowed without the complaint, a copy of the order shall be served with the summons.

(d) By Whom Served. Process may be served within the United States or its Territories by any person whose age is eighteen years or older, not a party to the action. Process served in a foreign country shall be according to any internationally agreed means reasonably calculated to give notice, the law of the foreign country, or as directed by the foreign authority or the court if not otherwise prohibited by international agreement.

(e) Personal Service. Personal service shall be as follows:

(1) Upon a natural person whose age is eighteen years or older by delivering a copy thereof to the person, or by leaving a copy thereof at the person's usual place of abode, with any person whose age is eighteen years or older and who is a member of the person's family, or at the person's usual workplace, with the person's secretary, administrative assistant, bookkeeper, or managing agent; or by delivering a copy to a person authorized by appointment or by law to receive service of process.

(2) Upon a natural person whose age is at least thirteen years and less than eighteen years, by delivering a copy thereof to the person and another copy thereof to the person's father, mother, or guardian, or if there be none in the state, then by delivering a copy thereof to any person in whose care or control the person may be; or with whom the person resides, or in whose service the person is employed; and upon a natural person under the age of thirteen years by delivering a copy to the person's father, mother, or guardian, or if there be none in the state, then by delivering a copy thereof to the person in whose care or control the person may be.

(3) Upon a person for whom a conservator has been appointed, by delivering a copy thereof to such conservator.

(4) Upon any form of corporation, partnership, association, cooperative, limited liability company, limited partnership association, trust, organization, or other form of entity that is recognized under the laws of this state or of any other jurisdiction, (including any such organization, association or entity serving as an agent for service of process for itself or for another entity) by delivering a copy thereof to the registered agent for service as set forth in the most recently filed document in the records of the secretary of state of this state or any other jurisdiction, or one of the following:

(A) An officer of any form of entity having officers;

(B) A general partner of any form of partnership;

(C) A manager of a limited liability company or limited partnership association in which management is vested in managers rather than members;

(D) A member of a limited liability company or limited partnership association in which management is vested in the members or in which management is vested in managers and there are no managers;

(E) A trustee of a trust;

(F) The functional equivalent of any person described in paragraphs (A) through (E) of this subsection (4), regardless of such person's title, under:

(I) the articles of incorporation, articles of organization, certificate of limited partnership, articles of association, statement of registration, or other document of similar import duly filed or recorded by which the entity or any or all of its owners obtains status as an entity or the attribute of limited liability, or

(II) the law pursuant to which the entity is formed or which governs the operation of the entity;

(G) If no person listed in subsection (4) of this rule can be found in this state, upon any person serving as a shareholder, member, partner, or other person having an ownership or similar interest in, or any director, agent, or principal employee of such entity, who can be found in this state, or service as otherwise provided by law.

(5) Repealed.

(6) Upon a municipal corporation, by delivering a copy thereof to the mayor, city manager, clerk, or deputy clerk.

(7) Upon a county, by delivering a copy thereof to the county clerk, chief deputy, or county commissioner.

(8) Upon a school district, by delivering a copy thereof to the superintendent.

(9) Upon the state by delivering a copy thereof to the attorney general.

(10) (A) Upon an officer, agent, or employee of the state, acting in an official capacity, by delivering a copy thereof to the officer, agent, or employee, and by delivering a copy to the attorney general.

(B) Upon a department or agency of the state, subject to suit, by delivering a copy thereof to the principal officer, chief clerk, or other executive employee thereof, and by delivering a copy to the attorney general.

(C) For all purposes the date of service upon the officer, agent, employee, department, or agency shall control, except that failure to serve copies upon the attorney general within three days of service upon the officer, agent, employee, department, or agency shall extend the time within which the officer, agent, employee, department, or agency must file a responsive pleading for sixty days beyond the time otherwise provided by these Rules.

(11) Upon other political subdivisions of the State of Colorado, special districts, or quasi-municipal entities, by delivering a copy thereof to any officer or general manager, unless otherwise provided by law.

(12) Upon any of the entities or persons listed in subsections (4) through (11) of this section (e) by delivering a copy to any designee authorized to accept service of process for such entity or person, or by delivery to a person authorized by appointment or law to receive service of process for such entity or person. The delivery shall be made in any manner permitted by such appointment or law.

(f) Substituted Service. In the event that a party attempting service of process by personal service under section (e) is unable to accomplish service, and service by publication or mail is not otherwise permitted under section (g), the party may file a motion, supported by an affidavit of the person attempting service, for an order for substituted service. The motion shall state (1) the efforts made to obtain personal service and the reason that personal service could not be obtained, (2) the identity of the person to whom the party wishes to deliver the process, and (3) the address, or last known address of the workplace and residence, if known, of the party upon whom service is to be effected. If the court is satisfied that due diligence has been used to attempt personal service under section (e), that further attempts to obtain service under section (e) would be to no avail, and that the person to whom delivery of the process is appropriate under the circumstances and reasonably calculated to give actual notice to the party upon whom service is to be effective, it shall:

(1) authorize delivery to be made to the person deemed appropriate for service, and

(2) order the process to be mailed to the address(es) of the party to be served by substituted service, as set forth in the motion, on or before the date of delivery. Service shall be complete on the date of delivery to the person deemed appropriate for service.

(g) Other Service. Except as otherwise provided by law, service by mail or publication shall be allowed only in actions affecting specific property or status or other proceedings in rem. When service is by publication, the complaint need not be published with the summons. The party desiring service of process by mail or publication under this section (g) shall file a motion verified by the oath of such party or of someone in the party's behalf for an order of service by mail or publication. It shall state the facts authorizing such service, and shall show the efforts, if any, that have been made to obtain personal service and shall give the address, or last known address, of each person to be served or shall state that the address and last known address are unknown. The court, if satisfied that due diligence has been used to obtain personal service or that efforts to obtain the same would have been to no avail, shall:

(1) Order the party to send by registered or certified mail a copy of the process addressed to such person at such address, requesting a return receipt signed by the addressee only. Such service shall be complete on the date of the filing of proof thereof, together with such return receipt attached thereto signed by such addressee, or

(2) Order publication of the process in a newspaper published in the county in which the action is pending. Such publication shall be made once each week for five successive weeks. Within fifteen days after the order the party shall mail a copy of the process to each person whose address or last known address has been stated in the motion and file proof thereof. Service shall be complete on the day of the last publication. If no newspaper is published in the county, the court shall designate one in some adjoining county.

(h) Manner of Proof. Proof of service shall be made as follows:

(1) If served personally, by a statement, certified by the sheriff, marshal or similar governmental official, or statement duly acknowledged under oath by any other person completing the service as to date, place, and manner of service;

(2) Repealed.

(3) If served by mail, by an affidavit showing the date of the mailing with the return receipt attached, where required;

(4) If served by publication, by the affidavit of publication, together with an affidavit as to the mailing of a copy of the process where required;

(5) If served by waiver, by the written admission or waiver of service by the person or persons served, duly acknowledged, or by their attorney;

(6) If served by substituted service, by a duly acknowledged statement as to the date, place, and manner of service, accompanied by an affidavit that the process was also mailed to the party to be served by substituted service, setting forth the address(es) where the process was mailed.

(i) Waiver of Service of Summons. A defendant who waives service of a summons does not thereby waive any objection to the venue or to the jurisdiction of the court over the defendant.

(j) Amendment. At any time in its discretion and upon such terms as it deems just, the court may allow any process or proof of service thereof to be amended, unless it clearly appears that material prejudice would result to the substantial rights of the party against whom the process is issued.

(k) Refusal of Copy. If a person to be served refuses to accept a copy of the process, service shall be sufficient if the person serving the process knows or has reason to identify the person who refuses to be served, identifies the documents being served, offers to deliver a copy of the documents to the person who refuses to be served, and thereafter leaves a copy in a conspicuous place.

Rule 304, C.R.C.P. Service of Process

(a) To What Applicable. This rule applies to all process except as otherwise provided by these rules.

(b) Initial Process. Except in cases of service by publication under Rule 304(f), the complaint and a blank copy of the answer form shall be served with the summons.

(c) By Whom Served. Process may be served within the United States or its Territories by any person whose age is eighteen years or older, not a party to the action. Process served in a foreign country shall be according to any internationally agreed means reasonably calculated to give notice, the law of the foreign country, or as directed by the foreign authority or the court if not otherwise prohibited by international agreement.

(d) Personal Service. Personal service shall be as follows:

(1) Upon a natural person whose age is eighteen years or older, by delivering a copy thereof to the person, or by leaving a copy thereof at the person's usual place of abode, with any person whose age is eighteen years or older and who is a member of the person's family, or at the person's usual workplace, with the person's secretary, administrative assistant, bookkeeper, managing agent, or by delivering a copy to a person authorized by appointment or by law to receive service of process.

(2) Upon a natural person whose age is at least thirteen years and less than eighteen years, by delivering a copy thereof to the person and another copy thereof to the person's father, mother, or guardian, or if there be none in the state, then by

delivering a copy thereof to any person in whose care or control the person may be, or with whom the person resides, or in whose service the person is employed, and upon a natural person under the age of thirteen years by delivering a copy to the person's father, mother, or guardian, or if there be none in the state, then by delivering a copy thereof to the person in whose care or control the person may be.

(3) Upon a person for whom a conservator has been appointed, by delivering a copy thereof to such conservator.

(4) Upon any form of corporation, partnership, association, cooperative, limited liability company, limited partnership association, trust, organization, or other form of entity that is recognized under the laws of this state or of any other jurisdiction, (including any such organization, association or entity serving as an agent for service of process for itself or for another entity) by delivering a copy thereof to the registered agent for service as set forth in the most recently filed document in the records of the secretary of state of this state or any other jurisdiction, or one of the following:

(A) an officer of any form of entity having officers;

(B) a general partner of any form of partnership;

(C) a manager of a limited liability company or limited partnership association in which management is vested in managers rather than members;

(D) a member of a limited liability company or limited partnership association in which management is vested in the members or in which management is vested in managers and there are no managers;

(E) a trustee of a trust;

(F) the functional equivalent of any person described in paragraphs (A) through (E) of this subsection (4), regardless of such person's title, under:

(I) the articles of incorporation, articles of organization, certificate of limited partnership, articles of association, statement of registration, or other document of similar import duly filed or recorded by which the entity or any or all of its owners obtains status as an entity or the attribute of limited liability, or

(II) the law pursuant to which the entity is formed or which governs the operation of the entity;

(G) if no person listed in subsection (4) of this rule can be found in this state, upon any person serving as a shareholder, member, partner, or other person having an ownership or similar interest in, or any director, agent, or principal employee of such entity, who can be found in this state, or service as otherwise provided by law.

(5) Repealed.

(6) Upon a municipal corporation, by delivering a copy thereof to the mayor, the city manager, the clerk, or deputy clerk.

(7) Upon a county, by delivering a copy thereof to the county clerk, chief deputy, or county commissioner.

(8) Upon a school district, by delivering a copy thereof to the superintendent.

(9) Upon the state by delivering a copy thereof to the attorney general.

(10) (A) Upon an officer, agent, or employee of the state, acting in an official capacity, by delivering a copy thereof to the officer, agent, or employee, and by delivering a copy to the attorney general.

(B) Upon a department or agency of the state, subject to suit, by delivering a copy thereof to the principal officer, chief clerk, or other executive employee thereof, and by delivering a copy to the attorney general.

(C) For purposes of service of an initial summons and complaint, the copies shall be delivered to both the party and the attorney general within the times as set forth in rule 312(a). For all other purposes, the effective date of service shall be the latter date of delivery.

(11) Upon other political subdivisions of the State of Colorado, special districts, or quasi-municipal entities, by delivering a copy thereof to any officer or general manager, unless otherwise provided by law.

(12) Upon any of the entities or persons listed in subsections (4) through (11) of this section (d) by delivering a copy to any designee authorized to accept service of process for such entity or person, or by delivery to a person authorized by appointment or law to receive service of process for such entity or person. The delivery shall be made in any manner permitted by such appointment or law.

(e) Substitute Service. In the event that a party attempting service of process by personal service under section (d) is unable to accomplish service, and service by publication or mail is not otherwise permitted under section (f), the party may file a motion, supported by an affidavit of the person attempting service, for an order for substituted service. The motion shall state (1) the efforts made to obtain personal service and the reason that personal service could not be obtained, (2) the identity of the person to whom the party wishes to deliver the process, and (3) the address, or last known address of the workplace and residence, if known, of the party upon whom service is to be effected. If the court is satisfied that due diligence has been used to attempt personal service under section (d), that further attempts to obtain service under section (d) would be to no avail, and that the person to whom delivery of the process is appropriate under the circumstances and reasonably calculated to give actual notice to the party upon whom service is to be effective, it shall:

(1) Authorize delivery to be made to the person deemed appropriate for service, and

(2) Order the process to be mailed to the address(es) of the party to be served by substituted service, as set forth in the motion, on or before the date of delivery.

Service shall be complete on the date of delivery to the person deemed appropriate for service.

(f) Other Service. Except as otherwise provided by law, service by mail or publication shall be allowed only in actions affecting specific property or status or other proceedings in rem. When service is by publication, the complaint need not be published with the summons. The party desiring service of process by mail or publication under this section (f) shall file a motion verified by the oath of such party or of someone in the party's behalf for an order of service by mail or publication. It shall state the facts authorizing such service, and shall show the efforts, if any, that have been made to obtain personal service and shall give the address, or last known address, of each person to be served or shall state that this address and last known address are unknown. The court, if satisfied that due diligence has been used to obtain personal service or that efforts to obtain the same would have been to no avail, shall:

(1) Order the party to send by registered or certified mail a copy of the summons and a copy of the complaint, addressed to such person at such address, requesting a return receipt signed by addressee only. Such service shall be complete on the date of the filing of proof thereof, together with such return receipt attached thereto signed by such addressee, or

(2) Order publication of the summons in a newspaper published in the county in which the action is pending. Such publication shall be made once each week for five successive weeks. Within fifteen days after the order the party shall mail a copy of the summons and complaint to each person whose address or last known address has been stated in the motion and file proof thereof. Service shall be completed on the day of the last publication. If no newspaper is published in the county, the court shall designate one in some adjoining county.

(g) Manner of Proof. Proof of service shall be made as follows:

(1) If served personally, by a statement, certified by the sheriff, marshal or similar governmental official, or statement duly acknowledged under oath by any other person completing the service as to date, place, and manner of service.

(2) Repealed.

(3) If served by mail, an affidavit showing the date of the mailing, with the return receipt attached, where applicable.

(4) If served by publication, by the affidavit of publication, together with an affidavit as to the mailing of a copy of the summons, complaint and answer form where required.

(5) If served by waiver, by the written admission or waiver of service by the person or persons to be served, duly acknowledged, or by their attorney.

(6) If served by substituted service, by a duly acknowledged statement as to the date, place, and manner of service, accompanied by an affidavit that the process was also mailed to the party to be served by substituted service, setting forth the address(es) where the process was mailed.

(h) Amendment. At any time in its discretion and upon such terms as it deems just, the court may allow any summons or proof of service thereof to be amended, unless it clearly appears that material prejudice would result to the substantial rights of the party against whom the summons issued.

(i) Waiver of Service of Summons. A defendant who waives service of a summons does not thereby waive any objection to the venue or to the jurisdiction of the court over the defendant.

(j) Refusal of Copy. If a person to be served refuses to accept a copy of the summons and complaint, service shall be sufficient if the person serving the documents knows or has reason to identify the person who refuses to be served, identifies the documents being served as a summons and complaint, offers to deliver a copy of the documents to the person who refuses to be served, and thereafter leaves a copy in a conspicuous place.

APPENDIX D

A Directory of Professionals in Alternative Dispute Resolutions is available by calling the Colorado Council of Mediators or the Colorado Bar Association.

Colorado Council of Mediators & Mediation Organizations
1212 Mariposa Street
Denver, CO 80204
(303) 322-9275 (800) 864-4317
www.coloradomediation.org

Colorado Bar Association
1900 Grant Street, 9th Floor
Denver, CO 80203
(303) 860-1115
www.cobar.org

Offices of Dispute Resolution
Colorado Judicial Department
1301 Pennsylvania, #300
Denver, CO 80203
(303) 837-3672 (800) 888-0001, Ext. 3672
www.courts.state.co.us

APPENDIX E

Websites of Interest

www.bradfordpublishing.com: Bradford Publishing Company. This site contains downloadable forms and many other resources with regard to evictions, and other areas of Colorado law.

www.courts.state.co.us: Colorado Judicial Branch. This site has information on court locations, policies and procedures. It also includes a very helpful "self-help" center with links to statutes, rules, forms, and FAQ's.

www.cobar.org: Colorado Bar Association. In addition to a "Find a Lawyer" link, this site has a "Legal Resource Directory" with numerous helpful legal links, legal research links for local, state and federal law, and limited access to recent Colorado Appellate Court cases.

www.colorado.edu/law/lawlib: University of Colorado Law School. Includes library catalogues and a wide range of research tools.

www.law.du.edu/library: University of Denver Law School. Selection of legal links for the public.

www.leg.state.co.us: Colorado Legislature. Access to Colorado legislation that is pending as well as current laws and history of previous legislation.

www.ci.boulder.co.us: City of Boulder. Search for "Landlord-Tenant Handbook" within site. Contains details on Boulder-specific ordinances, as well as general landlord/ tenant law.

www.cocourts.com: Access to Colorado court files on line.

www.denvergov.org: City and County of Denver, information on Denver courts as well as many other governmental resources.

Endnotes

Legal citations to cases, statutory law, and articles contained in the endnotes use the following abbreviations:

COLO. LAW. – The Colorado Lawyer magazine, published by the Colorado Bar Association.

C.R.E. – Colorado Rules of Evidence.

C.R.S. – Colorado Revised Statutes.

C.R.C.P. – Colorado Rules of Civil Procedure.

DENV. U. L. REV. – Denver University Law Review.

P.2d – Refers to cases from Pacific Case Reporter, 2nd Edition, West Publishing.

___ U.S. ___ – Refers to cases from the United States Supreme Court Reporter.

---

[1] § 38-10-108, C.R.S. Contracts for interests in land must be written. "Every contract for the leasing for a longer period than one year or for the sale of any lands or any interest in lands is void unless the contract or some note or memorandum thereof expressing the consideration is in writing and subscribed by the party by whom the lease or sale is to be made." § 38-10-108, C.R.S.

[2] Section 12-2-3 of the Boulder Revised Code (1981), requires a written lease in all situations in which the rental is for 30 days or more. The lease must be signed within 30 days of commencement of the rental, and the landlord must provide each tenant with a copy within 7 working days after all parties have signed or within 15 days after the date of signature by any tenant, whichever is sooner. The Boulder Revised Code can be accessed online at http://www.colocode.com/boulder2/index.htm.

[3] In the absence of fraud or concealment, a person executing a written contract will not be heard to say that he did not know its contents. Kovacheff v. Langhart, 147 Colo. 339, 363 P.2d 702 (1961); O'Brien v. Houston, 83 Colo. 109, 262 P. 1020 (1927).

[4] The "note or memorandum" required must show on its face or by reference to other writings: (1) the names of the parties; (2) the terms and conditions of the contract; (3) the interest or property affected; and (4) the consideration to be paid therefor. Micheli v. Taylor, 114 Colo. 258, 159 P.2d 912 (1945); Eppich v. Clifford, 6 Colo. 493 (1883).

[5] Groups that participated included the Colorado Association of Realtors, the Colorado Apartment Association, the Rocky Mountain Home Association, and affordable housing activists. Daily Camera, "GOP Lawmakers Fume Over Mediator For Tenant Rights" (Apr. 18, 2008), quoting Kathi Williams, Director of the Colorado Division of Housing. *See also* Jerry Kopel, "Warranty of Habitability" (Mar. 29, 2008), *available at* www.jerrykopel.com/2008/warranty-of-habitability.htm. The prior Colorado cases holding that there is no implied warranty are obviously superseded and overruled by the new Act. *See, e.g.*, Bedell v. Los Zapatistas, Inc., 805 P.2d 1198 (Colo. App. 1991).

[6] Since Colorado's adoption of this law, the only state that does not recognize an implied warranty of habitability either legislatively or judicially is Arkansas. *See* Jerry Kopel, "Warranty of Habitability" (Mar. 29, 2008), *available at* www.jerrykopel.com/2008/warranty-of-habitability.htm.

[7] § 38-12-501 to 38-12-511, C.R.S.

[8] The Act applies to "rental agreements entered into or extended or renewed on or after the effective date of this act." Laws 2008, Ch.387, §4(3). However, basic statutory and constitutional construction principles relating to contracts suggest that this Act would apply only to those rental agreements entered into on or after September 1, 2008; therefore, the "extended or renewed" language may be subject to question. *See generally*, Kuhn v. State, 924 P.2d 1053 (Colo. 1996).

[9] § 38-12-502, C.R.S. (definitions); § 38-12-503, C.R.S. (warranty of habitability); § 38-12-505, C.R.S. (uninhabitable premises).

[10] § 38-12-507, C.R.S. (tenant's remedies).

[11] § 38-12-504, C.R.S. (tenant's obligations).

[12] § 38-12-506, C.R.S. (opt-out).

[13] "Rental Agreement" is defined at § 38-12-502(4), C.R.S. Not all properties are subject to the new Act or covered under the Warranty of Habitability. Section 38-12-511, C.R.S. specifies which exceptions to the Act arise. More generally, the following are excepted from coverage under the Act: (1) college dormitories, religious residences, medical residences, geriatric residences (nursing, retirement homes), counseling residences or similar services; (2) properties under contract for sale to which the buyer is also the tenant; (3) residences provided as partial compensation for employment; (4) fraternities and sororities; (5) hostels, motels, hotels, in which occupancy lasts less than thirty days; (6) condominium owners; (7) residences in unincorporated areas of a county that do not provide "water, heat and sewer services from a public entity," which are rented for recreational purposes, such as "hunting cabins, yurts, huts or other similar structures"; (8) agricultural housing rentals; and (9) mobile home park lot leases. Common areas are also excluded from the Warranty of Habitability, unless the deficiency in the common area "materially and substantially limits the tenant's use of his or her dwelling unit." § 38-12-505(2), C.R.S.

[14] § 38-12-503(1), C.R.S.

[15] § 38-12-503(2), C.R.S.

[16] Additional research gathered from Community Housing has revealed that at least from pro-tenant advocates, "materially dangerous conditions" would include mold, fire, and flood (Personal Communication, 9/16/2008 with Community Housing and Claudia Abernathy, Esq.). However, as this was not drafted specifically into the Act, the diligent practitioner is directed toward relevant case law for more specific guidance. Additionally, Community Housing has indicated that if they were contacted about a "materially dangerous condition," they would refer complaining tenants to the Colorado Department of Health and Safety for further determination on the actual condition, including possible condemnation of the subject property (Personal Communication, 9/16/2008). Further, Community Housing has indicated that certain catastrophic events, including fire and flood, may give rise to "materially dangerous conditions." Such pro-

tenancy advocate declarations, however, are not supported by any language in the Act and it is arguable whether or not a court would construe such natural events, or Acts of God, to make the premises "uninhabitable" or "materially dangerous," given the non-involvement of a landlord in such occurrence. Diligent attorneys should be aware of this directive from Community Housing that could direct tenants in courses of action affecting their tenancy arrangements with their respective landlords, and are cautioned to proceed accordingly.

[17] § 38-12-503(2), C.R.S.

[18] § 38-12-505(1), C.R.S.

[19] § 38-12-503(2)(a), C.R.S. Guidance might also be gleaned from case law interpreting constructive eviction and breach of quiet enjoyment claims. The extent of the disturbance must be relatively extreme so that a reasonable person would deem the premises as unusable. *See, e.g.,* Radinsky v. Weaver, 170 Colo. 169, 460 P. 2d 218 (1969) (landlord's construction on the second story caused water and dust to fall on expensive printing and photo equipment through hole in roof of darkroom); Eskanos & Supperstein v. Irwin, 637 P. 2d 403 (Colo. App. 1981) (loud music from three different sources simultaneously at tenant's quiet photo studio, in violation of specific lease provisions). *See also* Bedell v. Los Zapatistas, Inc., 805 P.2d 1198 (Colo. App. 1991); Kirkland v. Allen, 678 P. 2d 568 (Colo. App. 1984); Isbill Assocs. v. City & County of Denver, 666 P. 2d 1117 (Colo. App. 1983).

[20] § 38-12-503(2)(b), C.R.S.

[21] § 38-12-503(2)(c), C.R.S.

[22] *See* J.C. Penney Co. v. Birrell, 95 Colo. 59, 32 P. 2d 805 (1934) (what constitutes a reasonable time is a factual determination).

[23] § 38-12-503(4), C.R.S.

[24] § 38-12-507(1)(a), C.R.S.

[25] § 38-12-507(1)(a), C.R.S.

[26] Unlike the FED law, which addresses "calendar days" and "business days" (*see* § 13-40-111, C.R.S.) the Act simply uses "days." Because the number of days is less than seven, Saturdays, Sundays, and legal holidays are excluded from computation. *See* C.R.C.P. 6(a) and 306(a).

[27] C.R.C.P. 65(b).

[28] Rathke v. MacFarlane, 648 P.2d 648 (Colo. 1982); Rivera v. Civil Serv. Comm'n, 34 Colo. App. 152, 529 P.2d 1347, 1348 (1974). *See also* C.R.C.P. 65.

[29] § 38-12-507(1)(b), C.R.S.

[30] § 38-12-507(1)(b), C.R.S.

[31] *See* C.R.C.P. 365.

[32] § 38-12-507(1)(b), C.R.S.

[33] § 38-12-507(1)(b), C.R.S.

[34] Rathke v. MacFarlane, 648 P.2d 648 (Colo. 1982).

[35] § 38-12-507(1)(b), C.R.S.

---

[36] § 38-12-508(3), C.R.S.
[37] § 38-12-508(5), C.R.S.
[38] § 38-12-507(1)(d), C.R.S.
[39] § 38-12-507(1)(d), C.R.S.
[40] §§ 38-12-507(2) and 13-40-123, C.R.S.
[41] § 38-12-503(6)(b), C.R.S.
[42] § 38-12-507(1)(c), C.R.S.
[43] § 38-12-508(4), C.R.S.
[44] § 38-12-508(2), C.R.S.
[45] § 38-12-508, C.R.S.
[46] § 38-12-508(1), C.R.S.
[47] § 38-12-508(5), C.R.S.
[48] § 38-12-504, C.R.S.
[49] § 38-12-504(1), C.R.S.
[50] § 38-12-504(2), C.R.S.
[51] §§ 38-12-504(1) and 38-12-504(3), C.R.S. Based on the statutory language, it appears that a violation by a tenant under this section would be the equivalent of a breach of the lease, giving the landlord the appropriate remedies.
[52] § 38-12-506, C.R.S.
[53] § 38-12-505(1)(f), C.R.S.
[54] § 38-12-505(1)(g), C.R.S.
[55] § 38-12-505(1)(h), C.R.S.
[56] § 38-12-506(1), C.R.S.
[57] § 38-12-506(1)(b), C.R.S.
[58] § 38-12-506(1)(a), C.R.S.
[59] § 38-12-506(2), C.R.S.
[60] § 38-12-506(2), C.R.S.
[61] The work must not be necessary to cure a failure to comply with §38-12-505(3), C.R.S. [initial condition of premises which fails to comply with the Implied Warranty of Habitability]. However, if the premises is a single family residence and the tenant has the requisite skills to perform the work required to cure a failure to comply with §38-12-505(3), C.R.S., then the parties may agree to the tenant's performance of such work.
[62] The work must not be necessary to cure a failure to comply with §38-12-505(3), C.R.S. [initial condition of Premises which fails to comply with the Implied Warranty of Habitability]. However if the premises is a single family residence and the tenant has the requisite skills to perform the work required to cure a failure to comply with § 38-12-505(3), C.R.S., then the parties may agree to the tenant's performance of such work.
[63] § 38-12-503(3), C.R.S.

[64] § 38-12-503(3), C.R.S.

[65] § 38-12-509(1), C.R.S.

[66] § 38-12-509(4), C.R.S.

[67] § 38-12-509(3), C.R.S.

[68] § 38-12-510, C.R.S.

[69] § 38-12-510, C.R.S.

[70] § 38-12-510, C.R.S.

[71] *See* §§ 13-32-101 *et seq.*, C.R.S. (clerk fees); §§ 30-1-104 *et seq.*, C.R.S. (sheriff fees). A list of current fees may be found at www.courts.state.co.us.

[72] § 30-1-104, C.R.S.

[73] The City and County of Denver and Boulder County are two of the more progressive courts in this area of alternative dispute mediation.

[74] § 13-22-308(1), C.R.S.; Nat'l Union Fire Ins. Co. v. Price, 78 P.3d 1138 (Colo. App. 2003). *See also* § 13-22-311(1), C.R.S., which grants the court express authority to refer a matter to mediation.

[75] Montgomery v. Tufford, 165 Colo. 18, 437 P.2d 36 (1968) (trespass and conversion); Chryar v. Wolf, 21 P.3d 428 (Colo. App. 2000) (conversion and outrageous conduct); Danyew v. Phelps, 676 P.2d 707 (Colo. App. 1983) (outrageous conduct); Deeb v. Canniff, 29 Colo. App. 510, 488 P.2d 93 (1971) (conversion). *See also* Christopher J . Koenigs, *Enforcement of Leases Through Unlawful Detainer Actions*, 20 COLO. LAW. No. 2, 251–252 (1991).

[76] *See, e.g.*, Montgomery v. Tufford, 165 Colo. 18, 437 P.2d 36 (1968); Clark v. Morris, 710 P.2d 1130 (Colo. App. 1985).

[77] For example, an apartment lease previously available from Bradford Publishing (Form No. 1045) contained the language: "Landlord may, at his option, without liability for trespass or for damages, enter into and upon said premises...repossess the said premises...expel and remove the tenant...and their effects...all without prejudice to any other remedies available to the landlord for arrears of rent or breach of covenant."

[78] *See, e.g.*, Clark v. Morris, 710 P.2d 1130 (Colo. App. 1985) (implying that if a landlord complies with specific provisions of the lease, self-help would be okay). *Compare* MANUEL A. RAMOS, RIGHTS AND OBLIGATIONS: COLORADO LANDLORD-TENANT LAW FROM THE PROSPECTIVE OF A TENANT ADVOCATE p. 46 (3rd ed. 2002), ("Landlord 'Self-Help' has not been condoned by Colorado courts"); D. Cypser, *Survey of Colorado Landlord and Tenant Law*, 20 COLO. LAW. 2023, 2026 (Oct. 1991) ("However, recent cases have held that an unlawful detainer action and a writ of restitution executed by an officer of the law are the only lawful means of evicting a tenant. Lockouts and other 'self-help' evictions are not lawful."). *See also* Christopher J . Koenigs, *Enforcement of Leases Through Unlawful Detainer Actions*, 20 COLO. LAW. No. 2, 251, 252 (1991); D. Rubin, *Representation of the Landlord in an Unlawful Detainer Action*, 12 COLO. LAW. 69, 72 (Oct. 1983) (both cautioning against self-help actions). *See also* Martinez v. Steinbaum, 623 P 2d 49 (Colo. 1981); Ruston v. Centennial Real Estate & Inv. Co., 166 Colo. 377, 445 P.2d 64 (1966) (both addressing self-help situations).

[79] § 38-12-510, C.R.S.

[80] § 38-12-510, C.R.S.

[81] § 38-12-510, C.R.S.

[82] § 38-12-510, C.R.S. *See, e.g.*, Clark v. Morris, 710 P.2d 1130 (Colo. App. 1985).

[83] § 38-12-510, C.R.S.

[84] § 38-12-510, C.R.S.

[85] *See* Martinez v. Steinbaum, 623 P 2d 49 (Colo. 1981); Ruston v. Centennial Real Estate & Inv. Co., 166 Colo. 377, 445 P.2d 64 (1966).

[86] *See* Martinez v. Steinbaum, 623 P 2d 49 (Colo. 1981) (tenant who reported he would be back in two or three days and who did not return for eight weeks had abandoned the property). *Compare* Berae Co. v. Gorman, 168 Colo. 551, 452 P.2d 379 (1969) (meat market was closed, not abandoned, for ten days).

[87] *See, e.g.*, Clark v. Morris, 710 P.2d 1130 (Colo. App. 1985).

[88] Martinez v. Steinbaum, 623 P 2d 49, 53 (Colo. 1981); Berae Co. v. Gorman, 168 Colo. 551, 452 P.2d 379 (1969).

[89] Berae Co. v. Gorman, 168 Colo. 551, 452 P.2d 379, 380 (1969); *see also* School Dist. RE-2(J) v. Panucci, 30 Colo. App. 184, 187, 490 P.2d 711 (1971) (holding that "intent cannot be presumed from or proved solely by the fact of nonuse for a period less than that set by the statute of limitations").

[90] Berae Co. v. Gorman, 168 Colo. 551, 452 P.2d 379 (1969); *see also* Deeb v. Canniff, 29 Colo. App. 510, 488 P.2d 93 (1971).

[91] Martinez v. Steinbaum, 623 P 2d 49 (Colo. 1981); *see also* Ruston v. Centennial Real Estate & Inv. Co., 166 Colo. 377, 445 P.2d 64 (1966).

[92] D. Rubin, *Representation of the Landlord in an Unlawful Detainer Action*, 12 COLO. LAW. 69, 72 (Oct. 1983) ("It is preferable to get the judgment . . . to avoid any doubt as to the legality of the actions by the landlord. Often in an effort to save time and costs the landlord places himself in a more precarious position than before.").

[93] §§ 38-20-101 *et seq.* C.R.S. This applies to residential premises. *See generally* J. Gigax, *Rights of Landlords in Tenant's Personal Property*, 57 DENV. U. L. REV. 685 (1980). *See also* Senn & Jones, *Self Help for Commercial Landlords*, 19 COLO. LAW. 479 (March 1990).

[94] § 38-20-102(3)(c), C.R.S. Assertion of a lien in a forcible manner or manner that interferes with tenant's right of occupancy is wrongful.

[95] J. Gigax, *Rights of Landlords in Tenant's Personal Property*, 57 DENV. U. L. REV. 685, 693 (1980); M. Ramos, *Colorado's Landlord Lien Statute: Equal Protection and Due Process Infirmities*, 11 COLO. LAW. 1867 (July 1982); MANUEL A. RAMOS, RIGHTS AND OBLIGATIONS: COLORADO LANDLORD-TENANT LAW FROM THE PROSPECTIVE OF A TENANT ADVOCATE pp. 52–53 (3rd ed. 2002).

[96] § 38-20-116, C.R.S. *See generally* J. Gigax, *Rights of Landlords in Tenant's Personal Property*, 57 DENV. U. L. REV. 685 (1980).

[97] § 8-4-123, C.R.S.

[98] § 8-4-123, C.R.S.

[99] § 13-40-104(1)(d), C.R.S.

[100] The designation of "Demand for Possession" is actually misleading because the landlord is more properly giving the tenant a "notice to pay or quit." *See* Aigner v. Cowell Sales Co., 660 P.2d 907, 908 (Colo. 1983); Barlow v. Hoffman, 103 Colo. 286, 291, 86 P.2d 239, 241 (1938); GTM Investments v. Depot, Inc., 694 P.2d 379, 382 (Colo. App. 1984). This book will refer to this document as a "Demand for Compliance or Possession" because this is what the form employed is entitled. "Demand for Compliance or Right To Possession Notice" is the term employed on the Colorado Judiciary form.

[101] *See* Magliocco v. Olson, 762 P.2d 681 (Colo. App. 1987); *but see* Duran v. Housing Authority, 761 P.2d 180 (Colo. 1988) (requiring two notices).

[102] Duran v. Housing Authority, 761 P.2d 180 (Colo. 1988) (discussing the difference between waiver and estoppel in the context of an eviction).

[103] § 38-12-504, C.R.S.

[104] § 13-40-104(1)(e), C.R.S.

[105] § 13-40-104(1)(e.5), C.R.S.

[106] §§ 13-40-107.5 and 13-40-104(1)(d.5), C.R.S.

[107] *See* Doss v. Craig, 1 Colo. 177 (Colo. Terr. 1869) (a party cannot be guilty of unlawful detainer until after a demand has been made upon him; by requiring a prior demand, the legislature intended to give the tenant an opportunity to surrender possession and avoid expensive litigation); *see also* Audubon Commercial Area Co. v. Skelly Oil Co., 268 F. Supp. 883 (D. Colo. 1967) (demand for payment was a prerequisite to declaring forfeiture where the right to demand was not waived).

[108] Francam Bldg. Corp. v. Fail, 646 P.2d 345 (Colo. 1982).

[109] *See also* Rocky Mountain Props. v. Purified H2O To Go Co., 3 P.3d 485 (Colo. App. 2000) (service of a timely demand is a condition precedent to filing an FED action); Grombone v. Krekel, 754 P.2d 777 (Colo. App. 1988); Wu v. Good, 720 P.2d 1005 (Colo. App. 1986).

[110] Note, however, the above language applies only to the nonpayment of rent defaults under paragraph (d) and is not referenced to paragraph (e) which relates to "any other condition or covenant." Query: Does this mean *Francam Bldg. Corp. v. Fail*, 646 P.2d 345 (Colo. 1982), is still good law as applied to notice requirement in (e)? This question is unanswered by case law or the legislature. The more conservative approach would be to serve a defaulting tenant a Three Day Notice even if a default is under paragraph (e) and the lease contains a waiver. This will assure that the case will not be dismissed under a broad reading of Section 13-40-104(1)(d) and (e), C.R.S.

[111] § 13-40-104(1)(d), C.R.S.

[112] § 13-40-104(1)(d), C.R.S. The Demand for Compliance or Possession must be addressed to all tenants on the property or it is not effective to those not named. *See* Danyew v. Phelps, 676 P.2d 707 (Colo. App. 1983). If you believe there are other tenants of whose identity you may not be aware, it is advisable to include the phrase "any other parties occupying the premises."

[113] § 13-40-104(1)(d), C.R.S. *See also* Tumbarello v. Byers, 37 Colo. App. 61, 543 P.2d 1278 (1975). If the notice does not demand payment of rent or possession in the

alternative, it is defective. The landlord should attempt to specify in the notice exactly how much rent is due. However, a demand for the incorrect amount does not void the notice. Barlow v. Hoffman, 103 Colo. 286, 86 P.2d 239 (1938); Perry v. White, 69 Colo. 234, 193 P. 543 (1920).

[114] §§ 13-40-104(1)(e), C.R.S.

[115] § 13-40-106, C.R.S. *See also* Danyew v. Phelps, 676 P.2d 707 (Colo. App. 1983).

[116] § 13-40-106, C.R.S.

[117] § 13-40-106, C.R.S. *See also* Hix v. Roy, 139 Colo. 457, 340 P.2d 438 (1959) (a six-month demand was defective because it failed to unequivocally terminate the lease).

[118] § 13-40-106, C.R.S. *See also* Hix v. Roy, 139 Colo. 457, 340 P.2d 438, 440 (1959) (all joint owners must sign the demand; one tenant in common cannot give notice for all co-lessors without consent). *But compare* Didamo v. Tyrol Sport Arms Co., 680 P.2d 1328, 1330 (Colo. App. 1984).

[119] Hix v. Roy, 139 Colo. 457, 340 P.2d 438 (1959).

[120] § 13-40-108, C.R.S.

[121] Magliocco v. Olson, 762 P.2d 681 (Colo. App. 1987).

[122] § 13-40-108, C.R.S. *See* Danyew v. Phelps, 676 P.2d 707 (Colo. App. 1983).

[123] § 13-40-108, C.R.S.

[124] § 13-40-108, C.R.S. *See* Magliocco v. Olson, 762 P.2d 681 (Colo. App. 1987) (notice by posting is adequate even if the tenant does not see the notice). D. Rubin, *Representation of the Landlord in an Unlawful Detainer Action*, 12 COLO. LAW. 69, 72 (Oct. 1983); Christopher J . Koenigs, *Enforcement of Leases Through Unlawful Detainer Actions*, 20 COLO. LAW. No. 2, 251, 252 (1991); C. KRENDL, COLORADO METHODS OF PRACTICE, VOL. 2A, § 71.19 (West Publishing, 4th ed. 1998). If there is a question of proper posting, it is a question of fact, which may be determined by the trial court based on an assessment of the credibility of witnesses. Rocky Mountain Props. v. Purified H2O To Go Co., 3 P.3d 485 (Colo. App. 2000).

[125] D. Rubin, *Representation of the Landlord in an Unlawful Detainer Action*, 12 COLO. LAW. 69, 72 (Oct. 1983); Christopher J . Koenigs, *Enforcement of Leases Through Unlawful Detainer Actions*, 20 COLO. LAW. No. 2, 251, 252 (1991); C. KRENDL, COLORADO METHODS OF PRACTICE, VOL. 2A, § 71.19 (West Publishing, 4th ed. 1998).

[126] This would comport with the requirement of C.R.C.P. 4(d). This rule implies that people over age 18 are more responsible and credible.

[127] C.R.C.P. 6(a) and 306(a). *See* D. Rubin, *Representation of the Landlord in an Unlawful Detainer Action*, 12 COLO. LAW. 69, 72 (Oct. 1983).

[128] § 13-40-111, C.R.S. (definition of "business days").

[129] § 13-40-104(1)(e.5), C.R.S.

[130] §§ 13-40-104(1)(e.5), 13-40-106, 13-40-107, C.R.S.

[131] § 13-40-107.5, C.R.S.

[132] § 13-40-107.5(3), C.R.S.

[133] § 13-40-107.5(4)(a), C.R.S.

---

[134] § 13-40-107.5(5)(a), C.R.S. *See* Carder, Inc. v. Cash, 97 P.3d 174 (Colo. App. 2003).

[135] § 13-40-107.5(5)(c)(I), C.R.S. *See* Chapter XIII for further discussion of domestic violence issues. The law provides very specific protections for victims of domestic violence. See §§ 13-40-104(4) and 38-12-402, C.R.S. If you are a victim of domestic violence, or if you are a landlord involved with premises where domestic violence may be occurring, you are strongly encouraged to review these laws.

[136] § 13-40-107.5(5)(b)(II), C.R.S. *See* Boulder County Apartment Ass'n v. Boulder, 97 P.3d 332 (Colo. App. 2004).

[137] § 13-40-107(4), C.R.S.; July Bldg. Corp. v. Heathrow & Co., 679 P.2d 1120 (Colo. App. 1984); Didamo v. Tyrol Sport Arms Co., 680 P.2d 1328 (Colo. App. 1984); C. KRENDL, COLORADO METHODS OF PRACTICE, VOL. 2A, § 71.22 (West Publishing, 4th ed. 1998) (see additional cases cited therein).

[138] Sinclair Refining Co. v. Shakespeare, 115 Colo. 520, 175 P.2d 389 (1946). *See also* First Interstate Bank v. Tanktech, Inc., 864 P.2d 116 (Colo. 1993); Blazis v. Orlinski, 738 P.2d 62 (Colo. App. 1987). For an in-depth discussion, see F. Anes, *Holdover Tenants in Colorado*, 34 ROCKY MT. L. REV. 320 (1962).

[139] For example, typical language might be: "If after the expiration of this lease, the tenant, with the permission of the landlord, shall remain in possession of said premises, the tenant shall be regarded as a tenant from month-to-month."

[140] Hurd v. Whitsett, 4 Colo. 77 (1878).

[141] Sinclair Refining Co. v. Shakespeare, 115 Colo. 520, 175 P.2d 389 (1946).

[142] F. Anes, *Holdover Tenants in Colorado*, 34 ROCKY MT. L. REV. 320, 324 (1962). *See also* In Re Van Vleet, 383 B.R. 782 (Bankr. D. Colo. 2008) (a periodic tenancy does not expire every month but continues until terminated).

[143] The Notice to Vacate is also known as "Notice to Quit" and informally called a "10 Day Notice" because the ten-day notice period is the most common period required. In this book we will refer to this document as the Notice to Vacate because that is what the form is captioned.

[144] § 13-40-107(1)(a), (c), (d), C.R.S.

[145] § 13-40-107(1), C.R.S. (emphasis added).

[146] § 13-40-107, C.R.S.

[147] C.R.C.P. 6(a) and 306(a).

[148] § 13-40-110, C.R.S. If there are conflicts between the FED law and the rules of civil procedure, the FED law takes precedence. § 13-40-119, C.R.S.; Beeghly v. Mack, 20 P.3d 610 (Colo. 2001); Butler v. Farner, 704 P.2d 853 (Colo. 1985).

[149] C.R.C.P. 10 and 310(a).

[150] § 13-40-110, C.R.S. *See* Klopfer v. Keller, 1 Colo. 410 (Colo. Terr. 1871) (substantial facts must be set forth).

[151] § 13-40-110, C.R.S.

[152] C.R.C.P. 310; Doss v. Craig, 1 Colo. 177 (Colo. Terr. 1869).

[153] C.R.C.P. 311. However, it is advisable to have the complaint verified because it will aid you if a default judgment is sought. Christopher J . Koenigs, *Enforcement of Leases Through Unlawful Detainer Actions*, 20 COLO. LAW. No. 2, 251, 253 (1991).

[154] C.R.C.P. 38 and 338; Husar v. Larimer County Court, 629 P.2d 1104 (Colo. App. 1981).

[155] As of the time of publication of this book, the fee is $98.

[156] *See* § 12-5-112, C.R.S.

[157] *See* § 13-1-127, C.R.S. In the event of such representation, the court must receive evidence, such as a written resolution, that the party has the authority to represent the entity. If proceeding under this law, review the language of the statute and note the $10,000 limit (not $15,000, as in the County Court jurisdictional limit).

[158] *See* §§ 7-60-109 and 7-60-110, C.R.S.

[159] § 13-40-111, C.R.S.; C.R.C.P. 4 and 304.

[160] §§ 13-40-111 and 13-40-112, C.R.S. This is a requirement under the due process clauses of the United States and Colorado Constitutions. The courts take this requirement very seriously, and it should be strictly complied with.

[161] § 13-40-111, C.R.S.

[162] § 13-40-111(1), C.R.S. In 2008, new language was added to the required statutory language in § 13-40-111(1), C.R.S. to comply with § 38-12-507(1)(c), C.R.S., concerning the landlord's failure to repair and deposit of rent: "If you are claiming that the landlord's failure to repair the residential premises is a defense to the landlord's allegation of nonpayment of rent, the court will require you to pay into the registry of the court, at the time of filing your answer, the rent due less any expenses you have incurred based upon the landlord's failure to repair the residential premises."

[163] C.R.C.P. 304; § 13-40-111 C.R.S.

[164] C.R.C.P. 3 and 303.

[165] C.R.C.P. 3 and 303.

[166] § 13-40-109, C.R.S.

[167] § 13-40-112(1), C.R.S.

[168] C.R.C.P. 4(e) and 304(d).

[169] § 13-40-112(2), C.R.S.

[170] § 13-40-112(2), C.R.S.

[171] § 13-40-112, C.R.S. It is advisable that a copy of the complaint and answer form also be mailed at that time. Mailing in addition to posting constitutes compliance with due process requirements. Greene v. Lindsey, 456 U.S. 444 (1982). Use regular first class mail, not certified mail. C. KRENDL, COLORADO METHODS OF PRACTICE, VOL. 2A, § 71.22 (West Publishing, 4th ed. 1998). *See also* Dodge v. Meyer, 793 P.2d 639 (Colo. App. 1990).

[172] The requirement of mailing immediately after filing the complaint, before the plaintiff even knows if the defendant, after diligent attempts, may be served personally or by posting, is problematic. Unlike other civil actions in which an attorney may first issue and

serve the summons, and then file a complaint (see C.R.C.P. 3 and 303), the statute appears clear that the summons may only be issued "upon filing the complaint ..." (see § 13-40-111, C.R.S.). Thus, under a strict reading of the statute, the plaintiff is required to mail the notice the business day after filing the complaint, thus allowing for only one day of "diligent effort."

[173] § 13-40-115, C.R.S. Typically, an "alias" summons will be issued for personal service upon the defendant because the case may be continued until the defendant is served. At that point, the court will consider economic claims.

[174] § 13-40-112(4), C.R.S.

[175] C.R.C.P. 304(f).

[176] *See* Rocky Mountain Props. v. Purified H2O To Go Co., 3 P.3d 485 (Colo. App. 2000) (posting the demand is sufficient); Magliocco v. Olson, 762 P.2d 681 (Colo. App. 1987) (posting the demand is sufficient).

[177] Continuing liability for subsequent rent after vacating the premises depends solely on the language of the lease. Read the lease carefully. McArthur v. Rostek, 483 P.2d 1351 (Colo. App. 1971). *See* Robert A. McNeil Corp. v. Paul, 757 P.2d 165 (Colo. App. 1988); Emrich v. Joyce's Submarine Sandwiches, Inc., 751 P.2d 651 (Colo. App. 1987); First Nat'l Bank of Boston v. Dykstra, 684 P.2d 957 (Colo. App. 1984) (all holding the tenant liable). *Compare* Aigner v. Cowell Sales Co., 660 P.2d 907 (Colo. 1983) (tenant not liable). *See also* Christopher J . Koenigs, *Enforcement of Leases Through Unlawful Detainer Actions*, 20 COLO. LAW. No. 2, 251, fn 7 (1991).

[178] Barlow v. Hoffman, 103 Colo. 286, 86 P.2d 239 (1938). Additionally, the offer to cure must be unconditional. *See* Duran v. Housing Authority, 761 P.2d 180 (Colo. 1988).

[179] §§ 13-40-112 and 13-40-113, C.R.S.

[180] § 13-40-113, C.R.S. Note that an unqualified general appearance or filing of an Answer may waive the defective process defense. *See* Tyler v. McKenzie, 43 Colo. 233, 95 P. 943 (1908); Behr v. Burge, 940 P.2d 1084 (Colo. App. 1996).

[181] C.R.C.P. County Court Form No. 3; C.R.C.P. District Court Form No. 17. With minor modification, the forms presented in this book will be acceptable for District Court.

[182] Spar Consol. Mining & Dev. Co. v. Aasgaard, 33 Colo. App. 35, 516 P.2d 127 (1973).

[183] McCrimmon v. Raymond, 77 Colo. 81, 234 P. 1058 (1925); Bonnell v. Gill, 41 Colo. 59, 92 P. 13 (1907).

[184] § 13-40-113, C.R.S.; C.R.C.P. 312. Any defense not included in the answer is deemed waived (except subject matter jurisdiction). § 13-40-113, C.R.S.; C.R.C.P. 312. The law also permits defenses to be raised by motions filed simultaneously with the Answer form. In the event that the tenant intends to argue that improper service of process was effected, a motion to dismiss pursuant to C.R.C.P. 312 and § 13-40-113, C.R.S. should be filed and addressed before the Answer.

[185] *See* Tyler v. McKenzie, 43 Colo. 233, 95 P. 943 (1908); Behr v. Burge, 940 P.2d 1084 (Colo. App. 1996).

[186] All defenses, other than defective notice, are typically applicable only to default evictions (as opposed to a termination of tenancy situation). For additional information

on defenses, see MANUEL A. RAMOS, RIGHTS AND OBLIGATIONS: COLORADO LANDLORD-TENANT LAW FROM THE PROSPECTIVE OF A TENANT ADVOCATE (3rd ed. 2002).

[187] Duran v. Housing Authority, 761 P.2d 180 (Colo. 1988); Aigner v. Cowell Sales Co., 660 P.2d 907 (Colo. 1983); Barlow v. Hoffman, 103 Colo. 286, 86 P.2d 239 (1938).

[188] *See* D. Cypser, *Survey of Colorado Landlord and Tenant Law*, 20 COLO. LAW. 2023 (Oct. 1991).

[189] Werner v. Baker, 693 P.2d 385 (Colo. App. 1984). Even if a lease requires that all modifications be in writing, this requirement too may be waived orally or by conduct. Williams v. Colorado Springs College of Business, Inc., 736 P.2d 419 (Colo. App. 1987).

[190] *See* MANUEL A. RAMOS, RIGHTS AND OBLIGATIONS: COLORADO LANDLORD-TENANT LAW FROM THE PROSPECTIVE OF A TENANT ADVOCATE pp. 54–57 (3rd ed. 2002).

[191] Williams v. Colorado Springs College of Business, Inc., 736 P.2d 419 (Colo. App. 1987).

[192] Blazis v. Orlinski, 738 P.2d 62 (Colo. App. 1987); Zarlengo v. Farrer, 683 P.2d 1208 (Colo. App. 1984); Werner v. Baker, 693 P.2d 385 (Colo. App. 1984); Kimmick v. Santilli, 42 Colo. App. 341, 596 P.2d 1223 (1979); Kelley v. Morgan, 42 Colo. App. 223, 595 P.2d 1058 (1979).

[193] Duran v. Housing Authority, 761 P.2d 180 (Colo. 1988) (good discussion on difference between waiver and estoppel in the context of an eviction).

[194] §§ 13-40-106, 13-40-107, C.R.S. *See* Chapters IV and V. *See also* Audubon Commercial Area Co. v. Skelly Oil Co., 268 F. Supp 883 (D. Colo. 1967).

[195] §§ 13-40-104 and 13-40-107, C.R.S. However, if an improper time is specified in the notice but the landlord waits the appropriate time before bringing the action, specifying an improper time in the notice will not be considered a defense. *See* Western Cities Broadcasting, Inc. v. Schueller, 830 P.2d 1074 (Colo. App. 1991), *aff'd*, 849 P.2d 44 (Colo. 1993).

[196] Danyew v. Phelps, 676 P.2d 707 (Colo. App. 1983).

[197] § 13-40-104(1), C.R.S.; MANUEL A. RAMOS, RIGHTS AND OBLIGATIONS: COLORADO LANDLORD-TENANT LAW FROM THE PROSPECTIVE OF A TENANT ADVOCATE pp. 7, 8 (3rd ed. 2002).

[198] Tumbarello v. Byers, 37 Colo. App. 61, 543 P.2d 1278 (1975).

[199] Barlow v. Hoffman, 103 Colo. 286, 86 P.2d 239 (1938) (amount); Hepp Wall Paper & Mercantile Co. v. Deahl, 53 Colo. 274, 125 P. 491 (1912) (form). *See also* Hemberger v. Hagemann, 120 Colo. 431, 210 P.2d 995 (1949) ("Sufficiency of the notice or the manner of service thereof cannot be questioned where notice was conceded to have been received.").

[200] *See* MANUEL A. RAMOS, RIGHTS AND OBLIGATIONS: COLORADO LANDLORD-TENANT LAW FROM THE PROSPECTIVE OF A TENANT ADVOCATE p. 37 (3rd ed. 2002), interpreting *Kirkland v. Allen*, 678 P.2d 568 (Colo. App. 1984) as implying that the landlord's breach occurring before a tenant's refusal to pay rent relieves the tenant from the duty to pay rent.

[201] The extent of the disturbance must be relatively extreme so that a reasonable person would deem the premises as unusable. *See, e.g.*, Radinsky v. Weaver, 170 Colo. 169, 460

P. 2d 218 (1969) (landlord's construction on the second story caused water and dust to fall on expensive printing and photo equipment through hole in roof of darkroom); Copeland v. Lincoln, 166 P.3d 245 (Colo. App. 2007) (hazardous condition of furnace); Eskanos & Supperstein v. Irwin, 637 P. 2d 403 (Colo. App. 1981) (loud music from three different sources simultaneously at tenant's quiet photo studio was in violation of specific lease provisions).

[202] Candell v. Western Fed. Sav. & Loan Ass'n of Denver, 156 Colo. 552, 400 P.2d 909 (1965). What a reasonable time is depends on the facts. *See, e.g.*, H & K Automotive Supply Co. v. Moore & Co., 657 P.2d 986 (Colo. App. 1982) (three years was "unreasonable as a matter of law"); Eskanos & Supperstein v. Irwin, 637 P. 2d 403 (Colo. App. 1981) (tenant's decision to stay on after making complaints and make a "good-faith effort" to find a solution was reasonable). *See also* J.C. Penney Co. v. Birrell, 95 Colo. 59, 32 P. 2d 805 (1934) (what constitutes a reasonable time is a factual determination); Copeland v. Lincoln, 166 P.3d 245 (Colo. App. 2007).

[203] Bedell v. Los Zapatistas, Inc., 805 P.2d 1198 (Colo. App. 1991); Kirkland v. Allen, 678 P.2d 568 (Colo. App. 1984); Isbill Assocs. v. City & County of Denver, 666 P.2d 1117 (Colo. App. 1983). *See also* D. Cypser, *Survey of Colorado Landlord and Tenant Law*, 20 COLO. LAW. 2023, 2024 (Oct. 1991); note, however, that a lack of abandonment does not allow for a constructive eviction claim as stated in Cypser's article.

[204] Western Stock Center, Inc. v. Sevit, Inc., 195 Colo. 372, 578 P.2d 1045 (1978); Radinsky v. Weaver, 170 Colo. 169, 460 P. 2d 218 (1969); Carder, Inc. v. Cash, 97 P.3d 174 (Colo. App. 2003). Most leases do not waive a right to quiet enjoyment, but one should check the particular lease.

[205] Shanahan v. Collins, 189 Colo. 169, 539 P.2d 1261 (1975) (covenants dependent, defense allowed); GTM Investments v. Depot, Inc., 694 P.2d 379, 382 (Colo. App. 1984) (covenants independent, defense not allowed). A contract with "dependent covenants" means that the breach of one promise by a landlord (e.g., to provide promised space or services) allows a tenant to suspend performance on tenant's promise (e.g., to pay rent). A contract with "independent covenants" means that despite the breach of promise by one party, the other party may not suspend performance but must perform and seek a separate remedy.

[206] § 38-12-508(4), C.R.S.

[207] § 38-12-507(1)(c), C.R.S.

[208] Aigner v. Cowell Sales Co., 660 P.2d 907 (Colo. 1983); Robert A. McNeil Corp. v. Paul, 757 P.2d 165 (Colo. App. 1988); Emrich v. Joyce's Submarine Sandwiches, Inc., 751 P.2d 651 (Colo. App. 1987); GTM Investments v. Depot, Inc., 694 P.2d 379, 382 (Colo. App. 1984); Grolier Society, Inc. v. Int'l Realty Co., 482 P.2d 394 (Colo. App. 1971).

[209] La Casa Nino, Inc. v. Plaza Esteban, 762 P.2d 669 (Colo. 1988); Schneiker v. Gordon, 732 P.2d 603 (Colo. 1987). *See also* CMCB Enterprises, Inc. v. Ferguson, 114 P.3d 90 (Colo. App. 2005) (the burden of proof is on the tenant to demonstrate the landlord's failure to mitigate).

[210] Cafeteria Operators L.P. v. AMCAP/Denver Ltd. P'ship, 972 P.2d 276 (Colo. App. 1998); Basnett v. Vista Village Mobile Home Park, 699 P.2d 1343 (Colo. App. 1984), *rev'd on other grounds*, 731 P.2d 700 (Colo. 1987).

---

[211] La Casa Nino, Inc. v. Plaza Esteban, 762 P.2d 669 (Colo. 1988).

[212] C.R.C.P. 313(a). Almost every claim that a tenant could bring in an eviction action would be deemed compulsory. A "compulsory" claim is one that involves the same parties, events, or transactions as the eviction claim. All compulsory claims must be brought with the original claim for eviction, or they will be barred forever.

[213] "If the tenant is entitled to an abatement of the rent, the rent is abated to the amount of that proportion of the rent which the fair rental value after the event giving the right to abate bears to the fair rental value before the event. Abatement is allowed until the default is eliminated or the lease terminates, whichever first occurs." Bedell v. Los Zapatistas, Inc., 805 P.2d 1198, 1200 (Colo. App. 1991), quoting the Restatement (Second) of Property § 11.1 (1977). In other words, what rent is the property worth with a defect (e.g., no hot water) compared to what the property rents for without the defect (e.g., working hot water)? The difference between the two is the amount of rent to be abated (subtracted) while the defect remains.

[214] Radinsky v. Weaver, 170 Colo. 169, 460 P. 2d 218 (1969).

[215] Cablevision of Breckenridge, Inc. v. Tannhauser Condo. Ass'n, 649 P.2d 1093 (Colo. 1982); McCrea & Co. Auctioneers, Inc. v. Dwyer Auto Body, 799 P.2d 394 (Colo. App. 1989).

[216] Hurricane v. Kanover, Ltd., 651 P.2d 1218 (Colo. 1982); Rugg v. McCarty, 173 Colo. 170, 476 P.2d 753 (1970); Danyew v. Phelps, 676 P.2d 707 (Colo. App. 1983). These torts require some very extreme or outrageous wrongful conduct on the part of defendant. For example, in *Danyew v. Phelps*, an elderly woman was evicted without statutory notice while she was incapacitated in the hospital. She was forced to spend more time in the hospital because she was "extremely upset and weakened by the knowledge of the eviction." And in *Chryar v. Wolf*, 21 P.3d 428 (Colo. App. 2000), which involved both conversion and outrageous conduct, the landlord wrongfully removed the tenant's property and placed it on the street with a sign saying, "Free Take." Finally, the court in *Carder, Inc. v. Cash*, 97 P.3d 174 (Colo. App. 2003) rejected a claim for conversion based on the "economic loss rule." (Under the economic loss rule, when parties address duties and potential claims in a contract, and they have suffered only economic loss relative to those claims, the parties cannot also attempt to recover by filing a separate tort claim.)

[217] § 38-12-507(1)(d), C.R.S.

[218] § 38-12-507(1)(d), C.R.S.

[219] § 13-40-113, C.R.S.; C.R.C.P. 311, 312, and 313.

[220] When a tenant files an answer *pro se*, the answer must contain the tenant's telephone number. If the answering tenant is represented by an attorney, the answer must contain the attorney's phone number. C.R.C.P. 311.

[221] McCrimmon v. Raymond, 77 Colo. 81, 234 P. 1058 (1925); Bonnell v. Gill, 41 Colo. 59, 92 P. 13 (1907); Spar Consol. Mining & Dev. Co. v. Aasgaard, 33 Colo. App. 35, 516 P.2d 127 (1973).

[222] § 13-40-113(1), C.R.S.

[223] These forms can be found at www.courts.state.co.us. The "Motion to File without Payment and Supporting Financial Affidavit" is form JDF 205. You will also need an Order form JDF 206.

[224] C.R.C.P. 5 and 305.

[225] C.R.C.P. 38(b).

[226] *See* §§ 13-40-113 and 13-40-114, C.R.S.

[227] C.R.C.P. 38 and 338. *See* Husar v. Larimer County Court, 629 P.2d 1104 (Colo. App. 1981) (addressing the right to a jury trial in an FED action). A jury trial makes the presentation of a case much more complex. If a jury is desired, a party would do well to retain an experienced trial attorney for the hearing.

[228] Beeghly v. Mack, 20 P.3d 610 (Colo. 2001); Butler v. Farner, 704 P.2d 853 (Colo. 1985).

[229] § 13-40-114, C.R.S. Some commentators have construed Section 13-40-114, C.R.S. as requiring trial within five days, but the cases and practice do not bear this out. Some courts may not allow a trial to occur until after five days, and there is no prohibition against a longer length. *See* D. Rubin, *Representation of the Landlord in an Unlawful Detainer Action*, 12 COLO. LAW. 69, 71 (Oct. 1983). *Compare* MANUEL A. RAMOS, RIGHTS AND OBLIGATIONS: COLORADO LANDLORD-TENANT LAW FROM THE PROSPECTIVE OF A TENANT ADVOCATE p. 14 (3rd ed. 2002); D. Cypser, *Survey of Colorado Landlord and Tenant Law*, 20 COLO. LAW. 2023, 2026 (Oct. 1991). *See also* Beeghly v. Mack, 20 P.3d 610 (Colo. 2001).

[230] § 13-40-114, C.R.S.; Christopher J . Koenigs, *Enforcement of Leases Through Unlawful Detainer Actions*, 20 COLO. LAW. No. 2, 251, 253 (1991); MANUEL A. RAMOS, RIGHTS AND OBLIGATIONS: COLORADO LANDLORD-TENANT LAW FROM THE PROSPECTIVE OF A TENANT ADVOCATE p. 21 (3rd ed. 2002). Ramos points out that this requirement is misread by many courts. If a party is required to post bond and does not do so, then the correct action for the court is to require an immediate trial. It is not proper to order a default judgment. Beeghly v. Mack, 20 P.3d 610 (Colo. 2001).

[231] C.R.C.P. 355. Note that if the defendant was not personally served (i.e., served by posting), the court only has jurisdiction to enter an order for possession and not monetary damages. §13-40-115, C.R.S.. However, there is also authority stating that if defendants appear in the proceeding and participate in a substantive manner, they subject themselves to the court's jurisdiction. County of Adams v. Hibbard, 918 P.2d 212 (Colo. 1996); Brown v. Amen, 147 Colo. 468, 364 P.2d 735 (1961).

[232] C.R.C.P. 307(b) and 312(b). Certain exceptions exist to this rule but should not be of concern in the typical eviction.

[233] The procedure for default judgment in district court is somewhat different. *See* C.R.C.P. 55. If your case is in district court, be sure to comply with C.R.C.P. 121, § 1-14, which requires that a number of specific documents be prepared.

[234] § 13-40-112, C.R.S. An alias summons may be issued, and the court may continue the case for purpose of establishing monetary damages. § 13-40-115, C.R.S.

[235] C.R.C.P. 355.

[236] It is within the discretion of the trial court to decide what type of hearing it requires in an FED default; no evidentiary hearing is required. Orebaugh v. Doskocil, 145 Colo.

484, 359 P.2d 671 (1961). The Colorado State Judicial Branch website provides a form for a default motion (JDF 104). This form can be found at www.courts.state.co.us. While this would appear to be contrary to C.R.C.P. 307(b), which bars written motions in county court, some courts prefer to use this form because it can also be a form of affidavit.

237 DAVID R. DEMURO, COLORADO CIVIL TRIAL PRACTICE § 384 (West Publishing 1986). *See, e.g.*, C.R.C.P. Chapter 33 (Rules of Evidence).

238 JACK H. FRIEDENTHAL, MARY KAY KANE, & ARTHUR R. MILLER, CIVIL PROCEDURE § 10.1 (West Group 1985); DAVID R. DEMURO, COLORADO CIVIL TRIAL PRACTICE § 384 (West Publishing 1986); THOMAS A. MAUET, FUNDAMENTALS OF TRIAL TECHNIQUES pp. 1–21 (Little, Brown & Co., 2d ed. 1988).

239 *See generally* THOMAS A. MAUET, FUNDAMENTALS OF TRIAL TECHNIQUES pp. 45–74 (Little, Brown & Co., 2d ed. 1988).

240 C.R.E. 1001, 1002, 1003, and 1004. If the original lease is unavailable, the landlord must present proof showing the reason for its unavailability.

241 C.R.C.P. 343; C.R.E. 101 *et seq.*

242 C.R.E. 401.

243 C.R.E. 602, 801–803.

244 C.R.C.P. 343; C.R.E. 1002 and 1003.

245 C.R.E. 901 and 902.

246 *See* C.R.E. 101 *et seq.* The rules of evidence are extremely complex and this discussion does not even scratch the surface.

247 C.R.C.P. 41(b)(1); § 13-40-116, C.R.S. This is also applicable to counterclaims by the defendant. *See also* C.R.C.P. 350 regarding County Court motions for directed verdict.

248 C.R.C.P. 41 and 341. A defendant who is successful may recover against the plaintiff for his or her costs. § 13-40-110, C.R.S.

249 C.R.C.P. 352 (this applies to non-jury county court cases only). However, in "exceptional" cases, the court may take cases under advisement.

250 § 13-40-115(2), C.R.S.

251 § 13-40-115(2), C.R.S.

252 §§ 13-40-115(2) and 13-40-123, C.R.S.; C.R.C.P. 354(d).

253 §§ 13-40-115(2) and 13-40-123, C.R.S. *See also* Magliocco v. Olson, 762 P.2d 681 (Colo. App. 1987); Del E. Webb Realty & Mgmt. Co. v. Wessbecker, 628 P.2d 114 (Colo. App. 1980); Collins v. Shanahan, 34 Colo. App. 82, 523 P.2d 999 (1974), *aff'd*, 539 P.2d 1261 (Colo. 1976). Although the statute provides for recovery of attorney fees in practice, judges have seemed unwilling to enforce these provisions or have unilaterally reduced the claimed fees. *See* MANUEL A. RAMOS, RIGHTS AND OBLIGATIONS: COLORADO LANDLORD-TENANT LAW FROM THE PROSPECTIVE OF A TENANT ADVOCATE p. 24 (3rd ed. 2002); C. KRENDL, COLORADO METHODS OF PRACTICE, VOL. 2A, § 71.27 (West Publishing, 4th ed. 1998). The recent cases of *Integra Financial, Inc. v. Grynberg Petroleum Co.*, 74 P.3d 347 (Colo. App. 2002) and *Wilcox v. Clark*, 42 P.3d 29 (Colo. App. 2001) add further guidance by providing that the party who obtains (or retains) possession is deemed the

prevailing party and further that award of attorney fees is mandatory and not discretionary.

[254] § 13-40-123, C.R.S.

[255] § 13-40-115(2), C.R.S.

[256] § 13-40-122, C.R.S.

[257] § 13-40-122(1), C.R.S.

[258] § 13-40-122(a), C.R.S.

[259] Christensen v. Hoover, 643 P.2d 525 (Colo. 1982).

[260] Christensen v. Hoover, 643 P.2d 525, 528 (Colo. 1982).

[261] *See, e.g.*, §§ 13-40-117 to 13-40-121, C.R.S.; C.R.C.P. 411; C.R.C.P. App. to Ch. 25, County Court Forms 4 and 5. Morgan v. Dist. Court, 192 Colo. 418, 559 P.2d 712 (1977).

[262] §§ 13-40-118 and 13-40-120, C.R.S. These payments may be distributed to landlord upon order of court. § 13-40-121, C.R.S. If the defendant fails to pay any of these, the appeal will be dismissed. §§ 13-40-118 and 13-40-120, C.R.S.

[263] § 13-40-117(3), C.R.S. For a further discussion of appeal requirements, see MANUEL A. RAMOS, RIGHTS AND OBLIGATIONS: COLORADO LANDLORD-TENANT LAW FROM THE PROSPECTIVE OF A TENANT ADVOCATE pp. 24–28 (3rd ed. 2002); C. KRENDL, COLORADO METHODS OF PRACTICE, VOL. 2A, § 71.26 (West Publishing, 4th ed. 1998).

[264] § 38-12-103(7), C.R.S.; Ingold v. AIMCO/Bluffs L.L.C. Apartments, 159 P.3d 116 (Colo. 2007).

[265] § 38-12-103(1), C.R.S. Some local ordinances may require landlords to pay interest on security deposits, but no such state law exists.

[266] § 38-12-103(1), C.R.S.

[267] § 38-12-103(1), C.R.S.; Chew v. Int'l Society for Krishna Consciousness of Colorado, 738 P.2d 57 (Colo. App. 1987) ("ordinary wear and tear" defined).

[268] § 38-12-102(1), C.R.S.

[269] Mishkin v. Young, 107 P.3d 393, 399 (Colo. 2005).

[270] It is doubtful that a security deposit claim would exceed $15,000. But if it does, it must be filed in the District Court.

[271] *See generally* §§ 13-6-401 *et seq.*, C.R.S.; C.R.C.P. 501 *et seq.*

[272] § 13-6-403(1), C.R.S.

[273] § 13-6-407, C.R.S.

[274] §§ 13-6-404 and 13-6-407, C.R.S.

[275] Guzman v. McDonald, 194 Colo. 160, 570 P.2d 532 (1977); *see also* Martinez v. Steinbaum, 623 P 2d 49 (Colo. 1981). For a detailed discussion of the "willful" and "wrongful" requirements, see *Mishkin v. Young*, 107 P.3d 393 (Colo. 2005).

[276] Mishkin v. Young, 107 P.3d 393 (Colo. 2005); Turner v. Lyon, 189 Colo. 234, 539 P.2d 1241 (1975).

---

[277] Mishkin v. Young, 107 P.3d 393 (Colo. 2005); Heatherridge Mgmt. Co. v. Benson, 192 Colo. 190, 558 P.2d 435 (1977).

[278] § 38-12-104, C.R.S.

[279] § 38-12-104, C.R.S.

[280] Domestic abuse" and "domestic violence" are defined in § 38-12-401, C.R.S. with reference to other laws. "Domestic abuse" has the same meaning as provided in § 13-14-101, C.R.S. "Domestic violence" has the same meaning as provided in § 18-6-800.3(1), C.R.S. Essentially, these terms relate to violence or threats of violence against a person who is related or is (or was) in an intimate relationship with the perpetrator.

[281] §§ 13-40-104(4)(a), (b) and 13-40-107.5(5)(c)(I), C.R.S.

[282] § 13-40-104(4)(a)(I) and (II), C.R.S.

[283] §§ 13-40-104(4)(d) and 13-40-107.5(5)(c)(II), C.R.S.

[284] § 38-12-402(2)(a), C.R.S.

[285] § 38-12-402(2)(b), C.R.S.

[286] § 13-40-104(4)(c), C.R.S.

[287] § 38-12-402(1), C.R.S.

[288] § 38-12-503(3), C.R.S.

Bibliography

Note: COLO. LAW is an abbreviation for *The Colorado Lawyer Magazine* published monthly, and available from the Colorado Bar Association (1-800-332-6736).

F. Anes, "Holdover Tenants in Colorado," 34 ROCKY MOUNTAIN LAW REVIEW 320 (1962). In-depth discussion of holdover tenancy and termination thereof.

D. Cypser, "Survey of Colorado Landlord Tenant Law," 20 COLO. LAW 2023 (Oct. 1991). Contains discussions of many recent cases and statutes regarding all aspects of landlord/tenant relations. Especially good discussion on self-help and landlord's liens.

J. Gigax, "Rights of Landlords in Tenant's Personal Property," 57 DENV. U.L.J. 685 (1980). In-depth discussion of landlord's liens.

C. Koenigs, "Enforcement of Leases Through Unlawful Detainer Actions," 20 COLO. LAW 251 (Feb. 1991). This article contains a good, but brief, overview of the eviction process. Good "common sense" suggestions.

Cathleen Krendl, *Colorado Methods of Practice*, Volume 2A, West (4th Edition, 1998). The standard basic reference text among Colorado attorneys. Covers a wide variety of subjects. Chapter on eviction covers major steps. It is directed at attorneys already familiar with basic civil procedure.

David Kroll, "The Landlord/Tenant Warranty of Habitability and the Covenant of Quiet Enjoyment," 21 COLO. LAW 1159 (1992). This article contains a brief discussion of these concepts.

Manuel A. Ramos, *Rights and Obligations: Colorado Landlord-Tenant Law From the Perspective of a Tenant Advocate*, (2nd Edition 1995) (Published by and available through Continuing Legal Education of Colorado, Inc., Phone: 303-860-0608). Everything you ever wanted to know about tenant rights. Written in the style of a legal brief, filled with comprehensive information with citations to cases. May be too technical for the layman.

M. Ramos, "Colorado's Landlord Lien Statute: Equal Protection and Due Process Infirmities," 11 COLO. LAW 1867 (July 1982). Tenant's rights advocate view of landlord's lien statute. Constitutional law perspective.

D. Rubin, "Representation of the Landlord in an Unlawful Detainer Action," 12 COLO. LAW 69 (Oct. 1973). Landlord's perspective on evictions. Suggestion to protect landlord and attorney representing landlord from liability.

Alan Sweetbaum and E. James Wilder, "Forcible Entry and Detainer: A Primer," 29 COLO. LAW 89 (2000). Contains a basic rundown of FED procedures.

Index